Interactive Data Visualization with Python

Second Edition

Present your data as an effective and
compelling story

Abha Belorkar

Sharath Chandra Guntuku

Shubhangi Hora

Anshu Kumar

Interactive Data Visualization with Python

Second Edition

Authors: Abha Belorkar, Sharath Chandra Guntuku, Shubhangi Hora, and Anshu Kumar

Technical Reviewer: Saurabh Dorle

Managing Editor: Ranu Kundu

Acquisitions Editor: Kunal Sawant

Production Editor: Shantanu Zagade

Editorial Board: Shubhopriya Banerjee, Bharat Botle, Ewan Buckingham, Mahesh Dhyani, Manasa Kumar, Alex Mazonowicz, Bridget Neale, Dominic Pereira, Shiny Poojary, Abhisekh Rane Erol Staveley, Ankita Thakur, Nitesh Thakur, and Jonathan Wray.

First published: October 2019

Second edition: April 2020

Production Reference: 1130420

ISBN: 978-1-80020-094-4

Published by Packt Publishing Ltd.

Livery Place, 35 Livery Street

Birmingham B3 2PB, UK

Table of Contents

Chapter 2: Static Visualization – Global Patterns and Summary Statistics   47

Chapter 3: From Static to Interactive Visualization 85

Chapter 4: Interactive Visualization of Data across Strata 121

Chapter 5: Interactive Visualization of Data across Time   169

Chapter 7: Avoiding Common Pitfalls to Create Interactive Visualizations   257

Preface

About

This section briefly introduces the authors, the coverage of this book, the technical skills you'll need to get started, and the hardware and software requirements required to complete all of the included activities and exercises.

About the Book

With so much data being continuously generated, developers who present data as impactful and interesting visualizations, are always in demand. *Interactive Data Visualization with Python, Second Edition,* sharpens your data exploration skills and provides an excellent takeoff in your remarkable journey of creating interactive data visualizations with Python.

You'll begin by learning how to draw various plots with `Matplotlib` and `Seaborn`, the non-interactive data visualization libraries. You'll study different types of visualizations, compare them, and learn how to select a particular type of visualization to suit your requirements. After you get a hang of the various non-interactive visualization libraries, you'll learn the principles of intuitive and persuasive data visualization, and use `Altair`, `Bokeh` and `Plotly` to transform your visuals into strong stories.

By the end of the book, you'll have a new skill set that'll make you the go-to person for transforming data visualizations into engaging and interesting stories.

About the Authors

Abha Belorkar is an educator and researcher in computer science. She received her bachelor's degree in computer science from Birla Institute of Technology and Science Pilani, India and her Ph.D. from the National University of Singapore. Her current research work involves the development of methods powered by statistics, machine learning, and data visualization techniques to derive insights from heterogeneous genomics data on neurodegenerative diseases.

Sharath Chandra Guntuku is a researcher in natural language processing and multimedia computing. He received his bachelor's degree in computer science from Birla Institute of Technology and Science, Pilani, India and his Ph.D. from Nanyang Technological University, Singapore. His research aims to leverage large-scale social media image and text data to model social health outcomes and psychological traits. He uses machine learning, statistical analysis, natural language processing, and computer vision to answer questions pertaining to health and psychology in individuals and communities.

Shubhangi Hora is a Python developer, artificial intelligence enthusiast, data scientist, and writer. With a background in computer science and psychology, she is particularly passionate about mental health-related AI. Apart from this, she is interested in the performing arts and is a trained musician.

Anshu Kumar is a data scientist with over 5 years of experience in solving complex problems in natural language processing and recommendation systems. He has an M.Tech. from Indian Institute of Technology, Madras in computer science. He is also a mentor at SpringBoard. His current interests are building semantic search, text summarization, and content recommendations for large-scale multilingual datasets.

Learning Objectives

By the end of this book, you will be able to:

- Explore and apply different static and interactive data visualization techniques
- Make effective use of plot types and features from the Matplotlib, Seaborn, Altair, Bokeh, and Plotly libraries
- Master the art of selecting appropriate plotting parameters and styles to create attractive plots
- Choose meaningful and informative ways to present your stories through data
- Customize data visualization for specific scenarios, contexts, and audiences
- Avoid common errors and slip-ups in visualizing data

Audience

This book intends to provide a solid training ground for Python developers, data analysts, and data scientists to enable them to present critical data insights in a way that best captures the user's attention and imagination. It serves as a simple step-by-step guide that demonstrates the different types and components of visualization, the principles and techniques of effective interactivity, as well as common pitfalls to avoid when creating interactive data visualizations.

Students should have an intermediate level of competency in writing Python code, as well as some familiarity with using libraries such as pandas.

Approach

Resources for learning interactive data visualization are scarce. Moreover, the materials that are available either deal with tools other than Python (for example, Tableau), or focus on a single Python library for visualization. This book is the first of its kind to present a variety of options for building interactive data visualizations with Python. Moreover, the method of presentation is simple and accessible for anyone who is well versed in Python.

The book follows an engaging syllabus as the reader is systematically led through the various steps and aspects of interactive visualization with a series of realistic case studies. The book is packed with actionable information throughout, and programming activities are supplemented with helpful tips and advice on the capabilities and limitations of the tools being used.

Hardware Requirements

For an optimal experience, we recommend the following hardware configuration:

- Intel® Core™ i5 processor 4300M at 2.60 GHz or 2.59 GHz (1 socket, 2 cores, 2 threads per core) and 8 GB of DRAM

- Intel® Xeon® processor E5-2698 v3 at 2.30 GHz (2 sockets, 16 cores each, 1 thread per core) and 64 GB of DRAM

- Intel® Xeon Phi™ processor 7210 at 1.30 GHz (1 socket, 64 cores, 4 threads per core), 32 GB of DRAM, and 16 GB of MCDRAM (flat mode enabled)

- Disk space: 2 to 3 GB

- Operating systems: Windows® 10, macOS, and Linux

Minimum System Requirements:

- Processors: Intel Atom® processor or Intel® Core™ i3 processor

- Disk space: 1 GB

- Operating systems: Windows 7 or later, macOS, and Linux

Software Requirements

We also recommend that you have the following software installed in advance:

- Browser: Google Chrome or Mozilla Firefox

- The latest version of Git

- Anaconda 3.7 Python distribution

- Python 3.7

- The following Python libraries installed: **numpy**, **pandas**, **matplotlib**, **seaborn**, **plotly**, **bokeh**, **altair**, and **geopandas**

Conventions

Code words in text, database table names, folder names, filenames, file extensions, pathnames, dummy URLs, user input, and Twitter handles are shown as follows:

"Python performs advanced numerical and scientific computations with libraries such as **numpy** and **scipy**, hosts a wide array of machine learning methods owing to the availability of the **scikit-learn** package, provides a great interface for big data manipulation due to the availability of the **pandas** package and its compatibility with Apache Spark, and generates aesthetically pleasing plots and figures with libraries such as **seaborn**, **plotly**, and more."

A block of code is set as follows:

```
#import the python modules
import seaborn as sns
#load the dataset
diamonds_df = sns.load_dataset('diamonds')
#Plot a histogram
diamonds_df.hist(column='carat')
```

New terms and important words are shown in bold:

"The **kernel density estimation** is a non-parametric way to estimate the probability density function of a random variable."

Installation and Setup

Before we begin this journey of visualizing various types of data through different graphs and interactive features, we need to be prepared with the most productive environment. Follow these notes to learn how to do that:

Installing the Anaconda Python Distribution

Find the Anaconda version for your operating system on the official installation page at https://www.anaconda.com/distribution/.

After the download is complete, double-click on the file to open the installer and follow the prompts displayed on your screen.

Installing pip

1. To install pip, go to the following link and download the **get-pip.py** file: https://pip.pypa.io/en/stable/installing/.

2. Then, use the following command to install it: **python get-pip.py**.

You might need to use the **python3 get-pip.py** command, as previous versions of Python on your computer already use the Python command.

Installing the Python Libraries

Use the following command in your Anaconda terminal to install **Seaborn**:

```
pip install seaborn
```

Use the following command in your Anaconda terminal to install **Bokeh**:

```
pip install bokeh
```

Use the following command in your Anaconda terminal to install **Plotly**:

```
pip install plotly==4.1.0
```

Working with JupyterLab and Jupyter Notebook

You'll be working on different exercises and activities in Jupyter Lab or Notebook. These exercises and activities can be downloaded from the related GitHub repository.

You can download the repository here: https://github.com/TrainingByPackt/Interactive-Data-Visualization-with-Python.

You can either download it using GitHub or as a zipped folder by clicking on the green clone or download button in the top-right corner. In order to open Jupyter Notebooks, you have to traverse into the directory with your terminal. To do that, type the following:

```
cd Interactive-Data-Visualization-with-Python/<your current chapter>.
```

For example:

```
cd Interactive-Data-Visualization-with-Python/Chapter01/
```

To complete the process, perform the following steps:

1. To reach each activity and exercise, you have to use **cd** once more to go into each folder, like so:

   ```
   cd Activity01
   ```

2. Once you are in the folder of your choice, simply call the following:

   jupyter-lab to start up JupyterLab. Similarly, for Jupyter Notebook, call **jupyter notebook**

Importing the Python Libraries

Every exercise and activity in this book will make use of various libraries. Importing libraries into Python is very simple. Here's how we do it:

- To import libraries, such as **seaborn** and **pandas**, we have to run the following code:
  ```
  #import the python modules
  import seaborn
  import pandas
  ```

  This will import the whole **numpy** library into our current file.

- In the first cells of the exercises and activities of this book, you will see the following code. We can use **sns** instead of **seaborn** in our code to call methods from **seaborn**:
  ```
  # import seaborn and assign alias sns
  import seaborn as sns
  ```

Installing Git

To install Git, go to https://git-scm.com/downloads and follow the instructions that are specific to your platform.

Additional Resources

The code bundle for this book is also hosted on GitHub at https://github.com/TrainingByPackt/Interactive-Data-Visualization-with-Python.

The high-quality color images used in book can be found at: https://github.com/TrainingByPackt/Interactive-Data-Visualization-with-Python/tree/master/Graphics.

We also have other code bundles from our rich catalog of books and videos available at https://github.com/PacktPublishing/. Check them out!

1

Introduction to Visualization with Python – Basic and Customized Plotting

Learning Objectives

By the end of this chapter, you will be able to:

- Explain the concept of data visualization
- Analyze and describe the pandas DataFrame
- Use the basic functionalities of the pandas DataFrame
- Create distributional plots using matplotlib
- Generate visually appealing plots using seaborn

In this chapter, we will explore the basics of data visualization using Python programming.

Introduction

Data visualization is the art and science of telling captivating stories with data. Today's developers and data scientists, irrespective of their operational domain, agree that communicating insights effectively using data visualization is very important.

Data scientists are always looking for better ways to communicate their findings through captivating visualizations. Depending on their domain, the type of visualization varies, and often, this means employing specific libraries and tools that will best suit the visualization needs. Thus, developers and data scientists are looking for a comprehensive resource containing quick, actionable information on this topic. The resources for learning interactive data visualization are scarce. Moreover, the available materials either deal with tools other than Python (for example, Tableau) or focus on a single Python library for visualization. This book is designed to be accessible for anyone who is well-versed in Python.

Why Python? While most languages have associated packages and libraries built specifically for visualization tasks, Python is uniquely empowered to be a convenient tool for data visualization. Python performs advanced numerical and scientific computations with libraries such as `numpy` and `scipy`, hosts a wide array of machine learning methods owing to the availability of the `scikit-learn` package, provides a great interface for big data manipulation due to the availability of the `pandas` package and its compatibility with Apache Spark, and generates aesthetically pleasing plots and figures with libraries such as `seaborn`, `plotly`, and more.

The book will demonstrate the principles and techniques of effective interactive visualization through relatable case studies and aims to enable you to become confident in creating your own context-appropriate interactive data visualizations using Python. Before diving into the different visualization types and introducing interactivity features (which, as we will see in this book, will play a very useful role in certain scenarios), it is essential to go through the basics, especially with the `pandas` and `seaborn` libraries, which are popularly used in Python for data handling and visualization.

This chapter serves as a refresher and one-stop resource for reviewing these basics. Specifically, it illustrates creating and handling `pandas` DataFrame, the basics of plotting with `pandas` and `seaborn`, and tools for manipulating plotting style and enhancing the visual appeal of your plots.

> **Note**
>
> Some of the images in this chapter have colored notations, you can find high-quality color images used in this chapter at: https://github.com/TrainingByPackt/Interactive-Data-Visualization-with-Python/tree/master/Graphics/Lesson1.

Handling Data with pandas DataFrame

The **pandas** library is an extremely resourceful open source toolkit for handling, manipulating, and analyzing structured data. Data tables can be stored in the DataFrame object available in **pandas**, and data in multiple formats (for example, `.csv`, `.tsv`, `.xlsx`, and `.json`) can be read directly into a DataFrame. Utilizing built-in functions, DataFrames can be efficiently manipulated (for example, converting tables between different views, such as, long/wide; grouping by a specific column/feature; summarizing data; and more).

Reading Data from Files

Most small-to medium-sized datasets are usually available or shared as delimited files such as **comma-separated values** (**CSV**), **tab-separated values** (**TSV**), **Excel** (**.xslx**), and JSON files. Pandas provides built-in I/O functions to read files in several formats, such as, **read_csv**, **read_excel**, and **read_json**, and so on into a DataFrame. In this section, we will use the **diamonds** dataset (hosted in book GitHub repository).

> **Note**
>
> The datasets used here can be found in https://github.com/TrainingByPackt/Interactive-Data-Visualization-with-Python/tree/master/datasets.

Exercise 1: Reading Data from Files

In this exercise, we will read from a dataset. The example here uses the **diamonds** dataset:

1. Open a jupyter notebook and load the **pandas** and **seaborn** libraries:

    ```
    #Load pandas library
    import pandas as pd
    import seaborn as sns
    ```

2. Specify the URL of the dataset:

    ```
    #URL of the dataset
    diamonds_url = "https://raw.githubusercontent.com/TrainingByPackt/
    Interactive-Data-Visualization-with-Python/master/datasets/diamonds.
    csv"
    ```

3. Read files from the URL into the **pandas** DataFrame:

```
#Yes, we can read files from a URL straight into a pandas DataFrame!
diamonds_df = pd.read_csv(diamonds_url)
# Since the dataset is available in seaborn, we can alternatively
read it in using the following line of code
diamonds_df = sns.load_dataset('diamonds')
```

The dataset is read directly from the URL!

> **Note**
>
> Use the **usecols** parameter if only specific columns need to be read.

The syntax can be followed for other datatypes using, as shown here:

```
diamonds_df_specific_cols = pd.read_csv(diamonds_url,
usecols=['carat','cut','color','clarity'])
```

Observing and Describing Data

Now that we know how to read from a dataset, let's go ahead with observing and describing data from a dataset. **pandas** also offers a way to view the first few rows in a DataFrame using the **head()** function. By default, it shows **5** rows. To adjust that, we can use the argument **n**—for instance, **head(n=5)**.

Exercise 2: Observing and Describing Data

In this exercise, we'll see how to observe and describe data in a DataFrame. We'll be again using the **diamonds** dataset:

1. Load the **pandas** and **seaborn** libraries:

```
#Load pandas library
import pandas as pd
import seaborn as sns
```

2. Specify the URL of the dataset:

```
#URL of the dataset
diamonds_url = "https://raw.githubusercontent.com/TrainingByPackt/
Interactive-Data-Visualization-with-Python/master/datasets/diamonds.
csv"
```

3. Read files from the URL into the **pandas** DataFrame:

```
#Yes, we can read files from a URL straight into a pandas DataFrame!
diamonds_df = pd.read_csv(diamonds_url)
# Since the dataset is available in seaborn, we can alternatively
read it in using the following line of code
diamonds_df = sns.load_dataset('diamonds')
```

4. Observe the data by using the **head** function:

```
diamonds_df.head()
```

The output is as follows:

	carat	cut	color	clarity	depth	table	price	x	y	z
0	0.23	Ideal	E	SI2	61.5	55.0	326	3.95	3.98	2.43
1	0.21	Premium	E	SI1	59.8	61.0	326	3.89	3.84	2.31
2	0.23	Good	E	VS1	56.9	65.0	327	4.05	4.07	2.31
3	0.29	Premium	I	VS2	62.4	58.0	334	4.20	4.23	2.63
4	0.31	Good	J	SI2	63.3	58.0	335	4.34	4.35	2.75

Figure 1.1: Displaying the diamonds dataset

The data contains different features of diamonds, such as **carat**, **cut quality**, **color**, and **price**, as columns. Now, **cut**, **clarity**, and **color** are **categorical variables**, and **x**, **y**, **z**, **depth**, **table**, and **price** are **continuous variables**. While categorical variables take unique categories/names as values, continuous values take real numbers as values.

cut, **color**, and **clarity** are ordinal variables with **5**, **7**, and **8** unique values (can be obtained by **diamonds_df.cut.nunique()**, **diamonds_df.color. nunique()**, **diamonds_df.clarity.nunique()** – try it!), respectively. **cut** is the quality of the cut, described as **Fair**, **Good**, **Very Good**, **Premium**, or **Ideal**; **color** describes the diamond color from **J (worst)** to **D (best)**. There's also **clarity**, which measures how clear the diamond is–the degrees are **I1 (worst)**, **SI1**, **SI2**, **VS1**, **VS2**, **VVS1**, **VVS2**, and **IF (best)**.

5. Count the number of rows and columns in the DataFrame using the **shape** function:

```
diamonds_df.shape
```

The output is as follows:

```
(53940, 10)
```

The first number, **53940**, denotes the number of rows and the second, **10**, denotes the number of columns.

6. Summarize the columns using **describe()** to obtain the distribution of variables, including **mean**, **median**, **min**, **max**, and the different quartiles:

```
diamonds_df.describe()
```

The output is as follows:

	carat	depth	table	price	x	y	z
count	53940.000000	53940.000000	53940.000000	53940.000000	53940.000000	53940.000000	53940.000000
mean	0.797940	61.749405	57.457184	3932.799722	5.731157	5.734526	3.538734
std	0.474011	1.432621	2.234491	3989.439738	1.121761	1.142135	0.705699
min	0.200000	43.000000	43.000000	326.000000	0.000000	0.000000	0.000000
25%	0.400000	61.000000	56.000000	950.000000	4.710000	4.720000	2.910000
50%	0.700000	61.800000	57.000000	2401.000000	5.700000	5.710000	3.530000
75%	1.040000	62.500000	59.000000	5324.250000	6.540000	6.540000	4.040000
max	5.010000	79.000000	95.000000	18823.000000	10.740000	58.900000	31.800000

Figure 1.2: Using the describe function to show continuous variables

This works for continuous variables. However, for categorical variables, we need to use the **include=object** parameter.

7. Use **include=object** inside the **describe** function for categorical variables (**cut, color, clarity**):

```
diamonds_df.describe(include=object)
```

The output is as follows:

	cut	color	clarity
count	53940	53940	53940
unique	5	7	8
top	Ideal	G	SI1
freq	21551	11292	13065

Figure 1.3: Use the describe function to show categorical variables

Now, what if you would want to see the column types and how much memory a DataFrame occupies?

8. To obtain information on the dataset, use the **info()** method:

```
diamonds_df.info()
```

The output is as follows:

```
<class 'pandas.core.frame.DataFrame'>
RangeIndex: 53940 entries, 0 to 53939
Data columns (total 10 columns):
carat       53940 non-null float64
cut         53940 non-null object
color       53940 non-null object
clarity     53940 non-null object
depth       53940 non-null float64
table       53940 non-null float64
price       53940 non-null int64
x           53940 non-null float64
y           53940 non-null float64
z           53940 non-null float64
dtypes: float64(6), int64(1), object(3)
memory usage: 4.1+ MB
```

Figure 1.4: Information on the diamonds dataset

The preceding figure shows the data type (**float64**, **object**, **int64**..) of each of the columns, and memory (**4.1MB**) that the DataFrame occupies. It also tells the number of rows (**53940**) present in the DataFrame.

Selecting Columns from a DataFrame

Let's see how to select specific columns from a dataset. A column in a **pandas** DataFrame can be accessed in two simple ways: with the . operator or the [ ] operator. For example, we can access the **cut** column of the **diamonds_df** DataFrame with **diamonds_df.cut** or **diamonds_df['cut']**. However, there are some scenarios where the . operator cannot be used:

- When the column name contains spaces
- When the column name is an integer
- When creating a new column

Now, how about selecting all rows corresponding to diamonds that have the **Ideal** cut and storing them in a separate DataFrame? We can select them using the **loc** functionality:

```
diamonds_low_df = diamonds_df.loc[diamonds_df['cut']=='Ideal']

diamonds_low_df.head()
```

The output is as follows:

	carat	cut	color	clarity	depth	table	price	x	y	z
0	0.23	Ideal	E	SI2	61.5	55.0	326	3.95	3.98	2.43
11	0.23	Ideal	J	VS1	62.8	56.0	340	3.93	3.90	2.46
13	0.31	Ideal	J	SI2	62.2	54.0	344	4.35	4.37	2.71
16	0.30	Ideal	I	SI2	62.0	54.0	348	4.31	4.34	2.68
39	0.33	Ideal	I	SI2	61.8	55.0	403	4.49	4.51	2.78

Figure 1.5: Selecting specific columns from a DataFrame

Here, we obtain indices of rows that meet the criterion:

[diamonds_df['cut']=='Ideal' and then select them using **loc**.

Adding New Columns to a DataFrame

Now, we'll see how to add new columns to a DataFrame. We can add a column, such as, **price_per_carat**, in the **diamonds** DataFrame. We can divide the values of two columns and populate the data fields of the newly added column.

Exercise 3: Adding New Columns to the DataFrame

In this exercise, we are going to add new columns to the **diamonds** dataset in the **pandas** library. We'll start with the simple addition of columns and then move ahead and look into the conditional addition of columns. To do so, let's go through the following steps:

1. Load the **pandas** and **seaborn** libraries:

    ```
    #Load pandas library
    import pandas as pd
    import seaborn as sns
    ```

2. Specify the URL of the dataset:

    ```
    #URL of the dataset
    diamonds_url = "https://raw.githubusercontent.com/TrainingByPackt/
    Interactive-Data-Visualization-with-Python/master/datasets/diamonds.
    csv"
    ```

3. Read files from the URL into the **pandas** DataFrame:

    ```
    #Yes, we can read files from a URL straight into a pandas DataFrame!
    diamonds_df = pd.read_csv(diamonds_url)
    # Since the dataset is available in seaborn, we can alternatively
    read it in using the following line of code
    diamonds_df = sns.load_dataset('diamonds')
    ```

    Let's look at simple addition of columns.

4. Add a **price_per_carat** column to the DataFrame:

    ```
    diamonds_df['price_per_carat'] = diamonds_df['price']/diamonds_
    df['carat']
    ```

5. Call the DataFrame **head** function to check whether the new column was added as expected:

    ```
    diamonds_df.head()
    ```

    The output is as follows:

	carat	cut	color	clarity	depth	table	price	x	y	z	price_per_carat
0	0.23	Ideal	E	SI2	61.5	55.0	326	3.95	3.98	2.43	1417.391304
1	0.21	Premium	E	SI1	59.8	61.0	326	3.89	3.84	2.31	1552.380952
2	0.23	Good	E	VS1	56.9	65.0	327	4.05	4.07	2.31	1421.739130
3	0.29	Premium	I	VS2	62.4	58.0	334	4.20	4.23	2.63	1151.724138
4	0.31	Good	J	SI2	63.3	58.0	335	4.34	4.35	2.75	1080.645161

Figure 1.6: Simple addition of columns

Similarly, we can also use addition, subtraction, and other mathematical operators on two numeric columns.

Now, we'll look at *conditional addition of columns*. Let's try and add a column based on the value in **price_per_carat**, say anything more than **3500** as high (coded as **1**) and anything less than **3500** as low (coded as **0**).

6. Use the **np.where** function from Python's **numpy** package:

```
#Import numpy package for linear algebra
import numpy as np
diamonds_df['price_per_carat_is_high'] = np.where(diamonds_
df['price_per_carat']>3500,1,0)
diamonds_df.head()
```

The output is as follows:

	carat	cut	color	clarity	depth	table	price	x	y	z	price_per_carat	price_per_carat_is_high
0	0.23	Ideal	E	SI2	61.5	55.0	326	3.95	3.98	2.43	1417.391304	0
1	0.21	Premium	E	SI1	59.8	61.0	326	3.89	3.84	2.31	1552.380952	0
2	0.23	Good	E	VS1	56.9	65.0	327	4.05	4.07	2.31	1421.739130	0
3	0.29	Premium	I	VS2	62.4	58.0	334	4.20	4.23	2.63	1151.724138	0
4	0.31	Good	J	SI2	63.3	58.0	335	4.34	4.35	2.75	1080.645161	0

Figure 1.7: Conditional addition of columns

Therefore, we have successfully added two new columns to the dataset.

Applying Functions on DataFrame Columns

You can apply *simple functions* on a DataFrame column—such as, addition, subtraction, multiplication, division, squaring, raising to an exponent, and so on. It is also possible to apply more *complex functions* on single and multiple columns in a **pandas** DataFrame. As an example, let's say we want to round off the price of diamonds to its ceil (nearest integer equal to or higher than the actual price). Let's explore this through an exercise.

Exercise 4: Applying Functions on DataFrame columns

In this exercise, we'll consider a scenario where the price of diamonds has increased and we want to apply an increment factor of **1.3** to the price of all the diamonds in our record. We can achieve this by applying a simple function. Next, we'll round off the price of diamonds to its ceil. We'll achieve that by applying a complex function.Let's go through the following steps:

1. Load the **pandas** and **seaborn** libraries:

    ```
    #Load pandas library
    import pandas as pd
    import seaborn as sns
    ```

2. Specify the URL of the dataset:

    ```
    #URL of the dataset
    diamonds_url = "https://raw.githubusercontent.com/TrainingByPackt/
    Interactive-Data-Visualization-with-Python/master/datasets/diamonds.
    csv"
    ```

3. Read files from the URL into the **pandas** DataFrame:

    ```
    #Yes, we can read files from a URL straight into a pandas DataFrame!
    diamonds_df = pd.read_csv(diamonds_url)
    # Since the dataset is available in seaborn, we can alternatively
    read it in using the following line of code
    diamonds_df = sns.load_dataset('diamonds')
    ```

4. Add a **price_per_carat** column to the DataFrame:

    ```
    diamonds_df['price_per_carat'] = diamonds_df['price']/diamonds_
    df['carat']
    ```

5. Use the **np.where** function from Python's **numpy** package:

    ```
    #Import numpy package for linear algebra
    import numpy as np
    diamonds_df['price_per_carat_is_high'] = np.where(diamonds_
    df['price_per_carat']>3500,1,0)
    ```

6. Apply a simple function on the columns using the following code:

    ```
    diamonds_df['price']= diamonds_df['price']*1.3
    ```

7. Apply a complex function to round off the price of diamonds to its ceil:

    ```
    import math
    diamonds_df['rounded_price']=diamonds_df['price'].apply(math.ceil)
    diamonds_df.head()
    ```

The output is as follows:

	carat	cut	color	clarity	depth	table	price	x	y	z	price_per_carat	price_per_carat_is_high	rounded_price
0	0.23	Ideal	E	SI2	61.5	55.0	423.8	3.95	3.98	2.43	1417.391304	0	424
1	0.21	Premium	E	SI1	59.8	61.0	423.8	3.89	3.84	2.31	1552.380952	0	424
2	0.23	Good	E	VS1	56.9	65.0	425.1	4.05	4.07	2.31	1421.739130	0	426
3	0.29	Premium	I	VS2	62.4	58.0	434.2	4.20	4.23	2.63	1151.724138	0	435
4	0.31	Good	J	SI2	63.3	58.0	435.5	4.34	4.35	2.75	1080.645161	0	436

Figure 1.8: Dataset after applying simple and complex functions

In this case, the function we wanted for rounding off to the ceil was already present in an existing library. However, there might be times when you have to write your own function to perform the task you want to accomplish. In the case of small functions, you can also use the **lambda** operator, which acts as a one-liner function taking an argument. For example, say you want to add another column to the DataFrame indicating the rounded-off price of the diamonds to the nearest multiple of **100** (equal to or higher than the price).

8. Use the **lambda** function as follows to round off the price of the diamonds to the nearest multiple of **100**:

    ```
    import math
    diamonds_df['rounded_price_to_100multiple']=diamonds_df['price'].
    apply(lambda x: math.ceil(x/100)*100)
    diamonds_df.head()
    ```

The output is as follows:

	carat	cut	color	clarity	depth	table	price	x	y	z	price_per_carat	price_per_carat_is_high	rounded_price	rounded_price_to_100multiple
0	0.23	Ideal	E	SI2	61.5	55.0	423.8	3.95	3.98	2.43	1417.391304	0	424	500
1	0.21	Premium	E	SI1	59.8	61.0	423.8	3.89	3.84	2.31	1552.380952	0	424	500
2	0.23	Good	E	VS1	56.9	65.0	425.1	4.05	4.07	2.31	1421.739130	0	426	500
3	0.29	Premium	I	VS2	62.4	58.0	434.2	4.20	4.23	2.63	1151.724138	0	435	500
4	0.31	Good	J	SI2	63.3	58.0	435.5	4.34	4.35	2.75	1080.645161	0	436	500

Figure 1.9: Dataset after applying the lambda function

Of book, not all functions can be written as one-liners and it is important to know how to include user-defined functions in the **apply** function. Let's write the same code with a *user-defined function* for illustration.

9. Write code to create a user-defined function to round off the price of the diamonds to the nearest multiple of **100**:

```
import math

def get_100_multiple_ceil(x):
    y = math.ceil(x/100)*100
    return y

diamonds_df['rounded_price_to_100multiple']=diamonds_df['price'].
apply(get_100_multiple_ceil)
diamonds_df.head()
```

The output is as follows:

	carat	cut	color	clarity	depth	table	price	x	y	z	price_per_carat	price_per_carat_is_high	rounded_price	rounded_price_to_100multiple
0	0.23	Ideal	E	SI2	61.5	55.0	423.8	3.95	3.98	2.43	1417.391304	0	424	500
1	0.21	Premium	E	SI1	59.8	61.0	423.8	3.89	3.84	2.31	1552.380952	0	424	500
2	0.23	Good	E	VS1	56.9	65.0	425.1	4.05	4.07	2.31	1421.739130	0	426	500
3	0.29	Premium	I	VS2	62.4	58.0	434.2	4.20	4.23	2.63	1151.724138	0	435	500
4	0.31	Good	J	SI2	63.3	58.0	435.5	4.34	4.35	2.75	1080.645161	0	436	500

Figure 1.10: Dataset after applying a user-defined function

Interesting! Now, we had created an user-defined function to add a column to the dataset.

Exercise 5: Applying Functions on Multiple Columns

When applying a function on multiple columns of a DataFrame, we can similarly use **lambda** or user-defined functions. We will continue to use the **diamonds** dataset. Suppose we are interested in buying diamonds that have an **Ideal** cut and a **color** of **D** (entirely colorless). This exercise is for adding a new column, **desired** to the DataFrame, whose value will be **yes** if our criteria are satisfied and **no** if not satisfied. Let's see how we do it:

1. Import the necessary modules:

```
import seaborn as sns
import pandas as pd
```

2. Import the **diamonds** dataset from **seaborn**:

```
diamonds_df_exercise = sns.load_dataset('diamonds')
```

3. Write a function to determine whether a record, **x**, is desired or not:

```
def is_desired(x):
    bool_var = 'yes' if (x['cut']=='Ideal' and x['color']=='D') else
'no'
    return bool_var
```

4. Use the **apply** function to add the new column, **desired**:

```
diamonds_df_exercise['desired']=diamonds_df_exercise.apply(is_
desired, axis=1)
diamonds_df_exercise.head()
```

The output is as follows:

	carat	cut	color	clarity	depth	table	price	x	y	z	desired
0	0.23	Ideal	E	SI2	61.5	55.0	326	3.95	3.98	2.43	no
1	0.21	Premium	E	SI1	59.8	61.0	326	3.89	3.84	2.31	no
2	0.23	Good	E	VS1	56.9	65.0	327	4.05	4.07	2.31	no
3	0.29	Premium	I	VS2	62.4	58.0	334	4.20	4.23	2.63	no
4	0.31	Good	J	SI2	63.3	58.0	335	4.34	4.35	2.75	no

Figure 1.11: Dataset after applying the function on multiple columns

The new column **desired** is added!

Deleting Columns from a DataFrame

Finally, let's see how to delete columns from a **pandas** DataFrame. For example, we will delete the **rounded_price** and **rounded_price_to_100multiple** columns. Let's go through the following exercise.

Exercise 6: Deleting Columns from a DataFrame

In this exercise, we will delete columns from a **pandas** DataFrame. Here, we'll be using the **diamonds** dataset:

1. Import the necessary modules:

```
import seaborn as sns
import pandas as pd
```

2. Import the **diamonds** dataset from **seaborn**:

```
diamonds_df = sns.load_dataset('diamonds')
```

3. Add a **price_per_carat** column to the DataFrame:

```
diamonds_df['price_per_carat'] = diamonds_df['price']/diamonds_
df['carat']
```

4. Use the **np.where** function from Python's **numpy** package:

```
#Import numpy package for linear algebra
import numpy as np
diamonds_df['price_per_carat_is_high'] = np.where(diamonds_
df['price_per_carat']>3500,1,0)
```

5. Apply a *complex function* to round off the price of diamonds to its ceil:

```
import math
diamonds_df['rounded_price']=diamonds_df['price'].apply(math.ceil)
```

6. Write a code to create a *user-defined function*:

```
import math

def get_100_multiple_ceil(x):
    y = math.ceil(x/100)*100
    return y

diamonds_df['rounded_price_to_100multiple']=diamonds_df['price'].
apply(get_100_multiple_ceil)
```

7. Delete the **rounded_price** and **rounded_price_to_100multiple** columns using the **drop** function:

```
diamonds_df=diamonds_df.drop(columns=['rounded_price', 'rounded_
price_to_100multiple'])
diamonds_df.head()
```

The output is as follows:

	carat	cut	color	clarity	depth	table	price	x	y	z	price_per_carat	price_per_carat_is_high
0	0.23	Ideal	E	SI2	61.5	55.0	326	3.95	3.98	2.43	1417.391304	0
1	0.21	Premium	E	SI1	59.8	61.0	326	3.89	3.84	2.31	1552.380952	0
2	0.23	Good	E	VS1	56.9	65.0	327	4.05	4.07	2.31	1421.739130	0
3	0.29	Premium	I	VS2	62.4	58.0	334	4.20	4.23	2.63	1151.724138	0
4	0.31	Good	J	SI2	63.3	58.0	335	4.34	4.35	2.75	1080.645161	0

Figure 1.12: Dataset after deleting columns

> **Note**
>
> By default, when the **apply** or **drop** function is used on a **pandas** DataFrame, the original DataFrame is not modified. Rather, a copy of the DataFrame post modifications is returned by the functions. Therefore, you should assign the returned value back to the variable containing the DataFrame (for example, **diamonds_df=diamonds_df.drop(columns=['rounded_price', 'rounded_price_to_100multiple'])**).
>
> In the case of the **drop** function, there is also a provision to avoid assignment by setting an **inplace=True** parameter, wherein the function performs the column deletion on the original DataFrame and does not return anything.

Writing a DataFrame to a File

The last thing to do is write a DataFrame to a file. We will be using the **to_csv()** function. The output is usually a **.csv** file that will include column and row headers. Let's see how to write our DataFrame to a **.csv** file.

Exercise 7: Writing a DataFrame to a File

In this exercise, we will write a **diamonds** DataFrame to a **.csv** file. To do so, we'll be using the following code:

1. Import the necessary modules:

```
import seaborn as sns
import pandas as pd
```

2. Load the **diamonds** dataset from **seaborn**:

```
diamonds_df = sns.load_dataset('diamonds')
```

3. Write the diamonds dataset into a .csv file:

```
diamonds_df.to_csv('diamonds_modified.csv')
```

4. Let's look at the first few rows of the DataFrame:

```
print(diamonds_df.head())
```

The output is as follows:

```
   carat      cut color clarity  depth  table  price     x     y     z
0   0.23    Ideal     E     SI2   61.5   55.0    326  3.95  3.98  2.43
1   0.21  Premium     E     SI1   59.8   61.0    326  3.89  3.84  2.31
2   0.23     Good     E     VS1   56.9   65.0    327  4.05  4.07  2.31
3   0.29  Premium     I     VS2   62.4   58.0    334  4.20  4.23  2.63
4   0.31     Good     J     SI2   63.3   58.0    335  4.34  4.35  2.75
```

Figure 1.13: The generated .csv file in the source folder

By default, the **to_csv** function outputs a file that includes column headers as well as row numbers. Generally, the row numbers are not desirable, and an **index** parameter is used to exclude them:

5. Add a parameter **index=False** to exclude the row numbers:

```
diamonds_df.to_csv('diamonds_modified.csv', index=False)
```

And that's it! You can find this **.csv** file in the source directory. You are now equipped to perform all the basic functions on **pandas** DataFrames required to get started with data visualization in Python.

In order to prepare the ground for using various visualization techniques, we went through the following aspects of handling **pandas** DataFrames:

- Reading data from files using the **read_csv( )**, **read_excel( )**, and **readjson( )** functions

- Observing and describing data using the **dataframe.head( )**, **dataframe.tail( )**, **dataframe.describe( )**, and **dataframe.info( )** functions

- Selecting columns using the **dataframe.column__name** or **dataframe['column__name']** notation

- Adding new columns using the **dataframe['newcolumnname']=...** notation

- Applying functions to existing columns using the **dataframe.apply(func)** function

- Deleting columns from DataFrames using the `_dataframe.drop(column_list)` function

- Writing DataFrames to files using the `_dataframe.tocsv()` function

These functions are useful for preparing data in a format suitable for input to visualization functions in Python libraries such as **seaborn**.

Plotting with pandas and seaborn

Now that we have a basic sense of how to load and handle data in a **pandas** DataFrame object, let's get started with making some simple plots from data. While there are several plotting libraries in Python (including **matplotlib**, **plotly**, and **seaborn**), in this chapter, we will mainly explore the **pandas** and **seaborn** libraries, which are extremely useful, popular, and easy to use.

Creating Simple Plots to Visualize a Distribution of Variables

matplotlib is a plotting library available in most Python distributions and is the foundation for several plotting packages, including the built-in plotting functionality of **pandas** and **seaborn**. **matplotlib** enables control of every single aspect of a figure and is known to be verbose. Both **seaborn** and **pandas** visualization functions are built on top of **matplotlib**. The built-in plotting tool of **pandas** .is a useful exploratory tool to generate figures that are not ready for primetime but useful to understand the dataset you are working with. **seaborn**, on the other hand, has APIs to draw a wide variety of aesthetically pleasing plots.

To illustrate certain key concepts and explore the **diamonds** dataset, we will start with two simple visualizations in this chapter—histograms and bar plots.

Histograms

A histogram of a feature is a plot with the range of the feature on the x-axis and the count of data points with the feature in the corresponding range on the y-axis.

Let's look at the following exercise of plotting a histogram with **pandas**.

Exercise 8: Plotting and Analyzing a Histogram

In this exercise, we will create a histogram of the frequency of diamonds in the dataset with their respective **carat** specifications on the *x*-axis:

1. Import the necessary modules:

```
import seaborn as sns
import pandas as pd
```

2. Import the **diamonds** dataset from **seaborn**:

```
diamonds_df = sns.load_dataset('diamonds')
```

3. Plot a histogram using the **diamonds** dataset where **x axis = carat**:

```
diamonds_df.hist(column='carat')
```

The output is as follows:

```
array([[<matplotlib.axes._subplots.AxesSubplot object at 0x00000216D76A8DD8>]],
      dtype=object)
```

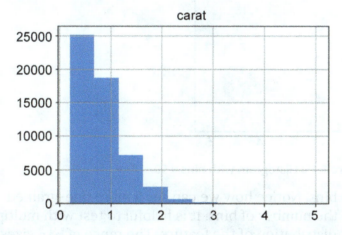

Figure 1.14: Histogram plot

The y axis in this plot denotes the number of diamonds in the dataset with the **carat** specification on the x-axis.

The **hist** function has a parameter called **bins**, which literally refers to the number of equally sized **bins** into which the data points are divided. By default, the bins parameter is set to **10** in **pandas**. We can change this to a different number, if we wish.

4. Change the **bins** parameter to **50**:

```
diamonds_df.hist(column='carat', bins=50)
```

The output is as follows:

```
array([[<matplotlib.axes._subplots.AxesSubplot object at 0x00000216D79E7898>]],
      dtype=object)
```

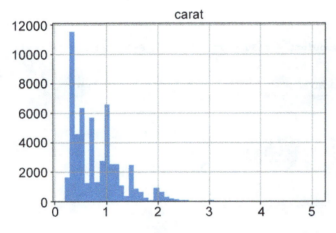

Figure 1.15: Histogram with bins = 50

This is a histogram with **50** bins. Notice how we can see a more fine-grained distribution as we increase the number of bins. It is helpful to test with multiple bin sizes to know the exact distribution of the feature. The range of **bin** sizes varies from **1** (where all values are in the same bin) to the number of values (where each value of the feature is in one bin).

5. Now, let's look at the same function using **seaborn**:

```
sns.distplot(diamonds_df.carat)
```

The output is as follows:

```
<matplotlib.axes._subplots.AxesSubplot at 0x216d7f01a58>
```

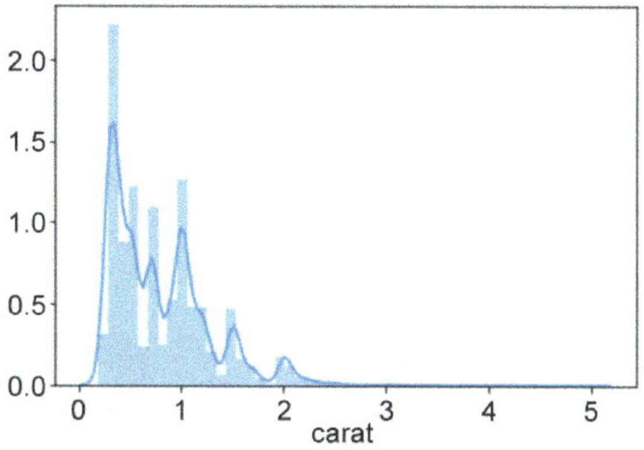

Figure 1.16: Histogram plot using seaborn

There are two noticeable differences between the **pandas hist** function and **seaborn distplot**:

- **pandas** sets the **bins** parameter to a default of **10**, but **seaborn** infers an appropriate bin size based on the statistical distribution of the dataset.

- By default, the **distplot** function also includes a smoothed curve over the histogram, called a **kernel density estimation**.

  The **kernel density estimation** (**KDE**) is a non-parametric way to estimate the probability density function of a random variable. Usually, a KDE doesn't tell us anything more than what we can infer from the histogram itself. However, it is helpful when comparing multiple histograms on the same plot. If we want to remove the KDE and look at the histogram alone, we can use the **kde=False** parameter.

6. Change **kde=False** to remove the KDE:

   ```
   sns.distplot(diamonds_df.carat, kde=False)
   ```

The output is as follows:

```
<matplotlib.axes._subplots.AxesSubplot at 0x216d800e390>
```

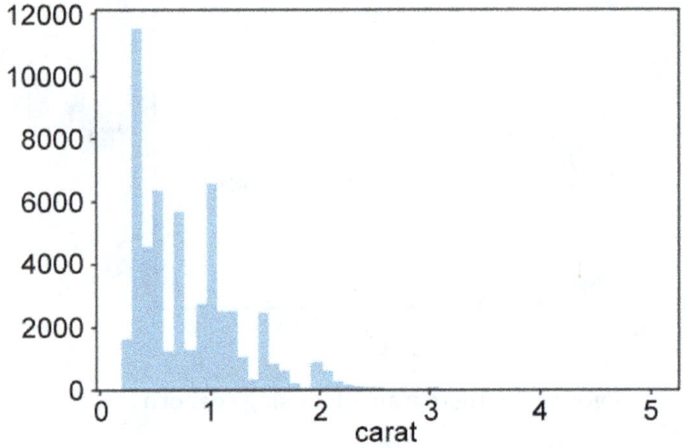

Figure 1.17: Histogram plot with KDE = false

Also note that the **bins** parameter seemed to render a more detailed plot when the bin size was increased from **10** to **50**. Now, let's try to increase it to 100.

7. Increase the **bins** size to **100**:

```
sns.distplot(diamonds_df.carat, kde=False, bins=100)
```

The output is as follows:

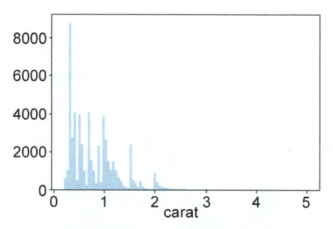

<matplotlib.axes._subplots.AxesSubplot at 0x216d80d35c0>

Figure 1.18: Histogram plot with increased bin size

The histogram with **100** bins shows a better visualization of the distribution of the variable—we see there are several peaks at specific carat values. Another observation is that most **carat** values are concentrated toward lower values and the **tail** is on the right—in other words, it is right-skewed.

A log transformation helps in identifying more trends. For instance, in the following graph, the x-axis shows log-transformed values of the **price** variable, and we see that there are two peaks indicating two kinds of diamonds—one with a high price and another with a low price.

8. Use a log transformation on the histogram:

```
import numpy as np
sns.distplot(np.log(diamonds_df.price), kde=False)
```

The output is as follows:

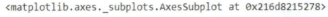

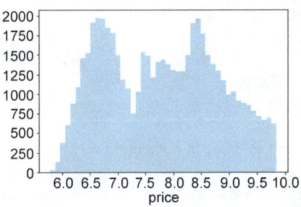

Figure 1.19: Histogram using a log transformation

That's pretty neat. Looking at the histogram, even a naive viewer immediately gets a picture of the distribution of the feature. Specifically, three observations are important in a histogram:

- Which feature values are more frequent in the dataset (in this case, there is a peak at around 6.8 and another peak between **8.5** and **9**—note that **log(price) = values**, in this case,

- How many *peaks* exist in the data (the peaks need to be further inspected for possible causes in the context of the data)

- Whether there are any outliers in the data

Bar Plots

Another type of plot we will look at in this chapter is the bar plot.

In their simplest form, *bar plots* display counts of categorical variables. More broadly, bar plots are used to depict the relationship between a categorical variable and a numerical variable. Histograms, meanwhile, are plots that show the statistical distribution of a continuous numerical feature.

Let's see an exercise of bar plots in the **diamonds** dataset. First, we shall present the counts of diamonds of each cut quality that exist in the data. Second, we shall look at the price associated with the different types of cut quality (**Ideal**, **Good**, **Premium**, and so on) in the dataset and find out the mean price distribution. We will use both **pandas** and **seaborn** to get a sense of how to use the built-in plotting functions in both libraries.

Before generating the plots, let's look at the unique values in the **cut** and **clarity** columns, just to refresh our memory.

Exercise 9: Creating a Bar Plot and Calculating the Mean Price Distribution

In this exercise, we'll learn how to create a table using the **pandas crosstab** function. We'll use a table to generate a bar plot. We'll then explore a bar plot generated using the **seaborn** library and calculate the mean price distribution. To do so, let's go through the following steps:

1. Import the necessary modules and dataset:

   ```
   import seaborn as sns
   import pandas as pd
   ```

2. Import the **diamonds** dataset from **seaborn**:

   ```
   diamonds_df = sns.load_dataset('diamonds')
   ```

3. Print the unique values of the **cut** column:

   ```
   diamonds_df.cut.unique()
   ```

   The output will be as follows:

   ```
   array(['Ideal', 'Premium', 'Good', 'Very Good', 'Fair'],
   dtype=object)
   ```

4. Print the unique values of the **clarity** column:

    ```
    diamonds_df.clarity.unique()
    ```

    The output will be as follows:

    ```
    array(['SI2', 'SI1', 'VS1', 'VS2', 'VVS2', 'VVS1', 'I1', 'IF'],
            dtype=object)
    ```

    > **Note**
    >
    > **unique()** returns an array. There are five unique **cut** qualities and eight unique values in **clarity**. The number of unique values can be obtained using **nunique()** in **pandas**.

5. To obtain the counts of diamonds of each cut quality, we first create a table using the **pandas crosstab()** function:

    ```
    cut_count_table = pd.crosstab(index=diamonds_
    df['cut'],columns='count')
    cut_count_table
    ```

    The output will be as follows:

col_0	count
cut	
Fair	1610
Good	4906
Ideal	21551
Premium	13791
Very Good	12082

Figure 1.20: Table using the crosstab function

6. Pass these counts to another **pandas** function, **plot(kind='bar')**:

    ```
    cut_count_table.plot(kind='bar')
    ```

    The output will be as follows:

    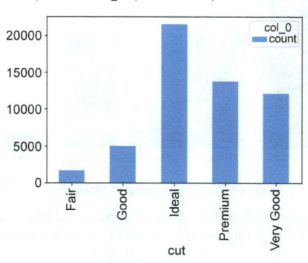

Figure 1.21: Bar plot using a pandas DataFrame

We see that most of the diamonds in the dataset are of the **Ideal** cut quality, followed by **Premium**, **Very Good**, **Good**, and **Fair**. Now, let's see how to generate the same plot using **seaborn**.

7. Generate the same bar plot using **seaborn**:

    ```
    sns.catplot("cut", data=diamonds_df, aspect=1.5, kind="count",
    color="b")
    ```

The output will be as follows:

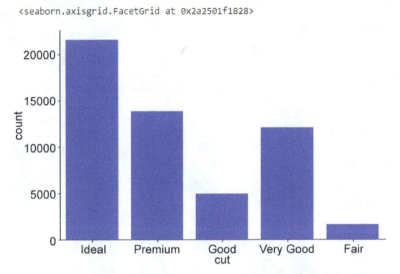

<seaborn.axisgrid.FacetGrid at 0x2a2501f1828>

Figure 1.22: Bar plot using seaborn

Notice how the **catplot()** function does not require us to create the intermediate count table (using **pd.crosstab()**), and reduces one step in the plotting process.

8. Next, here is how we obtain the mean price distribution of different cut qualities using **seaborn**:

```
import seaborn as sns
from numpy import median, mean
sns.set(style="whitegrid")
ax = sns.barplot(x="cut", y="price", data=diamonds_
df,estimator=mean)
```

The output will be as follows:

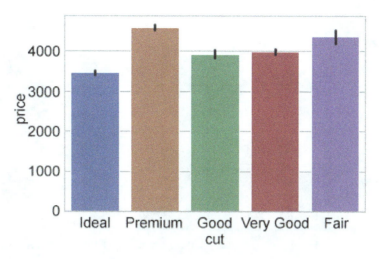

Figure 1.23: Bar plot with the mean price distribution

Here, the black lines (*error bars*) on the rectangles indicate the uncertainty (or spread of values) around the mean estimate. By default, this value is set to **95%** confidence. How do we change it? We use the **ci=68** parameter, for instance, to set it to **68%**. We can also plot the standard deviation in the prices using **ci=sd**.

9. Reorder the *x* axis bars using **order**:

    ```
    ax = sns.barplot(x="cut", y="price", data=diamonds_
    df, estimator=mean, ci=68, order=['Ideal','Good','Very
    Good','Fair','Premium'])
    ```

The output will be as follows:

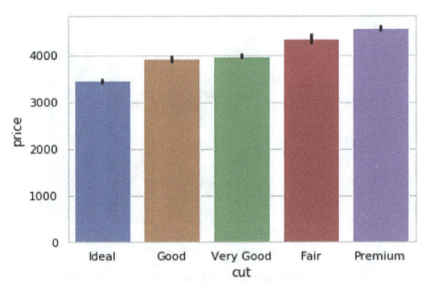

Figure 1.24: Bar plot with proper order

Grouped bar plots can be very useful for visualizing the variation of a particular feature within different groups. Now that you have looked into tweaking the plot parameters in a grouped bar plot, let's see how to generate a bar plot grouped by a specific feature.

Exercise 10: Creating Bar Plots Grouped by a Specific Feature

In this exercise, we will use the **diamonds** dataset to generate the distribution of prices with respect to **color** for each **cut** quality. In *Exercise 9, Creating a Bar Plot and Calculating the Mean Price Distribution*, we looked at the price distribution for diamonds of different cut qualities. Now, we would like to look at the variation in each color:

1. Import the necessary modules—in this case, only **seaborn**:

    ```
    #Import seaborn
    import seaborn as sns
    ```

2. Load the dataset:

    ```
    diamonds_df = sns.load_dataset('diamonds')
    ```

3. Use the **hue** parameter to plot nested groups:

```
ax = sns.barplot(x="cut", y="price", hue='color', data=diamonds_df)
```

The output is as follows:

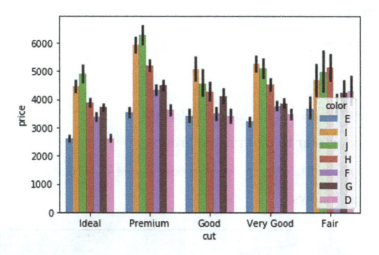

Figure 1.25: Grouped bar plot with legends

Here, we can observe that the price patterns for diamonds of different colors are similar for each cut quality. For instance, for **Ideal** diamonds, the price distribution of diamonds of different colors is the same as that for **Premium**, and other diamonds.

Tweaking Plot Parameters

Looking at the last figure in our previous section, we find that the legend is not appropriately placed. We can tweak the plot parameters to adjust the placements of the legends and the axis labels, as well as change the font-size and rotation of the tick labels.

Exercise 11: Tweaking the Plot Parameters of a Grouped Bar Plot

In this exercise, we'll tweak the plot parameters, for example, **hue**, of a grouped bar plot. We'll see how to place legends and axis labels in the right places and also explore the rotation feature:

1. Import the necessary modules—in this case, only **seaborn**:

   ```
   #Import seaborn
   import seaborn as sns
   ```

2. Load the dataset:

   ```
   diamonds_df = sns.load_dataset('diamonds')
   ```

3. Use the **hue** parameter to plot nested groups:

   ```
   ax = sns.barplot(x="cut", y="price", hue='color', data=diamonds_df)
   ```

   The output is as follows:

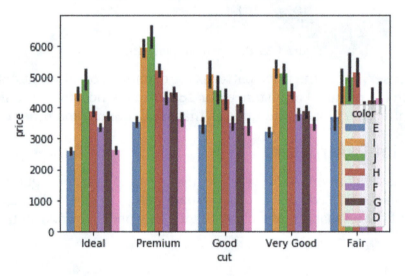

Figure 1.26: Nested bar plot with the hue parameter

4. Place the legend appropriately on the bar plot:

```
ax = sns.barplot(x='cut', y='price', hue='color', data=diamonds_df)
ax.legend(loc='upper right',ncol=4)
```

The output is as follows:

```
<matplotlib.legend.Legend at 0x1d1d7320400>
```

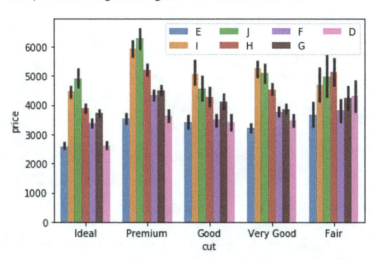

Figure 1.27: Grouped bar plot with legends placed appropriately

In the preceding **ax.legend()** call, the **ncol** parameter denotes the number of columns into which values in the legend are to be organized, and the **loc** parameter specifies the location of the legend and can take any one of eight values (*upper left*, *lower center*, and so on).

5. To modify the axis labels on the *x* axis and *y* axis, input the following code:

```
ax = sns.barplot(x='cut', y='price', hue='color', data=diamonds_df)
ax.legend(loc='upper right', ncol=4)
ax.set_xlabel('Cut', fontdict={'fontsize' : 15})
ax.set_ylabel('Price', fontdict={'fontsize' : 15})
```

The output is as follows:

```
Text(0, 0.5, 'Price')
```

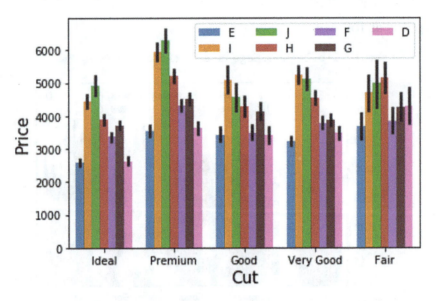

Figure 1.28: Grouped bar plot with modified labels

6. Similarly, use this to modify the font-size and rotation of the *x* axis of the tick labels:

```
ax = sns.barplot(x='cut', y='price', hue='color', data=diamonds_df)
ax.legend(loc='upper right',ncol=4)
# set fontsize and rotation of x-axis tick labels
ax.set_xticklabels(ax.get_xticklabels(), fontsize=13, rotation=30)
```

The output is as follows:

```
[Text(0, 0, 'Ideal'),
 Text(0, 0, 'Premium'),
 Text(0, 0, 'Good'),
 Text(0, 0, 'Very Good'),
 Text(0, 0, 'Fair')]
```

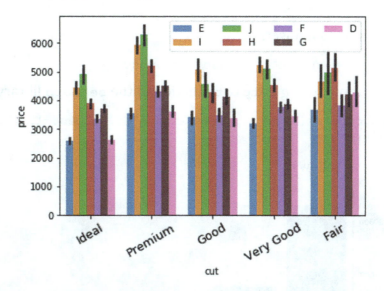

Figure 1.29: Grouped bar plot with the rotation feature of the labels

The *rotation feature* is particularly useful when the tick labels are long and crowd up together on the *x* axis.

Annotations

Another useful feature to have in plots is the annotation feature. In the following exercise, we'll make a simple bar plot more informative by adding some annotations. Suppose we want to add more information to the plot about *ideally* cut diamonds. We can do this in the following exercise:

Exercise 12: Annotating a Bar Plot

In this exercise, we will annotate a bar plot, generated using the `catplot` function of `seaborn`, using a note right above the plot. Let's see how:

1. Import the necessary modules:

    ```
    import matplotlib.pyplot as plt
    import seaborn as sns
    ```

2. Load the **diamonds** dataset:

    ```
    diamonds_df = sns.load_dataset('diamonds')
    ```

3. Generate a bar plot using **catplot** function of the **seaborn** library:

    ```
    ax = sns.catplot("cut", data=diamonds_df, aspect=1.5, kind="count",
    color="b")
    ```

    The output is as follows:

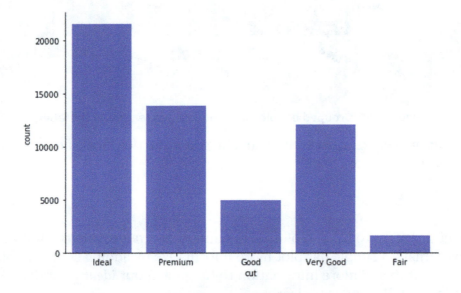

Figure 1.30: Bar plot with seaborn's catplot function

4. Annotate the column belonging to the **Ideal** category:

    ```
    # get records in the DataFrame corresponding to ideal cut
    ideal_group = diamonds_df.loc[diamonds_df['cut']=='Ideal']
    ```

5. Find the location of the *x* coordinate where the annotation has to be placed:

    ```
    # get the location of x coordinate where the annotation has to be
    placed
    x = ideal_group.index.tolist()[0]
    ```

6. Find the location of the *y* coordinate where the annotation has to be placed:

```
# get the location of y coordinate where the annotation has to be
placed
y = len(ideal_group)
```

7. Print the location of the *x* and *y* co-ordinates:

```
print(x)
print(y)
```

The output is:

```
0
21551
```

8. Annotate the plot with a note:

```
# annotate the plot with any note or extra information
sns.catplot("cut", data=diamonds_df, aspect=1.5, kind="count",
color="b")
plt.annotate('excellent polish and symmetry ratings;\nreflects almost
all the light that enters it', xy=(x,y), xytext=(x+0.3, y+2000),
arrowprops=dict(facecolor='red'))
```

The output is as follows:

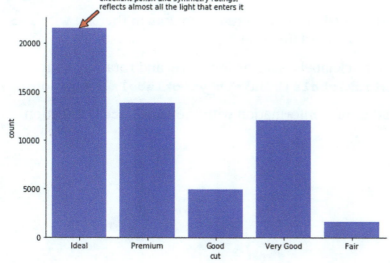

Figure 1.31: Annotated bar plot

Now, there seem to be a lot of parameters in the **annotate** function, but worry not! Matplotlib's https://matplotlib.org/3.1.0/api/_as_gen/matplotlib.pyplot.annotate.html official documentation covers all the details. For instance, the **xy** parameter denotes the point (**x,y**) on the figure to annotate. **xytext** denotes the position (x,y) to place the text at. If **None**, it defaults to **xy**. Note that we added an offset of **.3** for x and **2000** for y (since y is close to **20,000**) for the sake of readability of the text. The color of the arrow is specified using the **arrowprops** parameter in the **annotate** function.

There are several other bells and whistles associated with visualization libraries in Python, some of which we will see as we progress in the book. At this stage, we will go through a chapter activity to revise the concepts in this chapter.

So far, we have seen how to generate two simple plots using **seaborn** and **pandas**– histograms and bar plots:

- **Histograms**: Histograms are useful for understanding the statistical distribution of a numerical feature in a given dataset. They can be generated using the **hist()** function in **pandas** and **distplot()** in **seaborn**.

- **Bar plots**: Bar plots are useful for gaining insight into the values taken by a categorical feature in a given dataset. They can be generated using the **plot(kind='bar')** function in **pandas** and the **catplot(kind='count')**, and **barplot()** functions in **seaborn**.

With the help of various considerations arising in the process of plotting these two types of visualizations, we presented some basic concepts in data visualization:

- Formatting legends to present labels for different elements in the plot with **loc** and other parameters in the **legend** function

- Changing the properties of tick labels, such as font-size, and rotation, with parameters in the **set_xticklabels()** and **set_yticklabels()** functions

- Adding annotations for additional information with the **annotate()** function

Activity 1: Analyzing Different Scenarios and Generating the Appropriate Visualization

We'll be working with the **120 years of Olympic History** dataset acquired by Randi Griffin from https://www.sports-reference.com/ and made available on the GitHub repository of this book. Your assignment is to identify the top five sports based on the largest number of medals awarded in the year 2016, and then perform the following analysis:

1. Generate a plot indicating the number of medals awarded in each of the top five sports in 2016.

2. Plot a graph depicting the distribution of the age of medal winners in the top five sports in 2016.

3. Find out which national teams won the largest number of medals in the top five sports in 2016.

4. Observe the trend in the average weight of male and female athletes winning in the top five sports in 2016.

High-Level Steps

1. Download the dataset and format it as a pandas DataFrame.

2. Filter the DataFrame to only include the rows corresponding to medal winners from 2016.

3. Find out the medals awarded in 2016 for each sport.

4. List the top five sports based on the largest number of medals awarded. Filter the DataFrame one more time to only include the records for the top five sports in 2016.

5. Generate a bar plot of record counts corresponding to each of the top five sports.

6. Generate a histogram for the **Age** feature of all medal winners in the top five sports (2016).

7. Generate a bar plot indicating how many medals were won by each country's team in the top five sports in 2016.

8. Generate a bar plot indicating the average weight of players, categorized based on gender, winning in the top five sports in 2016.

The expected output should be:

After Step 1:

	ID	Name	Sex	Age	Height	Weight	Team	NOC	Games	Year	Season	City	Sport	Event	Medal
0	1	A Dijiang	M	24.0	180.0	80.0	China	CHN	1992 Summer	1992	Summer	Barcelona	Basketball	Basketball Men's Basketball	NaN
1	2	A Lamusi	M	23.0	170.0	60.0	China	CHN	2012 Summer	2012	Summer	London	Judo	Judo Men's Extra-Lightweight	NaN
2	3	Gunnar Nielsen Aaby	M	24.0	NaN	NaN	Denmark	DEN	1920 Summer	1920	Summer	Antwerpen	Football	Football Men's Football	NaN
3	4	Edgar Lindenau Aabye	M	34.0	NaN	NaN	Denmark/Sweden	DEN	1900 Summer	1900	Summer	Paris	Tug-Of-War	Tug-Of-War Men's Tug-Of-War	Gold
4	5	Christine Jacoba Aaftink	F	21.0	185.0	82.0	Netherlands	NED	1988 Winter	1988	Winter	Calgary	Speed Skating	Speed Skating Women's 500 metres	NaN

Figure 1.32: Olympics dataset

After Step 2:

	ID	Name	Sex	Age	Height	Weight	Team	NOC	Games	Year	Season	City	Sport	Event	Medal
3	4	Edgar Lindenau Aabye	M	34.0	NaN	NaN	Denmark/Sweden	DEN	1900 Summer	1900	Summer	Paris	Tug-Of-War	Tug-Of-War Men's Tug-Of-War	Gold
37	15	Arvo Ossian Aaltonen	M	30.0	NaN	NaN	Finland	FIN	1920 Summer	1920	Summer	Antwerpen	Swimming	Swimming Men's 200 metres Breaststroke	Bronze
38	15	Arvo Ossian Aaltonen	M	30.0	NaN	NaN	Finland	FIN	1920 Summer	1920	Summer	Antwerpen	Swimming	Swimming Men's 400 metres Breaststroke	Bronze
40	16	Juhamatti Tapio Aaltonen	M	28.0	184.0	85.0	Finland	FIN	2014 Winter	2014	Winter	Sochi	Ice Hockey	Ice Hockey Men's Ice Hockey	Bronze
41	17	Paavo Johannes Aaltonen	M	28.0	175.0	64.0	Finland	FIN	1948 Summer	1948	Summer	London	Gymnastics	Gymnastics Men's Individual All-Around	Bronze

Figure 1.33: Filtered Olympics DataFrame

After Step 3:

```
Athletics                  192
Swimming                   191
Rowing                     144
Football                   106
Hockey                      99
Handball                    89
Cycling                     84
Canoeing                    82
Water Polo                  78
Rugby Sevens                74
Basketball                  72
Volleyball                  72
Wrestling                   72
Gymnastics                  66
Fencing                     65
Judo                        56
Boxing                      51
Sailing                     45
Equestrianism               45
Shooting                    45
Weightlifting               45
Diving                      36
Taekwondo                   32
Synchronized Swimming       32
Table Tennis                24
Badminton                   24
Tennis                      24
Archery                     24
Rhythmic Gymnastics         18
Beach Volleyball            12
Modern Pentathlon            6
Trampolining                 6
Golf                         6
Triathlon                    6
Name: Sport, dtype: int64
```

Figure 1.34: The number of medals awarded

After Step 4:

	ID	Name	Sex	Age	Height	Weight	Team	NOC	Games	Year	Season	City	Sport	Event	Medal
158	62	Giovanni Abagnale	M	21.0	198.0	90.0	Italy	ITA	2016 Summer	2016	Summer	Rio de Janeiro	Rowing	Rowing Men's Coxless Pairs	Bronze
814	465	Matthew "Matt" Abood	M	30.0	197.0	92.0	Australia	AUS	2016 Summer	2016	Summer	Rio de Janeiro	Swimming	Swimming Men's 4 x 100 metres Freestyle Relay	Bronze
1228	690	Chantal Achterberg	F	31.0	172.0	72.0	Netherlands	NED	2016 Summer	2016	Summer	Rio de Janeiro	Rowing	Rowing Women's Quadruple Sculls	Silver
1529	846	Valerie Kasanita Adams-Vili (-Price)	F	31.0	193.0	120.0	New Zealand	NZL	2016 Summer	2016	Summer	Rio de Janeiro	Athletics	Athletics Women's Shot Put	Silver
1847	1017	Nathan Ghar-Jun Adrian	M	27.0	198.0	100.0	United States	USA	2016 Summer	2016	Summer	Rio de Janeiro	Swimming	Swimming Men's 50 metres Freestyle	Bronze

Figure 1.35: Olympics DataFrame

After Step 5:

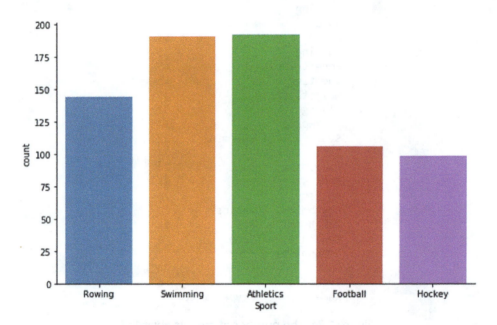

Figure 1.36: Generated bar plot

After Step 6:

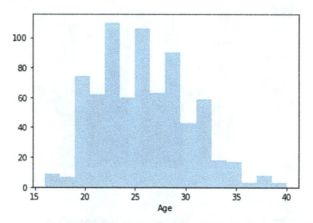

Figure 1.37: Histogram plot with the Age feature

After Step 7:

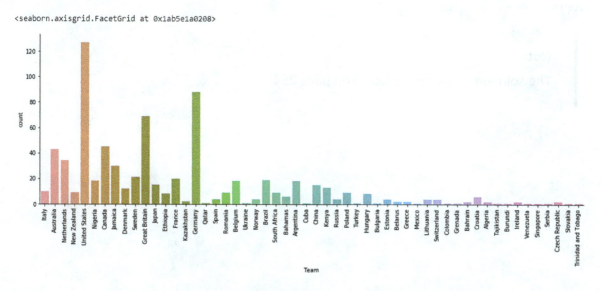

Figure 1.38: Bar plot with the number of medals won

After Step 8:

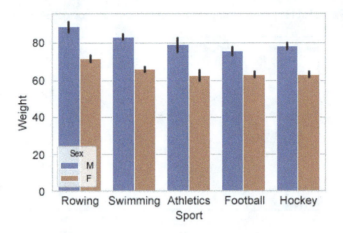

Figure 1.39: Bar plot with the average weight of players

The bar plot indicates the highest athlete weight in rowing, followed by swimming, and then the other remaining sports. The trend is similar across both male and female players.

> **Note**
>
> The solution steps can be found on page 254.

Summary

In this chapter, we covered the basics of handling **pandas** DataFrames to format them as inputs for different visualization functions in libraries such as **pandas**, **seaborn** and more, and we covered some essential concepts in generating and modifying plots to create pleasing figures.

The **pandas** library contains functions such as **read_csv()**, **read_excel()**, and **read_json()** to read structured text data files. Functions such as **describe()** and **info()** are useful to get information on the summary statistics and memory usage of the features in a DataFrame. Other important operations on **pandas** DataFrames include subletting based on user-specified conditions/constraints, adding new columns to a DataFrame, transforming existing columns with built-in Python functions as well as user-defined functions, deleting specific columns in a DataFrame, and writing a modified DataFrame to a file on the local system.

Once equipped with knowledge of these common operations on **pandas** DataFrames, we went over the basics of visualization and learned how to refine the visual appeal of the plots. We illustrated these concepts with the plotting of histograms and bar plots. Specifically, we learned about different ways of presenting labels and legends, changing the properties of tick labels, and adding annotations.

In the next chapter, we will learn about some popular visualization techniques and understand the interpretation, strengths, and limitations of each.

Static Visualization – Global Patterns and Summary Statistics

Learning Objectives

By the end of this chapter, you will be able to:

- Explain various visualization techniques for different contexts
- Identify global patterns of one or more features in a dataset
- Create plots to represent global patterns in data: scatter plots, hexbin plots, contour plots, and heatmaps
- Create plots that present summary statistics of data: histograms (revisited), box plots, and violin plots

In this chapter, we'll explore different visualization techniques for presenting global patterns and summary statistics of data.

Introduction

In the previous chapter, we learned how to handle **pandas** DataFrames as inputs for data visualization, how to plot with **pandas** and **seaborn**, and how to refine plots to increase their aesthetic appeal. The intent of this chapter is to acquire practical knowledge about the strengths and limitations of various visualization techniques. We'll practice creating plots for a variety of different contexts. However, you will notice that the variety in existing plot types and visualization techniques is huge, and choosing the appropriate visualization becomes confusing. There are times when a plot shows too much information for the reader to grasp or too little for the reader to get the necessary intuition regarding the data. There are times when a visualization is too esoteric for the reader to appreciate properly, and other times when an over-simplistic visualization just doesn't have the right impact. All these scenarios can be avoided by being armed with practical knowledge about the interpretation of different kinds of visualization techniques and their strengths and limitations.

This chapter is a primer on the different types of static visualization and the contexts in which they are most effective. Using **seaborn**, you will learn how to create a variety of plots and become proficient in selecting the right kind of visualization for the most suitable representation of your data. Combining these skills with the techniques learned in *Chapter 1, Introduction to Visualization with Python – Basic and Customized Plotting*, will help you make stellar plots that are both meaningful and attractive.

Let's first explore the right kind of visualization technique or plot to represent global patterns in data.

> **Note**
>
> Some of the images in this chapter have colored notations, you can find high-quality color images used in this chapter at: https://github.com/TrainingByPackt/Interactive-Data-Visualization-with-Python/tree/master/Graphics/Lesson2.

Creating Plots that Present Global Patterns in Data

In this section, we will study the context of plots that present global patterns in data, such as:

- Plots that show the variance in individual features in data, such as histograms
- Plots that show how different features present in data vary with respect to each other, such as scatter plots, line plots, and heatmaps

Most data scientists prefer to see such plots because they give an idea of the entire spectrum of values taken by the features of interest. Plots depicting global patterns are also useful because they make it easier to spot anomalies in data.

We will work with a dataset called **mpg**. It was published by the *StatLib* library, maintained at Carnegie Mellon University, and is available in the **seaborn** library. It was originally used to study the relationship of mileage – **Miles Per Gallon** (**MPG**) – with other features in the dataset; hence the name **mpg**. Since the dataset contains 3 discrete features and 5 continuous features, it is a good fit for illustrating multiple concepts in this chapter.

You can see what the dataset looks like using:

```
import seaborn as sns

# load a seaborn dataset

mpg_df = sns.load_dataset("mpg")

print(mpg_df.head())
```

The output is as follows:

```
   mpg  cylinders  displacement  ...  model_year  origin                       name
0  18.0          8         307.0  ...          70     usa  chevrolet chevelle malibu
1  15.0          8         350.0  ...          70     usa          buick skylark 320
2  18.0          8         318.0  ...          70     usa         plymouth satellite
3  16.0          8         304.0  ...          70     usa              amc rebel sst
4  17.0          8         302.0  ...          70     usa                ford torino

[5 rows x 9 columns]
```

Figure 2.1: mpg dataset

Now, let's take a look at a few different kinds of plots to present this data and derive statistical insights from it.

Scatter Plots

The first type of plot that we will generate is a scatter plot. A **scatter plot** is a simple plot presenting the values of two features in a dataset. Each datapoint is represented by a point with the x coordinate as the value of the first feature and the y coordinate as the value of the second feature. A scatter plot is a great tool to learn more about two such numerical attributes.

Scatter plots can help excavate relationships among different features in data such as weather and sales, nutrition intake, and health statistics in several contexts.

We will learn how to create a scatter plot with the help of an exercise.

Exercise 13: Creating a Static Scatter Plot

In this exercise, we will generate a scatter plot to examine the relationship between **weight** and **mileage (mpg)** of the vehicles from the **mpg** dataset. To do so, let's go through the following steps:

1. Open a Jupyter notebook and import the necessary Python modules:

   ```
   import seaborn as sns
   ```

2. Import the dataset from **seaborn**:

   ```
   mpg_df = sns.load_dataset("mpg")
   ```

3. Generate a scatter plot using the **scatterplot()** function:

   ```
   # seaborn ('version 0.9.0 is required')
   ax = sns.scatterplot(x="weight", y="mpg", data=mpg_df)
   ```

   The output is as follows:

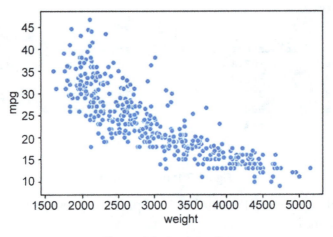

Figure 2.2: Scatter plot

Notice that the scatter plot shows a decline in **mileage (mpg)** with an increase in **weight**. That's a useful insight into the relationships between different features in the dataset.

Hexagonal Binning Plots

There's also a fancier version of scatter plots, called a **hexagonal binning plot** (**hexbin plot**) – this can be used when both rows and columns correspond to numerical attributes. Where there are lots of data points, the plotted points on a scatter plot can end up overlapping, resulting in a messy graph. It can be hard to infer trends in such cases. With a hexbin plot, a lot of data points in the same area can be shown using a darker shade. Hexbin plots use hexagons to represent clusters of data points. The darker bins indicate that there is a larger number of points in the corresponding ranges of features on the *x* and *y* axes. The lighter bins indicate fewer points. The white space corresponds to no points.This way, we end up with a cleaner graph that's clearer to read.

Let's see how to create a hexbin plot in the next exercise.

Exercise 14: Creating a Static Hexagonal Binning Plot

In this exercise, we will generate a hexagonal binning plot to get a better understanding of the relationship between **weight** and **mileage (mpg)**. Let's go through the following steps:

1. Import the necessary Python modules:

    ```
    import seaborn as sns
    ```

2. Import the dataset from **seaborn**:

    ```
    mpg_df = sns.load_dataset("mpg")
    ```

3. Plot a hexbin plot using **jointplot** with **kind** set to **hex**:

    ```
    ## set the plot style to include ticks on the axes.
    sns.set(style="ticks")
    ## hexbin plot
    sns.jointplot(mpg_df.weight, mpg_df.mpg, kind="hex",
    color="#4CB391")
    ```

Note the **jointplot** function of **seaborn** mentioned in the above code. It is defined where we provide the values for the x axis and y axis along with specifying the kind argument, which is set to **hex** here, to build the plot.

The output is as follows:

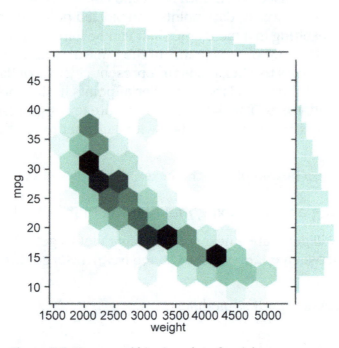

Figure 2.3: Hexagonal binning plot of weight versus mpg

As you might notice, the histogram on the top and right axes depict the variance in the features represented by the *x* and *y* axes respectively (**mpg** and **weight**, in this example). Also, you might have noticed in the previous scatter plot that data points overlapped heavily in certain areas, obscuring the actual distribution of the features. Hexbin plots are quite a nice data visualization tool when data points are very dense.

Contour Plots

Another alternative to scatter plots when data points are densely populated in specific region(s) is a **contour plot**. The advantage of using contour plots is the same as hexbin plots – accurately depicting the distribution of features in the visualization in cases where data points are likely to overlap heavily. Contour plots are commonly used to show the distribution of weather indicators such as temperature, rainfall, and others on maps of geographical regions.

Let's look at a contour plot in the following exercise.

Exercise 15: Creating a Static Contour Plot

In this exercise, we'll create a contour plot to show the relationship between `weight` and `mileage` in the `mpg` dataset. We'll be able to see that the relationship between `weight` and `mileage` is strongest when there are more data points. Let's go through the following steps:

1. Import the necessary Python modules:

    ```
    import seaborn as sns
    ```

2. Import the dataset from **seaborn**:

    ```
    mpg_df = sns.load_dataset("mpg")
    ```

3. Create a contour plot using the **set_style** method:

    ```
    # contour plot
    sns.set_style("white")
    ```

4. Generate a **Kernel Density Estimate** (**KDE**) (see *Chapter 1, Introduction to Visualization with Python-Basic and Customized Plotting*) plot:

    ```
    # generate KDE plot: first two parameters are arrays of X and Y
    coordinates of data points
    # parameter shade is set to True so that the contours are filled with
    a color gradient based on number of data points
    sns.kdeplot(mpg_df.weight, mpg_df.mpg, shade=True)
    ```

The output is as follows:

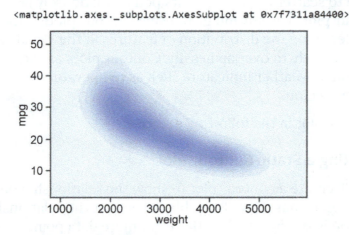

```
<matplotlib.axes._subplots.AxesSubplot at 0x7f7311a84400>
```

Figure 2.4: Contour plot showing weight versus mpg

Notice that the interpretation of contour plots is similar to that of hexbin plots – darker regions indicate more data points and lighter regions indicate fewer data points.

In our example of **weight** versus **mileage (mpg)**, the hexbin plot and the contour plot indicate that there is a certain curve along which the negative relationship between **weight** and **mileage** is strongest, as is evident by the larger number of data points. The negative relationship becomes relatively weaker as we move away from the curve (fewer data points).

Line Plots

Another kind of plot for presenting global patterns in data is a line plot.

Line plots represent information as a series of data points connected by straight-line segments. They are useful for indicating the relationship between a discrete numerical feature (on the x axis), such as **model_year**, and a continuous numerical feature (on the y axis), such as **mpg** from the **mpg** dataset.

Let's look at the succeeding exercise on creating a line plot with **model_year** versus **mpg**.

Exercise 16: Creating a Static Line Plot

In this exercise, we will create a scatter plot for a different pair of features, **model_year** and **mpg**. Then, we'll generate a line plot based on those discrete attributes – **model_year** and **mpg**. To do so, let's go through the following steps:

1. Import the necessary Python modules:

   ```
   import seaborn as sns
   ```

2. Import the dataset from **seaborn**:

   ```
   mpg_df = sns.load_dataset("mpg")
   ```

3. Create a contour plot:

   ```
   # contour plot
   sns.set_style("white")
   ```

4. Create a two dimensional scatter plot:

   ```
   # seaborn 2-D scatter plot
   ax1 = sns.scatterplot(x="model_year", y="mpg", data=mpg_df)
   ```

   The output is as follows:

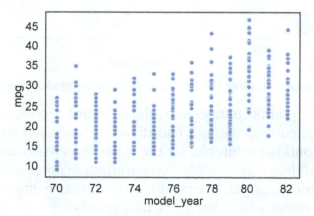

Figure 2.5: Two-dimensional line plot

In this example, we see that the **model_year** feature only takes discrete values between **70** and **82**. Now, when we have a discrete numerical feature like this (**model_year**), drawing a line plot joining the data points is a good idea. We can draw a simple line plot showing the relationship between **model_year** and **mileage** with the following code.

5. Draw a simple line plot to show the relationship between **model_year** and **mileage**:

```
# seaborn ('version 0.9.0 is required') line plot code
ax = sns.lineplot(x="model_year", y="mpg", data=mpg_df)
```

The output is as follows:

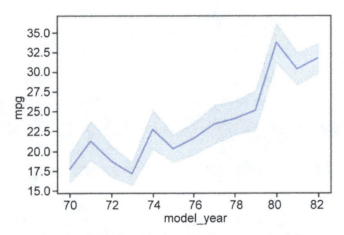

Figure 2.6: Line plot showing the relationship between model_year and mileage

As we can see, the points connected by the solid line represent the mean of the y axis feature at the corresponding *x* coordinate. The shaded area around the line plot shows the confidence interval for the *y* axis feature (by default, seaborn sets this to a **95%** confidence interval). The ci parameter can be used to change to a different confidence interval. The phrase **x%** confidence interval translates to a range of feature values where x% of the data points are present. An example of changing to a confidence interval of **68%** is shown in the code that follows.

6. Change the confidence interval to **68**:

```
sns.lineplot(x="model_year", y="mpg", data=mpg_df, ci=68)
```

The output is as follows:

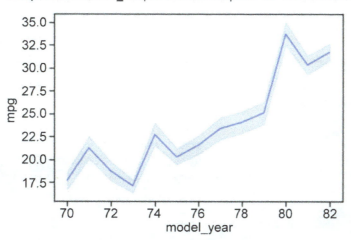

Figure 2.7: Line plot where ci = 68

As we can see from the preceding plot, the **68%** confidence interval translates to a range of feature values where **68%** of the data points are present. Line plots are great visualization techniques for scenarios where we have data that changes over time – the x axis could represent date or time, and the plot would help to visualize how a value varies over that period.

Speaking of presenting data across time using line plots, let's consider the example of the **flights** dataset from **seaborn**. The dataset is used to study a comparison between airlines, delay distribution, predicting flight delays, and more (this open source dataset is hosted on Packt's GitHub repository). Through the following example, we'll see how to generate line plots to represent this dataset.

Exercise 17: Presenting Data across Time with multiple Line Plots

In this example, we'll see how to present data across time with multiple line plots. We are using the **flights** dataset:

1. Import the necessary Python modules:

    ```
    import seaborn as sns
    ```

2. Load the flights dataset:

    ```
    flights_df = sns.load_dataset("flights")
    print(flights_df.head())
    ```

    The output is as follows:

    ```
          year     month  passengers
    0     1949   January         112
    1     1949  February         118
    2     1949     March         132
    3     1949     April         129
    4     1949       May         121
    ```

    Figure 2.8: Flights dataset

    Suppose you want to look at how the number of passengers varies between months in different years. *How would you display this information?*

    One option is to draw multiple line plots in a single figure. For example, let's look at the line plots for the months of December and January across different years. We can do this with the code that follows.

3. Create multiple plots for the months of **December** and **January**:

    ```
    #flights_df = flights_df.pivot("month", "year", "passengers")
    #ax = sns.heatmap(flights_df)
    # line plots for the planets dataset
    ax = sns.lineplot(x="year", y="passengers", data=flights_df[flights_
    df['month']=='January'], color='green')
    ax = sns.lineplot(x="year", y="passengers", data=flights_df[flights_
    df['month']=='February'], color='red')
    ax = sns.lineplot(x="year", y="passengers", data=flights_df[flights_
    df['month']=='March'], color='blue')
    ax = sns.lineplot(x="year", y="passengers", data=flights_df[flights_
    df['month']=='April'], color='cyan')
    ```

```
ax = sns.lineplot(x="year", y="passengers", data=flights_
df['month']=='May'], color='pink')
ax = sns.lineplot(x="year", y="passengers", data=flights_df[flights_
df['month']=='June'], color='black')
ax = sns.lineplot(x="year", y="passengers", data=flights_df[flights_
df['month']=='July'], color='grey')
ax = sns.lineplot(x="year", y="passengers", data=flights_df[flights_
df['month']=='August'], color='yellow')
ax = sns.lineplot(x="year", y="passengers", data=flights_df[flights_
df['month']=='September'], color='turquoise')
ax = sns.lineplot(x="year", y="passengers", data=flights_df[flights_
df['month']=='October'], color='orange')
ax = sns.lineplot(x="year", y="passengers", data=flights_df[flights_
df['month']=='November'], color='darkgreen')
ax = sns.lineplot(x="year", y="passengers", data=flights_df[flights_
df['month']=='December'], color='darkred')
```

The output is as follows:

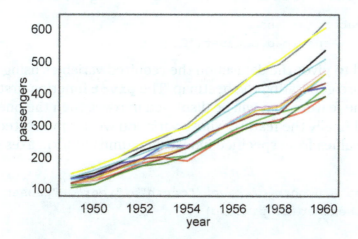

Figure 2.9: Multiple line plots for year versus passengers

With this example of 12 line plots, we can see how a figure with too many line plots quickly begins to get crowded and confusing. Thus, for certain scenarios, line plots are neither appealing nor useful.

So, what is the alternative for our use case?

Heatmaps

Enter heatmaps.

A *heatmap* is a visual representation of a specific continuous numerical feature as a function of two other discrete features (either a categorical or a discrete numerical) in the dataset. The information is presented in grid form – each cell in the grid corresponds to a specific pair of values taken by the two discrete features and is colored based on the value of the third numerical feature. A heatmap is a great tool to visualize high-dimensional data and even to tease out features that are particularly variable across different classes.

Let's go through a concrete exercise.

Exercise 18: Creating and Exploring a Static Heatmap

In this exercise, we will explore and create a heatmap. We will use the **flights** dataset from the **seaborn** library to generate a heatmap depicting the number of passengers per month across the years **1949–1960**:

1. Start by importing the **seaborn** module and loading the **flights** dataset:

    ```
    import seaborn as sns
    flights_df = sns.load_dataset('flights')
    ```

2. Now we need to pivot the dataset on the required variables using the **pivot()** function before generating the heatmap. The **pivot** function first takes as arguments the feature that will be displayed in rows, then the one displayed in columns, and finally the feature whose variation we are interested in observing. It uses unique values from specified indexes/columns to form axes of the resulting DataFrame:

    ```
    df_pivoted = flights_df.pivot("month", "year", "passengers")
    ax = sns.heatmap(df_pivoted)
    ```

The output is as follows:

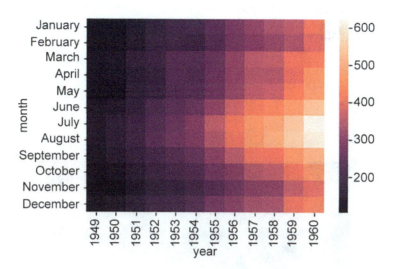

Figure 2.10: Generated heatmap

Here, we can note that the total number of yearly flights increased steadily from **1949** to **1960**. Moreover, the months of July and August seem to have the largest number of flights (compared to other months) across the years in observation. Now, that's an interesting trend to find from a simple visualization!

Plotting heatmaps is a very fun thing to explore, and there are lots of options available to tweak the parameters. You can learn more about them at https://seaborn.pydata.org/generated/seaborn.clustermap.html and https://seaborn.pydata.org/generated/seaborn.heatmap.html. However, we will only mention a few important aspects here – the *clustering option* and the *distance metric*.

Rows or columns in a heatmap can also be clustered based on the extent of their similarity. To do this in **seaborn**, use the **clustermap** option.

Exercise18 continued

3. Use **clustermap** option to cluster rows and columns:

```
ax = sns.clustermap(df_pivoted, col_cluster=False, row_cluster=True)
```

The output is as follows:

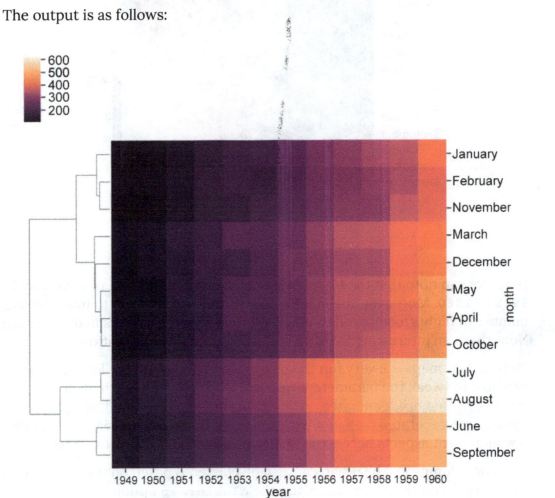

Figure 2.11: Heatmap using clustermap

Did you notice how the order of months got rearranged in the plots but some months (for example, July and August) stuck together because of their similar trends? In both July and August, the number of flights increased relatively more drastically in the last few years till **1960**.

> **Note**
>
> We can cluster the data by year by switching the parameter values (**row_cluster=False, col_cluster=True**) or cluster both by row and column (**row_cluster=True, col_cluster=True**).

At this point, you may be thinking, *But wait, how is the similarity between rows and columns computed?* The answer is that it depends on the distance metric – that is, how the distance between two rows or two columns is computed. The rows/columns with the least distance between them are clustered closer together than the ones with a greater distance between them. The user can set the distance metric to one of the many available options (**manhattan**, **euclidean**, **correlation**, and others) simply using the **metric** option as follows. You can read more about the distance **metric** options here: https://scikit-learn.org/stable/modules/generated/sklearn.neighbors.DistanceMetric.html.

> **Note**
>
> **seaborn** sets the metric to **euclidean** by default.

Exercise18 continued:

4. Set **metric** to **euclidean**:

```
# equivalent to ax = sns.clustermap(df_pivoted, row_cluster=False,
metric='euclidean')
ax = sns.clustermap(df_pivoted, col_cluster=False)
```

The output is as follows:

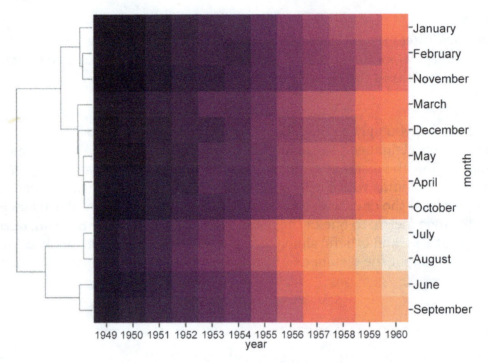

Figure 2.12: Heatmap with distance metric as euclidean

5. Change **metric** to **correlation**:

```
# change distance metric to correlation
ax = sns.clustermap(df_pivoted, row_cluster=False,
metric='correlation')
```

The output is as follows:

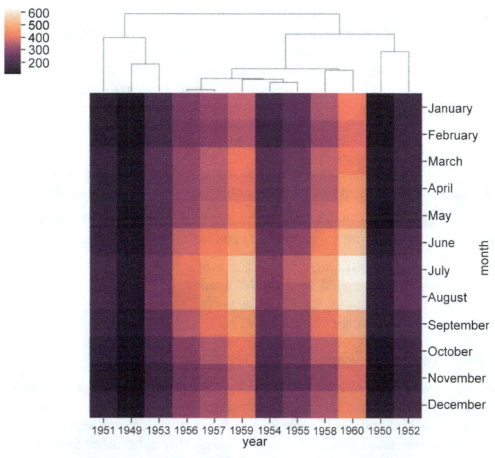

Figure 2.13: Heatmap with distance metric is correlation

On reading about *distance metric*, we learn that it defines the distance between two rows/columns. However, if we look carefully, we see that the heatmap also clusters not just individual rows or columns, but also groups of rows and columns. This is where linkage comes into the picture. But hold your breath for a moment before we come to that!

The Concept of Linkage in Heatmaps

The clustering seen in heatmaps is called agglomerative hierarchical clustering because it involves the sequential grouping of rows/columns until all of them belong to a single cluster, resulting in a hierarchy. Without loss of generality, let's assume we are clustering rows. The first step in hierarchical clustering is to compute the distance between all possible pairs of rows, and to select two rows, say, **A** and **B**, with the least distance between them. Once these rows are grouped, they are said to be *merged* into a single cluster. Once this happens, we need a rule that not only determines the distance between two rows but also the distance between any two clusters (even if the cluster contains a single point):

- If we define the distance between two clusters as the distance between the two points across the clusters closest to each other, the rule is called **single linkage**.

- If the rule is to define the distance between two clusters as the distance between the points farthest from each other, it is called **complete linkage**.

- If the rule is to define the distance as the average of all possible pairs of rows in the two clusters, it is called **average linkage**.

The same holds for clustering columns, too.

Exercise 19: Creating Linkage in Static Heatmaps

In this exercise, we'll generate a heatmap and understand the concept of single, complete, and average linkage in heatmaps using the **flights** dataset. We'll use the **cluster map** method and set the **method** parameter to different values, such as **average**, **complete**, and **single**. To do so, let's go throughout the following steps:

1. Start by importing the **seaborn** module and loading the **flights** dataset:

```
import seaborn as sns
flights_df = sns.load_dataset('flights')
```

2. Now we need to pivot the dataset on the required variables using the **pivot()** function before generating the heatmap:

```
df_pivoted = flights_df.pivot("month", "year", "passengers")
ax = sns.heatmap(df_pivoted)
```

The output is as follows:

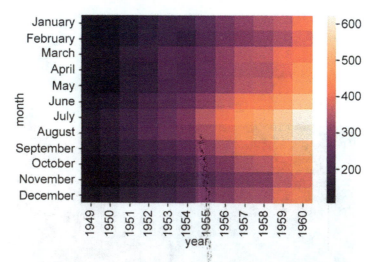

Figure 2.14: Generated heatmap for the flights dataset

3. Link the heatmaps using the code that follows:

```
ax = sns.clustermap(df_pivoted, col_cluster=False,
metric='correlation', method='average')
ax = sns.clustermap(df_pivoted, row_cluster=False,
metric='correlation', method='complete')
ax = sns.clustermap(df_pivoted, row_cluster=False,
metric='correlation', method='single')
```

The output is as follows:

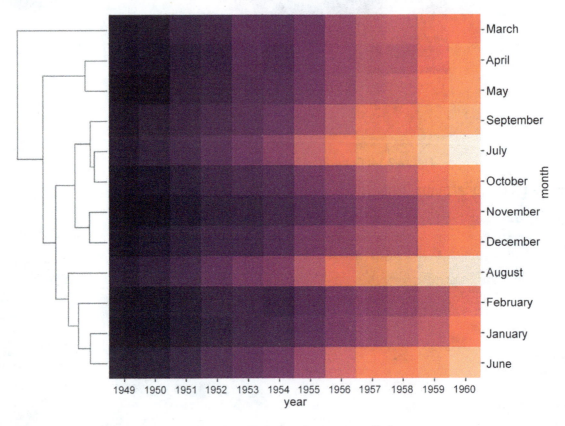

Figure 2.15a: Heatmap showing average linkage

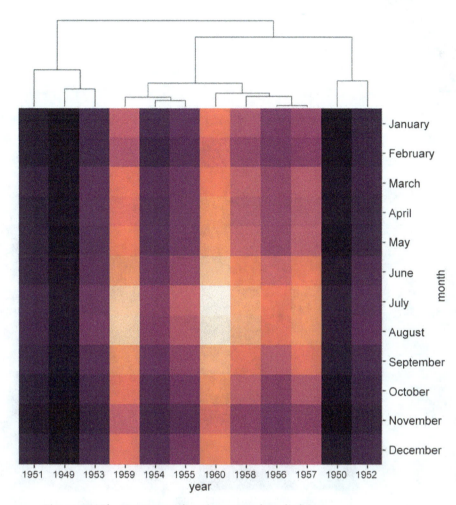

Figure 2.15b: Heatmap showing complete linkage

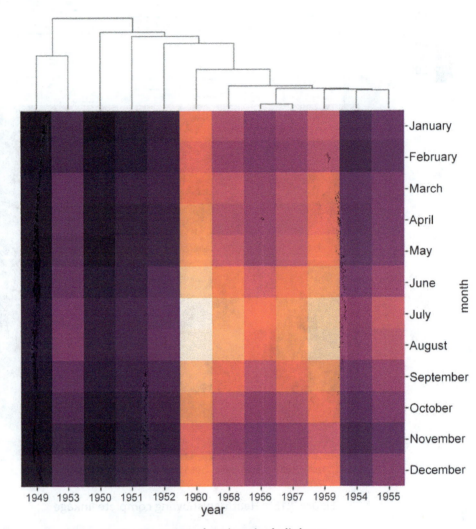

Figure 2.15c: Heatmap showing single linkage

Heatmaps are also a good way to visualize what happens in a 2D space. For example, they can be used to show where the most action is on the pitch in a soccer game. Similarly, for a website, heatmaps can be used to show the areas that are most frequently moussed over by users.

In this section, we have studied plots that present the global patterns of one or more features in a dataset. The following plots were specifically highlighted in the section:

- *Scatter plots*: Useful for observing the relationship between two potentially related features in a dataset

- *Hexbin plots and contour plots*: A good alternative for scatter plots when data is too dense in some parts of a feature space

- *Line plots*: Useful for indicating the relationship between a discrete numerical feature (on the x axis) and a continuous numerical feature (on the y axis)

- *Heatmaps*: Useful for examining the relationship between a continuous numerical feature of interest and two other features that are either a categorical or a discrete numerical

Creating Plots That Present Summary Statistics of Your Data

It's now time for a switch to our next section. When datasets are huge, it is sometimes useful to look at the summary statistics of a range of different features and get a preliminary idea of the dataset. For example, the summary statistics for any numerical feature include measures of central tendency, such as the mean, and measures of dispersion, such as the standard deviation.

When a dataset is too small, plots presenting summary statistics may actually be misleading because summary statistics are meaningful only when the dataset is big enough to draw statistical conclusions. For example, if somebody reports the variance of a feature using five data points, we cannot make any concrete conclusions regarding the *dispersion* of the feature.

Histogram Revisited

Let's revisit histograms from *Chapter 1, Introduction to Visualization with Python – Basic and Customized Plotting*. Although histograms show the distribution of a given feature in data, we can make a plot a little more informative by showing some summary statistics in the same plot. Let's go back to our **mpg** dataset and draw a histogram to analyze the spread of vehicle weights in the dataset.

Example 1: Histogram Revisited

We'll go through a histogram plot to revisit the concept we have learned in *Chapter 1, Introduction to Visualization with Python – Basic and Customized Plotting.* Let's go through the following:

Import the necessary Python modules; load the dataset; choose number of bins and whether the kernel density estimate should be shown or not; Use red color to show mean using a straight line on the x axis (parallel to y axis); define the location of legend:

```
# histogram using seaborn
import matplotlib.pyplot as plt
import seaborn as sns
import numpy as np
mpg_df = sns.load_dataset("mpg")
ax = sns.distplot(mpg_df.weight, bins=50, kde=False)
# `label` defines the name used in legend
plt.axvline(x=np.mean(mpg_df.weight), color='red', label='mean')
plt.axvline(x=np.median(mpg_df.weight), color='orange',
label='median')
plt.legend(loc='upper right')
```

The output is as follows:

<matplotlib.legend.Legend at 0x1a24a60358>

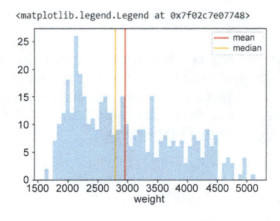

Figure 2.16: Histogram revisited

This histogram shows the distribution of the `weight` feature along with the mean and median. Notice that the mean is not equal to the median, which means that the feature is not *normally distributed*. Read more on this here: http://mathworld.wolfram.com/NormalDistribution.html.

Let's explore a few other plots to represent the summary statistics of data.

Box Plots

Box plots are an excellent way to examine the relationship between the summary statistics of a numerical feature in relation to other categorical features. Now, suppose we want to see the summary statistics of the `mpg` feature (`mileage`) classified by another feature – the number of cylinders. A popular way to show such information is to use box plots. This is very easy to do with the `seaborn` library.

Exercise 20: Creating and Exploring a Static Box Plot

In this exercise, we will create a box plot to analyze the relationship between `model_year` and `mileage` using the `mpg` dataset. We'll analyze manufacturing efficiency and the mileage of vehicles over a period of years. To do so, let's go through the following steps:

1. Import **seaborn** library:

    ```
    import seaborn as sns
    ```

2. Load the dataset:

    ```
    mpg_df = sns.load_dataset("mpg")
    ```

3. Create a box plot:

    ```
    # box plot: mpg(mileage) vs model_year
    sns.boxplot(x='model_year', y='mpg', data=mpg_df)
    ```

The output is as follows:

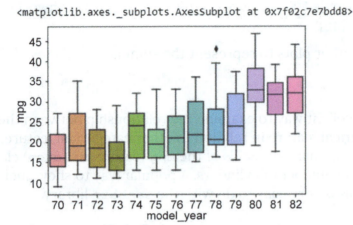

Figure 2.17: Box plot

As we can see, the box boundaries indicate the interquartile range, the upper boundary marks the **25%** quartile, and the lower boundary marks the **75%** quartile. The horizontal line inside the box indicates the median. Any solo points outside of the whiskers (the T-shaped bars above and below the box) mark outliers, while the whiskers themselves show the minimum and maximum values that are not outliers.

Apparently, **mileage** improved substantially in the 80s compared to the 70s. Let's add another feature to our **mpg** DataFrame that denotes whether the car was manufactured in the 70s or 80s.

4. Modify the **mpg** DataFrame by creating a new feature, **model_decade**:

```
import numpy as np
# creating a new feature 'model_decade'
mpg_df['model_decade'] = np.floor(mpg_df.model_year/10)*10
mpg_df['model_decade'] = mpg_df['model_decade'].astype(int)
mpg_df.tail()
```

The output is as follows:

	mpg	cylinders	displacement	horsepower	weight	acceleration	model_year	origin	name	model_decade
393	27.0	4	140.0	86.0	2790	15.6	82	usa	ford mustang gl	80
394	44.0	4	97.0	52.0	2130	24.6	82	europe	vw pickup	80
395	32.0	4	135.0	84.0	2295	11.6	82	usa	dodge rampage	80
396	28.0	4	120.0	79.0	2625	18.6	82	usa	ford ranger	80
397	31.0	4	119.0	82.0	2720	19.4	82	usa	chevy s-10	80

Figure 2.18:Modified mpg DataFrame

5. Now, let's redraw our box plot to look at **mileage** distribution for the two decades:

```
# a boxplot with multiple classes
sns.boxplot(x='model_decade', y='mpg', data=mpg_df)
```

The output is as follows:

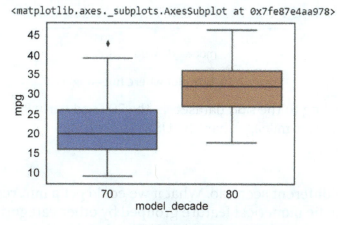

Figure 2.19: Redrawn Box plot

But wait – more can be done with boxplots. We can also add another feature, say, **region of origin**, and see how that affects the relationship between **mileage** and **manufacturing time**, the two features we have been considering so far.

6. Use the **hue** parameter to group by **origin**:

```
# boxplot: mpg (mileage) vs model_decade
# parameter hue is used to group by a specific feature, in this case
'origin'
sns.boxplot(x='model_decade', y='mpg', data=mpg_df, hue='origin')
```

The output is as follows:

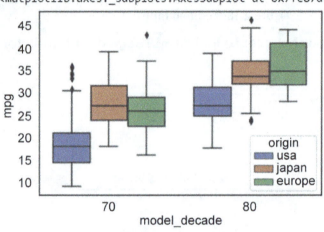

Figure 2.20: Box plot where hue=origin

As we can see, according to the **mpg** dataset, in the 70s and early 80s, Europe and Japan produced cars with better mileage than the USA. Interesting!

Violin Plots

Now let's consider a different scenario. What if we could get a hint regarding the entire distribution of a specific numerical feature grouped by other categorical features? The right kind of visualization technique here is a **violin plot**. A violin plot is similar to a box plot, but it includes more detail about variations in the data. The shape of a violin plot tells you the shape of the data distribution –where the data points cluster around a common value, the plot is fatter, and where there are fewer data points, the plot is thinner. We will look at a concrete example with the help of an exercise.

Exercise 21: Creating a Static Violin Plot

In this exercise, we will use the **mpg** dataset and generate a violin plot depicting the detailed variation of **mileage (mpg)** based on **model_decade** and **region of origin**:

1. Import the necessary Python modules:

```
import seaborn as sns
```

2. Load the dataset:

```
mpg_df = sns.load_dataset("mpg")
```

3. Generate the violin plot using the **violinplot** function in **seaborn**:

```
# creating the feature 'model_decade'
import numpy as np
mpg_df['model_decade'] = np.floor(mpg_df.model_year/10)*10
mpg_df['model_decade'] = mpg_df['model_decade'].astype(int)

# code for violinplots
# parameter hue is used to group by a specific feature, in this case
'origin', while x represents the model year and y represent mileage
sns.violinplot(x='model_decade', y='mpg', data=mpg_df, hue='origin')
```

The output is as follows:

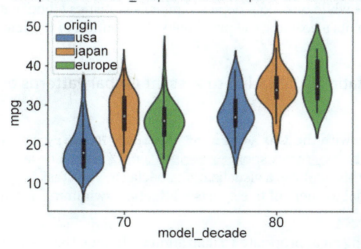

Figure 2.21: Violin plot

We can see here that, during the 70s, while most vehicles in the US had a median mileage of **19 mpg**, vehicles in Japan and Europe had median mileages of around **27** and **25 mpg**. While the mileages of vehicles in Europe and Japan jumped by **7** to **8** points in the 80s, the median mileage of vehicles in the US was still similar to that of the vehicles in Japan and Europe in the previous decade.

As we can see from the preceding plot, the fatter sections of the plot indicate ranges of higher probability of the y-axis feature, while the thinner sections indicate areas of lower probability. The thick solid line at the center of each distribution represents the interquartile range – the two ends are the **25%** and **75%** quantiles and the dot is the median. The thinner solid line shows **1.5** times the interquartile range.

> **Note**
>
> Since violin plots estimate a probability distribution based on the existing data, plots sometimes assign data points to negative values of the feature on the y axis. This may cause confusion and make readers doubt your results.

In this section, we have studied some plots that present summary statistics of various features in the dataset. These plots are especially useful representations of data when datasets are huge and it would be computationally expensive and time-intensive to generate plots that depict global patterns in the data. We learned how to add mean and median markers in the histogram of a given feature in the dataset. We also studied box plots and violin plots – while box plots depict summary statistics alone (with median and quartiles), violin plots also show the probability distribution of the feature across different value ranges.

Activity 2: Design Static Visualization to Present Global Patterns and Summary Statistics

We'll continue to work with the **120 years of Olympic History** dataset acquired by Randi Griffin from https://www.sports-reference.com/ and made available on the GitHub repository of this book. As a visualization specialist, your task is to create two plots for the 2016 medal winners of five sports – athletics, swimming, rowing, football, and hockey:

- Create a plot using an appropriate visualization technique that best presents the global pattern of the **height** and **weight** features of the 2016 medal winners of the five sports.

- Create a plot using an appropriate visualization technique that best presents the summary statistic for the height and weight of the players that won each type of medal (gold/silver/bronze) in the data.

You are encouraged to use your creativity and skills in bringing out important insights from the data.

High-Level Steps

1. Download the dataset and format it as a **pandas** DataFrame.

2. Filter the DataFrame to only include the rows corresponding to medal winners from 2016 for the sports mentioned in the activity description.

3. Look at the features in the dataset and note their data type – are they categorical or numerical?

4. Evaluate what the appropriate visualization(s) would be for a global pattern to depict the **height** and **weight** features.

5. Evaluate what the appropriate visualization(s) would be for depicting the medal-wise summary statistics of the **weight** and **height** features, further segregated by athlete gender.

The expected output should be:

After Step 1:

	ID	Name	Sex	Age	Height	Weight	Team	NOC	Games	Year	Season	City	Sport	Event	Medal
0	1	A Dijiang	M	24.0	180.0	80.0	China	CHN	1992 Summer	1992	Summer	Barcelona	Basketball	Basketball Men's Basketball	NaN
1	2	A Lamusi	M	23.0	170.0	60.0	China	CHN	2012 Summer	2012	Summer	London	Judo	Judo Men's Extra-Lightweight	NaN
2	3	Gunnar Nielsen Aaby	M	24.0	NaN	NaN	Denmark	DEN	1920 Summer	1920	Summer	Antwerpen	Football	Football Men's Football	NaN
3	4	Edgar Lindenau Aabye	M	34.0	NaN	NaN	Denmark/Sweden	DEN	1900 Summer	1900	Summer	Paris	Tug-Of-War	Tug-Of-War Men's Tug-Of-War	Gold
4	5	Christine Jacoba Aaftink	F	21.0	185.0	82.0	Netherlands	NED	1988 Winter	1988	Winter	Calgary	Speed Skating	Speed Skating Women's 500 metres	NaN

Figure 2.22: Olympic History dataset

After Step 2:

	ID	Name	Sex	Age	Height	Weight	Team	NOC	Games	Year	Season	City	Sport	Event	Medal
158	62	Giovanni Abagnale	M	21.0	198.0	90.0	Italy	ITA	2016 Summer	2016	Summer	Rio de Janeiro	Rowing	Rowing Men's Coxless Pairs	Bronze
814	465	Matthew "Matt" Abood	M	30.0	197.0	92.0	Australia	AUS	2016 Summer	2016	Summer	Rio de Janeiro	Swimming	Swimming Men's 4 x 100 metres Freestyle Relay	Bronze
1228	690	Chantal Achterberg	F	31.0	172.0	72.0	Netherlands	NED	2016 Summer	2016	Summer	Rio de Janeiro	Rowing	Rowing Women's Quadruple Sculls	Silver
1529	846	Valerie Kasanita Adams-Vili (-Price)	F	31.0	193.0	120.0	New Zealand	NZL	2016 Summer	2016	Summer	Rio de Janeiro	Athletics	Athletics Women's Shot Put	Silver
1847	1017	Nathan Ghar-Jun Adrian	M	27.0	198.0	100.0	United States	USA	2016 Summer	2016	Summer	Rio de Janeiro	Swimming	Swimming Men's 50 metres Freestyle	Bronze

Figure 2.23: Olympics history dataset with the medal winners

After Step 3:

	Age	Height	Weight
count	732.000000	729.000000	727.000000
mean	25.577869	180.023320	73.720770
std	4.451373	10.076398	14.279014
min	16.000000	150.000000	40.000000
25%	22.000000	173.000000	64.000000
50%	25.000000	180.000000	72.000000
75%	29.000000	187.000000	82.000000
max	40.000000	207.000000	136.000000

Figure 2.24: Olympics history dataset with the top sport winners

After Step 4:

Scatter plot–

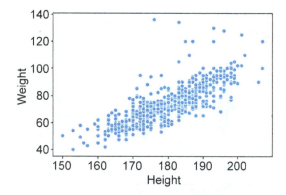

Figure 2.25: Scatter plot

Hexbin plot–

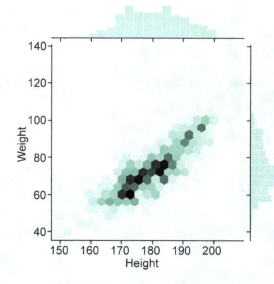

Figure 2.26: Hexagonal binning plot

After Step 5:

First Plot–

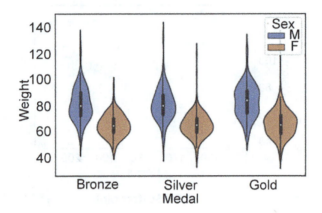

Figure 2.27: Violin plot showing medal versus weight

Second plot–

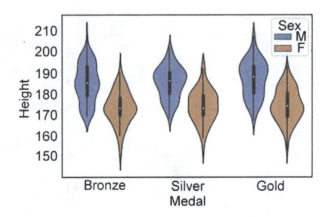

Figure 2.28: Violin plot showing medal versus height

Note

The solution steps can be found on page 259.

Summary

In this chapter, we learned how choosing the most appropriate visualization(s) depends on four key elements:

- The nature of the features in a dataset: categorical/discrete, numerical/ continuous numerical

- The size of the dataset: small/medium/large

- The density of the data points in the chosen feature space: whether too many or too few data points are set to certain feature values

- The context of the visualization: the source of the dataset and frequently used visualizations for the given application

For the purpose of explaining the concepts clearly and defining certain general guidelines, we classified visualizations into two categories:

- Plots representing the global patterns of the chosen features (for example, histograms, scatter plots, hexbin plots, contour plots, line plots,and heatmaps)

- Plots representing the summary statistics of the specific features (box plots and violin plots)

We are not implying that a single best visualization must be determined right away for any given application; for most datasets, the best visualizations will likely emerge from testing different kinds of plots and carefully examining the insights derived from each of them. This chapter provided the necessary resources to understand the interpretation and usage of various popular and less-used informative visualization types. In the next chapter, we will build on this foundation to introduce interactivity into our visualizations.

3

From Static
to Interactive
Visualization

Learning Objectives

By the end of this chapter, you will be able to:

- Explain the differences between static and interactive visualizations
- Explain the application of interactive visualizations in various sectors
- Create interactive plots with zoom, hover, and slide functionalities
- Use the Bokeh and Plotly (Express) Python libraries to create interactive data visualizations

In this chapter, we'll move from static to interactive visualizations and look into the applications of interactive visualizations for different scenarios.

Introduction

As we discussed in the previous chapters, data visualizations are graphical representations of information and data. Their purpose is to extract values from multiples rows and columns of numbers and data that are otherwise difficult to comprehend and represent them in graphically appealing plots. As a result, data visualizations can provide key insights regarding data at a glance. This is something that raw data, and even analyzed data in tabular form, is unable to do.

We discussed static data visualizations in the previous chapter – graphs and plots that are stagnant and cannot be modified or interacted with in real time by the audience.

Interactive data visualizations are a step ahead of static ones. Let's take a look at the term **interactive** to understand how. The definition of interactive is *something that involves communication between two or more things or people that work together.* Therefore, interactive visualizations are graphical representations of analyzed data (static or dynamic) that can react and respond to user actions in the moment. They are static visualizations that incorporate features to accept human inputs, thus enhancing and increasing the impact that data has.

> **Note**
>
> Some of the images in this chapter have colored notations, you can find high-quality color images used in this chapter at: https://github.com/TrainingByPackt/Interactive-Data-Visualization-with-Python/tree/master/Graphics/Lesson3.

The ability for a plot to provide you with more information about a datapoint when there's a user action, such as your mouse hovering above it, is what makes it interactive. An example of this can be seen in the following diagrams:

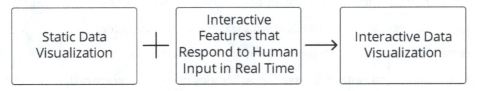

Figure 3.1: Interactive data visualization

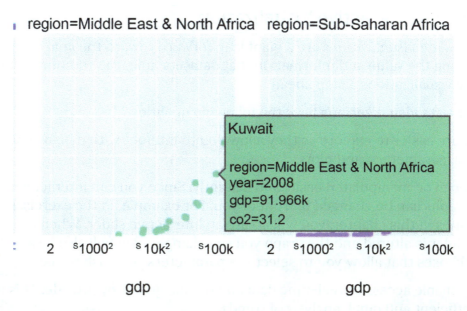

region=Middle East & North Africa   region=Sub-Saharan Africa

Kuwait

region=Middle East & North Africa
year=2008
gdp=91.966k
co2=31.2

2   $1000² $ 10k² $100k   2 $1000² $ 10k² $100k

gdp   gdp

Figure 3.2: Hovering over something provides you with more information about it

Interactive visualizations are often also built on dynamic data. The word dynamic is used to refer to something that is constantly changing, and when used with respect to data visualizations, it means that the input data that the visualization is built on is constantly changing as opposed to static data, which is stagnant and does not change. An example of interactive data visualization with dynamic data is visualizations depicting fluctuations in stock trends. The input data that's used to create these graphs is dynamic and constantly changing in real time, and so the visualizations are interactive. Static data is more for business intelligence, such as when data visualizations are used as part of a data science/machine learning process.

To understand the real capabilities of interactive visualization, let's compare it head to head with static visualization.

Static versus Interactive Visualization

While *static data visualizations* are a giant leap forward toward the goal of extracting and explaining the value and information that datasets hold, the addition of interactivity takes these visualizations a step ahead.

Interactive data visualizations have the following qualities:

- They are easier to explore as they allow you to interact with data by changing colors, parameters, and plots.

- They can be manipulated easily and instantly. Since you can interact with them, the graphs can be changed in front of you. For example, in the exercises and activities in this chapter, you will create an interactive slider. When the position of this slider is altered and the graph you see changes, you will also be able to create checkboxes that allow you to select the parameters you wish to see.

- They enable access to real-time data and the insights they provide. This allows for the efficient and quick analysis of trends.

- They are easier to comprehend, thereby allowing organizations to make better data-based decisions.

- They remove the requirement of having multiple plots for the same information – one interactive plot is able to convey the same insights.

- They allow you to observe relationships (for example, cause and effect).

Let's start with an example to understand what we can achieve through interactive visualization. Let's consider a dataset for members who are enrolled in a gym:

	age	weight	sex
0	29	88	2
1	45	96	1
2	35	91	0
3	37	79	1
4	27	62	0

Figure 3.3: Gym clients dataset

The following is a static data visualization in the form of a box plot that describes the weight of people categorized by their sex (**0** is male, **1** is female, and **2** is other):

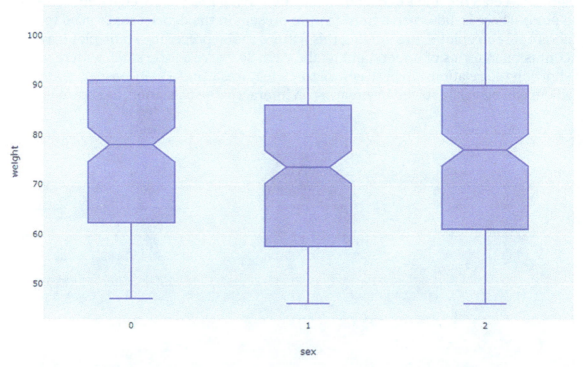

Figure 3.4 : A static visualization displaying weight versus the sex of gym clients

The only insight we can gain from this plot is the relationship between **weight** and **sex** – **male** clients visiting this gym weigh between **62kg** and **91kg**, **female** clients weigh between **57kg** and **86kg**, and clients identifying as **other** weigh between **61kg** and **90kg**. There is, however, a third feature present in the dataset that's used to generate this box plot – **age**. Adding this feature to the preceding static plot may lead to confusion in terms of understanding the data. So, we're a little stuck with regards to showing the relationship between all three features using a static visualization. This problem can be easily solved by creating an interactive visualization, as shown here:

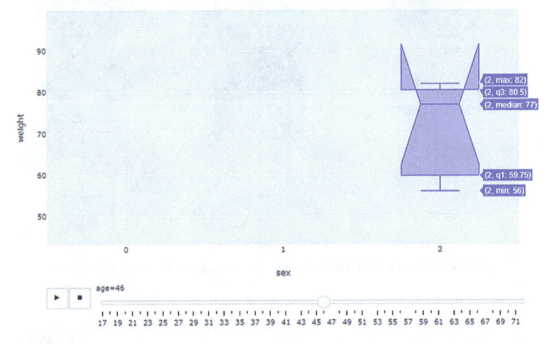

Figure 3.5: An interactive visualization displaying the weight and sex of 46-year-old gym clients

In the preceding box plot, a slider has been introduced for the **age** feature. The user can manually slide the position of the slider to observe the relationship between **weight, gender,** and **age** at different values of **age**. Additionally, there is a hover tool that allows the user to gain more information about the data.

The preceding box plot describes that, at this gym, the only **46**-year-old clients are those that identify as *other*, and the heaviest **46**-year-old weighs **82** kilograms, while the lightest weighs **56** kilograms.

The user can slide to another position to observe the relationship between `weight` and `sex` at a different `age`, as shown in the following plot:

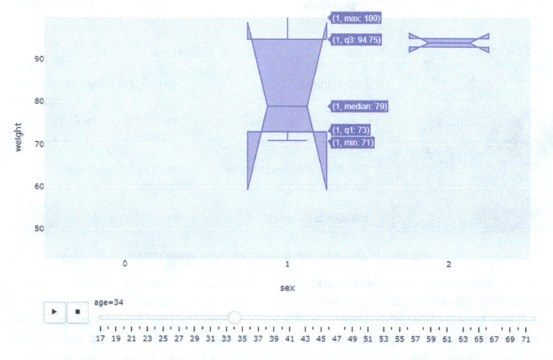

Figure 3.6: An interactive visualization displaying the weight and sex of 34-year-old gym clients

The preceding plot describes the data at the age of **34** – there are no male gym clients; however, the heaviest **34**-year old female client weights **100** `kilograms` while the lightest one weighs **71** `kilograms`.

But there are still more aspects to consider when differentiating between static and interactive visualizations. Let's look at the following table:

	Static Data Visualizations	Interactive Data Visualizations
Target Media/Fields	Best-suited for print media and presentations	Social media applications and websites, business intelligence, and so on
Cost to Create	Low	High
Connection to Data Source	Not required	Required in cases where data is dynamic; results in complicated systems involving online databases
Viewing	Render easily and can be saved as images	Might require advanced UI designs
Popular Python Libraries	Matplotlib, Seaborn	Bokeh, Plotly

Figure 3.7: Static versus interactive data visualizations

Ultimately, interactive data visualizations transform the discussion of data into the art of storytelling, thus simplifying the process of understanding what the data is trying to tell us. They benefit both the people creating the visualizations (since the messages and information they are trying to convey are put across efficiently and in a visually pleasing manner) and those who are viewing the visualizations (since they can understand and observe patterns and insights almost instantly). These aspects are what separate interactive visualizations from static visualizations.

Let's look at a few applications of interactive data visualizations.

Applications of Interactive Data Visualizations

Any industry that possesses large amounts of data can benefit from using interactive data visualizations. A few scenarios, such as those listed here, will help us understand how interactive visualizations help us get quick insights and facilitate our day-to-day activities:

- Let's say you wake up early in the morning and have time to hit the gym before you have to leave for work/school. You ate a pretty heavy meal last night with lots of carbs and sugar, so you want to do a workout that burns the most calories. You check your fitness app, which shows you a visualization describing your last couple of workouts, and with the help of the interactive graphs, you find a workout that helps you burn the most calories. Let's look at the following figure:

Figure 3.8: Fitness app

- Before leaving for work/school, you need to decide whether you should drive or take an Uber. You check Google Maps to see how much traffic there is on your route, and you see there's a lot. So, you decide to take an Uber to avoid the hassle of driving in a messy traffic situation. Let's look at an example app below:

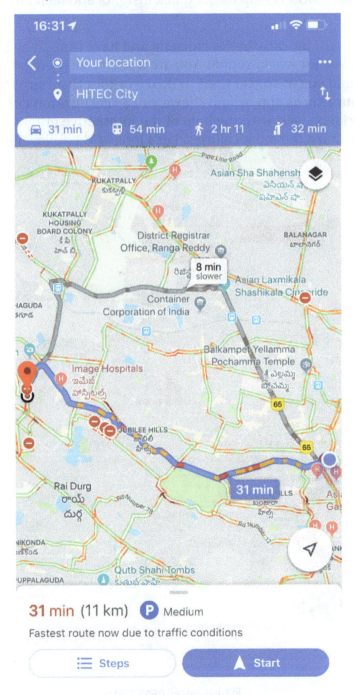

Figure 3.9: Google Maps app

- Uber drivers often decide what hours they should work and the areas they should work in based on peak hours, such as hours when there is a high demand for cabs in specific areas. They can judge this by observing an interactive data visualization.

- When you're at work/in school, you need to prepare a pitch for a client regarding a social media campaign, conveying the conclusion that Instagram is the app to target. To do this, you use data describing user habits on different social media platforms to create an interactive visualization, providing insights as to which app receives the most users and user time.

- You go to the cinema and ask the ticket vendor for a ticket for the most popular movie right now. The ticket vendor reviews the trends through an interactive visualization-based app pertaining to the movies currently in cinemas and gives you a ticket to Avengers: Endgame.

- When you go home after the movie, you add your review of the movie to the ticket-selling mobile app. Your review gets added to the data, which creates visualizations regarding movie trends.

The aforementioned examples involve fitness, Google Maps, transportation, social media, business intelligence, and the entertainment industry. These fields, along with many others, benefit from and use interactive data visualizations.

Getting Started with Interactive Data Visualizations

As we mentioned earlier, the key aspect of interactive data visualizations is its ability to respond and react to human inputs either in the moment or within a very short time span. Thus, human inputs themselves play an important role in interactive data visualizations. In this section, we'll look at some human inputs, how they can be introduced into data visualizations, and the impact that they have on the comprehension of data.

The following are some of the most popular forms of human input and interactive features:

- *Slider*: A slider allows the user to see data pertaining to a range of something. As the user changes the position of the slider, the plot changes in real time. This allows the user to see several plots in real time:

Figure 3.10: A slider tool

- *Hover*: Hovering a cursor above an element of a plot allows the user to receive more information about the datapoint than can be seen just by observing the plot. This is helpful when the information you wish to convey cannot fit in the plot itself (such as precise values or brief descriptions). Let's look at a hover tool:

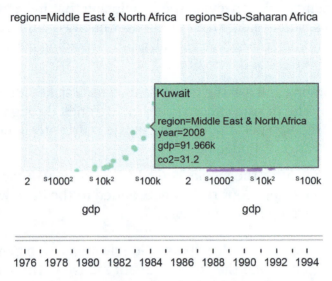

Figure 3.11: A hover tool

- *Zoom*: Zooming in and out of a plot is a feature that quite a few interactive data visualization libraries create on their own. They allow you to focus on specific datapoints of a plot and take a closer look at them.

- *Clickable parameters:*There are several types of clickable parameters, such as checkboxes and drop-down menus, that allow the user to pick and choose what aspects of the data they wish to analyze and view. An example is given here:

- region=South Asia
- region=Europe & Central Asia
- region=Middle East & North Africa
- region=Sub-Saharan Africa
- region=America
- region=East Asia & Pacific

Figure 3.12: Clickable parameters

There are Python libraries that are used to create these interactive features, which allow for the visualizations to take human input. Therefore, before we begin coding for and creating these interactive features, let's take a quick look at some of the most popular interactive data visualization Python libraries that exist.

In the previous chapters, we looked at two built-in Python libraries:

- **matplotlib**

- **seaborn**

Both are popular in the data visualization community.

With these, we can build a static visualization (a static scatter plot showing the relationship between two variables) like this:

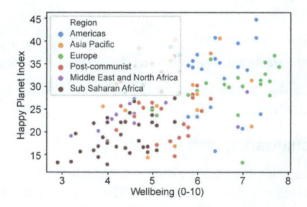

Figure 3. 13: Static data visualization

While both **matplotlib** and **seaborn** are great for *static data visualizations*, there are other libraries available that do a good job of designing interactive features.

Two of the most popular interactive data visualization Python libraries are as follows:

- **bokeh**

- **plotly**

These help us create visualizations such as the following:

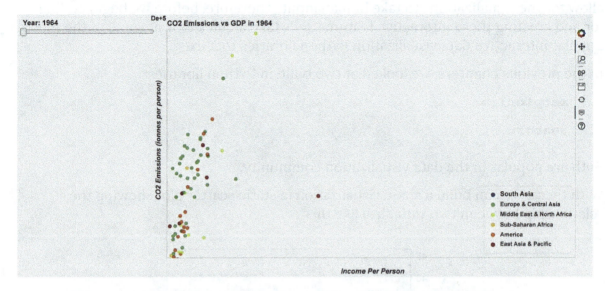

Figure 3.14: The interactive data visualization that we will be creating in this chapter

We will be using both **bokeh** and **plotly** in the exercises in this chapter to create interactive data visualizations.

Interactive Data Visualization with Bokeh

bokeh is a Python library for interactive data visualizations. The plots in Bokeh are created by stacking layers on top of each other. The first step is to create an empty figure, to which elements are added in layers. These elements are known as glyphs, which can be anything from lines to bars to circles. Attached to each glyph are properties such as color, size, and coordinates.

bokeh is popular because the visualizations are rendered using HTML and JavaScript, which is why it is commonly chosen when designing web-based interactive visualizations. Furthermore, the **bokeh.io** module creates a **.html** file that contains the basic static plot, along with the interactive features, and doesn't necessarily require a server to run, which makes the visualization super easy to deploy.

Let's get started with our visualizations!

The most important aspect of any kind of data visualization is the data itself – without it, there is nothing to convey. So, let's start our journey of interactive data visualizations by gathering and preparing our data so that we can visualize it in the most efficient manner.

In this chapter, Exercises 1 – 4 aim to create an interactive data visualization to represent the relationship between carbon dioxide emissions and the GDP of a country using the Python **bokeh** library.

> **Note**
>
> All the exercises and activities in this chapter will be developed on Jupyter Notebook. You will need Python 3.6, Bokeh, and Plotly installed on your system.

Exercise 22: Preparing Our Dataset

In this exercise, we will download and prepare our dataset using the built-in **pandas** and **numpy** libraries. By the end of this exercise, we will have a DataFrame on which we will build our interactive data visualizations. We'll be using the **co2.csv** and **gapminder.csv** datasets. The former consists of the carbon dioxide emissions per person per year per country, while the latter consists of the GDP per year per country. These files are available at https://github.com/TrainingByPackt/Interactive-Data-Visualization-with-Python/tree/master/datasets.

The following steps will help you prepare the data:

1. Import the **pandas** and **numpy** libraries:

    ```
    import pandas as pd
    import numpy as np
    ```

2. Store the **co2.csv** file in a DataFrame called **co2**, and the **gapminder.csv** file in a DataFrame called **gm**:

    ```
    url_co2 = 'https://raw.githubusercontent.com/TrainingByPackt/
    Interactive-Data-Visualization-with-Python/master/datasets/co2.csv'
    co2 = pd.read_csv(url_co2)

    url_gm = 'https://raw.githubusercontent.com/TrainingByPackt/
    Interactive-Data-Visualization-with-Python/master/datasets/
    gapminder.csv'
    gm = pd.read_csv(url_gm)
    ```

    We currently have two separate DataFrames, each consisting of data that we require to create our interactive data visualization. In order to create the visualization, we need to combine these two DataFrames and remove the unwanted columns.

3. Use **.drop_duplicates()** to remove the duplicate instances from the **gm** DataFrame and save this in a new DataFrame called **df_gm**:

```
df_gm = gm[['Country', 'region']].drop_duplicates()
```

4. Use **.merge()** to combine the **co2** DataFrame with the **df_gm** DataFrame. This **merge** function basically performs an inner join on the two DataFrames (the same as the inner join when used in databases). This merge is necessary to ensure that both the **co2** DataFrame and the **gm** DataFrame consist of the same countries, thus guaranteeing that the values of the CO2 emissions will correspond to their respective countries:

```
df_w_regions = pd.merge(co2, df_gm, left_on ='country', right_on ='Country', how ='inner')
```

> **Note**
>
> To find out more about merging and joining in Python, click here: https://www.shanelynn.ie/merge-join-DataFrames-python-pandas-index-1/.

5. Drop one of the country columns since there are two:

```
df_w_regions = df_w_regions.drop('Country', axis='columns')
```

6. Next, we're going to apply the **.melt()** function to this DataFrame and store it in a new DataFrame called **new_co2**. This function changes the format of a DataFrame into one that has identifier variables of our choice. In our case, we want the identifier variables to be **country** and **region** since they are the constants. We're also going to rename the columns:

```
new_co2 = pd.melt(df_w_regions, id_vars=['country', 'region'])
columns = ['country', 'region', 'year', 'co2']
new_co2.columns = columns
```

7. Set **1964** and onward as the range for the **year** column and **int64** as the data type. Set the lower limit for the **year** column as **1964** so that the column consists of **int64** values for **1964** and onward. Do this within the **new_co2** DataFrame we created in the previous step, and store this in a new DataFrame called **df_co2**. Sort the values of the **df_co2** DataFrame by the **country** column and then do the same for the **year** column using **.sort_values()**. Using the **head()** function, print the first five rows of the **df_co2** DataFrame:

```
df_co2 = new_co2[new_co2['year'].astype('int64') > 1963]
df_co2 = df_co2.sort_values(by=['country', 'year'])
df_co2['year'] = df_co2['year'].astype('int64')
df_co2.head()
```

The output is as follows:

	country	region	year	co2
28372	Afghanistan	South Asia	1964	0.0863
28545	Afghanistan	South Asia	1965	0.1010
28718	Afghanistan	South Asia	1966	0.1080
28891	Afghanistan	South Asia	1967	0.1240
29064	Afghanistan	South Asia	1968	0.1160

Figure 3.15: The first five rows of the df_co2 DataFrame

Now we have a DataFrame that consists of the carbon dioxide emissions per year per country! The serial numbers are not in ascending order because we have sorted the data by the **country** column and then the **year** column.

Next, we're going to create a similar table for the GDP per year per country.

8. Create a new DataFrame called **df_gdp** that consists of the **country**, **year**, and **gdp** columns from the **gm** DataFrame:

```
df_gdp = gm[['Country', 'Year', 'gdp']]
df_gdp.columns = ['country', 'year', 'gdp']
df_gdp.head()
```

The output is as follows:

	country	year	gdp
0	Afghanistan	1964	1182.0
1	Afghanistan	1965	1182.0
2	Afghanistan	1966	1168.0
3	Afghanistan	1967	1173.0
4	Afghanistan	1968	1187.0

Figure 3.16: The first five rows of the df_gdp DataFrame

We finally have two DataFrames that consist of the following:

The carbon dioxide emissions, the GDP

9. Merge the two DataFrames together by using the **.merge()** function on the **country** and **year** columns. Store this in a new DataFrame called **data**. Use the **dropna()** function to drop the **NaN** values and the **head()** function to print the first five rows. By doing this, we can see what the final dataset looks like:

```
data = pd.merge(df_co2, df_gdp, on=['country', 'year'], how='left')
data = data.dropna()
data.head()
```

The output is as follows:

	country	region	year	co2	gdp
0	Afghanistan	South Asia	1964	0.0863	1182.0
1	Afghanistan	South Asia	1965	0.1010	1182.0
2	Afghanistan	South Asia	1966	0.1080	1168.0
3	Afghanistan	South Asia	1967	0.1240	1173.0
4	Afghanistan	South Asia	1968	0.1160	1187.0

Figure 3.17:The first five rows of the final DataFrame that we are going to visualize

Finally, let's check the correlation between carbon dioxide emissions and the GDP to ensure we're analyzing data that is worth visualizing.

10. Create a **numpy** array of the **co2** and **gdp** columns:

```
np_co2 = np.array(data['co2'])
np_gdp = np.array(data['gdp'])
```

11. Use the **.corrcoef()** function to print the correlation between the carbon dioxide emissions and the GDP:

```
np.corrcoef(np_co2, np_gdp)
```

The output is as follows:

```
array([[1.        , 0.78219731],
       [0.78219731, 1.        ]])
```

Figure 3.18: Correlation between the carbon dioxide emissions and the GDP

As you can see from the preceding output, there is a high correlation between the carbon dioxide emissions and the GDP.

Exercise 23: Creating the Base Static Plot for an Interactive Data Visualization

In this exercise, we are going to create a static plot for our dataset and add circular glyphs to it. The following steps will help you with the solution:

1. Import the following:

- **curdoc** from **bokeh.io**: This returns the current default state of the document/plot.

- The figure from **bokeh.plotting**: This creates the figure for plotting.

- **HoverTool**, **ColumnDataSource**, **CategoricalColorMapper**, and **Slider** from **bokeh.models**: These are interactive tools and methods for mapping data from **pandas** DataFrames to a data source for plotting.

- **Spectral6** from **bokeh.palettes**: A color palette for the plot.

- **widgetbox** and **row** from **bokeh.layouts**: **widgetbox** creates a column of predefined tools (including zoom), while **row** creates a row of bokeh layout objects, forcing them to have the same **sizing_mode**:

```
from bokeh.io import curdoc, output_notebook
from bokeh.plotting import figure, show
from bokeh.models import HoverTool, ColumnDataSource,
CategoricalColorMapper, Slider
from bokeh.palettes import Spectral6
from bokeh.layouts import widgetbox, row
```

2. Run the **output_notebook()** function to load **BokehJS**. This is what enables the plot to be displayed within the notebook:

```
output_notebook()
```

3. We are going to color code our datapoints (which will be the individual countries) based on the region that they belong to. To do that, create a list of regions by applying the **.unique()** function on the **region** column in the DataFrame. Make this a list by using the **.tolist()** method:

```
regions_list = data.region.unique().tolist()
```

4. Use **CategoricalColorMapper** to assign a color from the **Spectral6** package to the different regions present in the **regions_list** list:

```
color_mapper = CategoricalColorMapper(factors=regions_list,
palette=Spectral6)
```

5. Next, we need to make a data source for the plot. Do this by creating a **ColumnDataSource** and storing it as **source**. The x axis will be the GDP per year while the y axis will be the carbon dioxide emissions per year:

```
source = ColumnDataSource(data={
    'x': data.gdp[data['year'] == 1964],
    'y': data.co2[data['year'] == 1964],
    'country': data.country[data['year'] == 1964],
    'region': data.region[data['year'] == 1964],
})
```

6. Store the minimum and maximum GDP values as **xmin** and **xmax** respectively:

```
xmin, xmax = min(data.gdp), max(data.gdp)
```

7. Repeat step 6 to determine the minimum and maximum carbon dioxide emission values:

```
ymin, ymax = min(data.co2), max(data.co2)
```

8. Create the empty figure:

- Set the title as CO2 Emissions versus GDP in **1964**.

- Set the plot height as **600**.

- Set the plot width as **1000**.

- Set the range of the x-axis from **xmin** to **xmax**.

- Set the range of the y-axis from **ymin** to **ymax**.

- Set the y-axis type as logarithmic:

```
plot = figure(title='CO2 Emissions vs GDP in 1964',
              plot_height=600, plot_width=1000,
              x_range=(xmin, xmax),
              y_range=(ymin, ymax), y_axis_type='log')
```

9. Add circular glyphs to the plot:

```
plot.circle(x='x', y='y', fill_alpha=0.8, source=source,
legend='region', color=dict(field='region', transform=color_mapper),
size=7)
```

10. Set the location of the legend to the bottom-right corner of the plot:

```
plot.legend.location = 'bottom_right'
```

11. Set the x-axis title as **Income Per Person**:

```
plot.xaxis.axis_label = 'Income Per Person'
```

12. Set the y-axis title as **CO2 Emissions (tons per person)**:

```
plot.yaxis.axis_label = 'CO2 Emissions (tons per person)'
```

Now we have our basic plot created!

13. Display the plot:

```
show(plot)
```

The output is as follows:

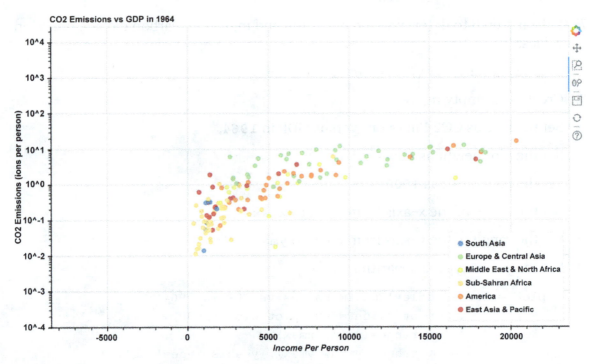

Figure 3.19: The static plot with circular glyphs. Right now, this is a static data visualization

Exercise 24: Adding a Slider to the Static Plot

In this exercise, we are going to add a slider for the **year** column of the **DataFrame** to our plot. The following steps will help you with the solution:

1. Create a slider object:

   - Set the start as the first year in the year column.

   - Set the end as the last year in the year column.

   - Set the step as 1. Since with each movement of the slider, we want the year to increment with the value of 1.

   - Set the value as the minimum value of the year column.

   - Set the title as Year:

   ```
   slider = Slider(start=min(data.year), end=max(data.year), step=1,
   value=min(data.year), title='Year')
   ```

2. Create a function called **update_plot** that will update the plot every time the slider is moved:

   ```
   def update_plot(attr, old, new):
   yr = slider.value
   new_data = {
           'x': data.gdp[data['year'] == yr],
           'y': data.co2[data['year'] == yr],
           'country': data.country[data['year'] == yr],
           'region': data.region[data['year'] == yr],
   }
   source.data = new_data
   plot.title.text = 'CO2 Emissions vs GDP in %d' % yr
   ```

   slider.value is the value of the current position of the slider, and thus is the year whose data we need to display in the plot. This value is stored as **yr**. Create a dictionary called **new_data** that is structured the way **source** is structured (from Exercise 2, Creating the Base Static Plot for an Interactive Data Visualization step 4), except instead of **1964**, the year is **yr**. **source.data** is set to **new_data**, and the plot title is modified.

3. Apply the `.on_change()` function with **value** and **update_plot** as the parameters to tell the plot that once the value of the slider changes, update the plot using the method described in the **update_plot** function:

```
slider.on_change('value', update_plot)
```

4. Create a row layout of the slider:

```
layout = row(widgetbox(slider), plot)
```

5. Add the layout to the current plot:

```
curdoc().add_root(layout)
```

We have successfully added a slider to our plot! Our visualization is now interactive.

Once again, you can't view the plot just yet, but this is what the slider will look like once we display our plot:

Figure 3.20: The slider tool

Exercise 25: Adding a Hover Tool

In this exercise, we are going to allow the user to hover above a datapoint on our plot to see the name of the country, the carbon dioxide emissions, and the GDP. The following steps will help you with the solution:

1. Create a hover tool called **hover**:

```
hover = HoverTool(tooltips=[('Country', '@country'), ('GDP', '@x'),
('CO2 Emission', '@y')])
```

2. Add the hover tool to the plot:

```
plot.add_tools(hover)
```

Once again, you can't view the plot just yet, but this is what hovering over a datapoint will look like:

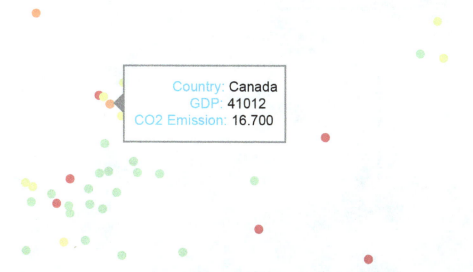

Figure 3.21: Information about the Canada datapoint upon hovering above it

Now that we've added the hover tool, let's display our plot.

3. Go back to cmd or your Terminal and traverse to the folder that contains this Jupyter notebook. Type the following command and wait until the plot is displayed in your web browser:

```
bokeh serve --show name_of_your_notebook.ipynb
```

The output is as follows:

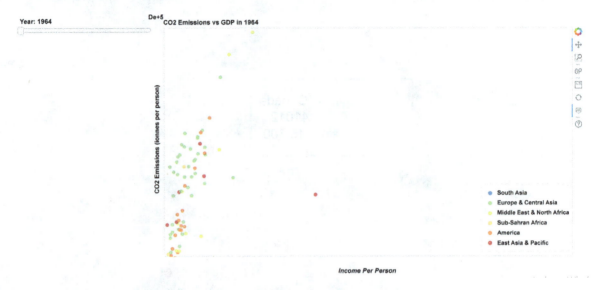

Figure 3.22: The plot when the slider is at the year 1964

The preceding plot displays the carbon dioxide emissions versus the GDP per country in the year 1964. As you move the slider, you will see the plot change in real time:

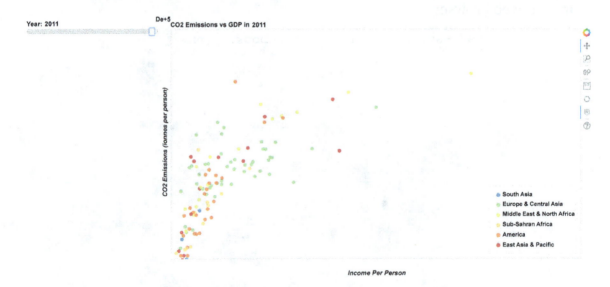

Figure 3.23:The plot when the slider is at the year 2011

As you can see, in the right-hand corner, there are several tools. These are automatically generated by Bokeh when you create a plot:

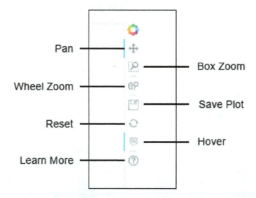

Figure 3.24: The automatically generated features

These tools are as follows:

- Pan: The pan tool allows you to move and shift the view of your plot.

- Box Zoom: This allows you to zoom in to a particular square-shaped section of the plot:

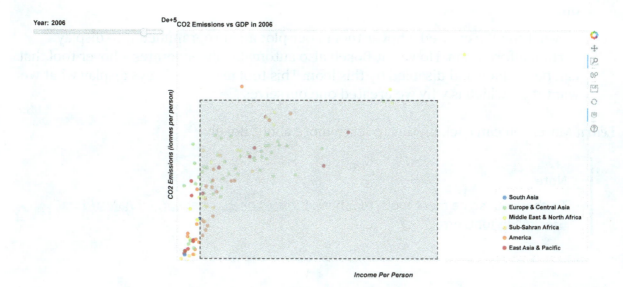

Figure 3.25a: Box zoom on the plot

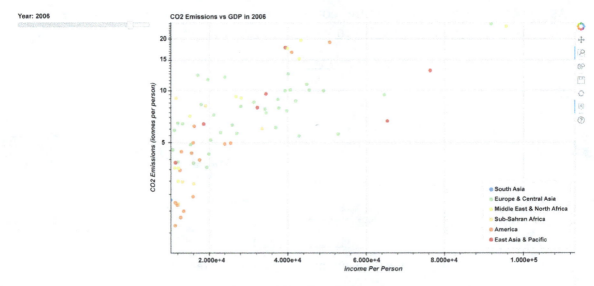

Figure 3.25b: Plot after pan

- Wheel Zoom: This allows you to arbitrarily zoom in to any point of the plot.

- Save Plot: This allows you to save the current plot.

- Reset: This resets the plot and takes you back to the original plot that you landed on.

- Hover Tool: We created a hover tool in our plot and programmed it to display certain information. However, Bokeh also automatically generates a hover tool that can be enabled and disabled by this icon. This tool may not always display what we want it to, which is why we created one ourselves.

Learn More: You can click on this to learn more about Bokeh:

> **Note**
>
> To check out some more tools, click here: https://bokeh.pydata.org/en/latest/docs/user_guide/tools.html.

Interactive Data Visualization with Plotly Express

Plotly is a very popular Python library and is used to create amazing and informative interactive data visualizations. It is a JSON-based plotting tool, and so every plot is defined by two JSON objects – data and layout. Deploying a **Plotly** visualization requires a little more effort than a **Bokeh** visualization does because we need to build a separate application (most commonly a Flask application) using the Dash framework.

Compared with **Bokeh**, the tools and syntax of **Plotly** are much more straightforward. However, the code that's required to create these interactive data visualizations is still quite lengthy and tedious. Therefore, the creators of **Plotly** invented **Plotly Express**!

Plotly Express is a high-level API. Basically, it creates a high-level wrapper around the base **Plotly** code. As a result, the syntax and commands that are required to create interactive data visualizations are minimized immensely.

Exercise 26: Creating an Interactive Scatter Plot

In this exercise, we are going to create an interactive data visualization of the DataFrame we created in *Exercise 1, Preparing Our Dataset* of this chapter – the carbon dioxide emissions and GDP DataFrame.

The following steps will help you with the solution:

1. Open a new Jupyter notebook.

2. Import the following libraries and packages:

- **Pandas**: To prepare the DataFrame

- **plotly.express**: To create the plots:

```
import pandas as pd
import plotly.express as px
```

3. Create the carbon dioxide emissions and GDP DataFrame from *Exercise 1* in this notebook:

```
co2 = pd.read_csv('co2.csv')
gm = pd.read_csv('gapminder.csv')
df_gm = gm[['Country', 'region']].drop_duplicates()
df_w_regions = pd.merge(co2, df_gm, left_on='country', right_
on='Country', how='inner')
df_w_regions = df_w_regions.drop('Country', axis='columns')
new_co2 = pd.melt(df_w_regions, id_vars=['country', 'region'])
columns = ['country', 'region', 'year', 'co2']
new_co2.columns = columns
df_co2 = new_co2[new_co2['year'].astype('int64') > 1963]
df_co2 = df_co2.sort_values(by=['country', 'year'])
df_co2['year'] = df_co2['year'].astype('int64')
df_gdp = gm[['Country', 'Year', 'gdp']]
df_gdp.columns = ['country', 'year', 'gdp']
data = pd.merge(df_co2, df_gdp, on=['country', 'year'], how='left')
data = data.dropna()
data.head()
```

The output is as follows:

	country	region	year	co2	gdp
0	Afghanistan	South Asia	1964	0.0863	1182.0
1	Afghanistan	South Asia	1965	0.1010	1182.0
2	Afghanistan	South Asia	1966	0.1080	1168.0
3	Afghanistan	South Asia	1967	0.1240	1173.0
4	Afghanistan	South Asia	1968	0.1160	1187.0

Figure 3.26: The first five rows of the final DataFrame that we are going to visualize

4. Store the minimum and maximum GDP values as **xmin** and **xmax** respectively:

```
xmin, xmax = min(data.gdp), max(data.gdp)
```

5. Repeat step 4 for the minimum and maximum carbon dioxide emission values:

```
ymin, ymax = min(data.co2), max(data.co2)
```

6. Create the scatter plot and save it as **fig**:

- The **data** parameter will be the name of our DataFrame, that is, **data**.

- Assign the **gdp** column to the x-axis.

- Assign the **co2** column to the y-axis.

- Set the **animation_frame** parameter as the **year** column.

- Set the **animation_group** parameter as the **country** column.

- Set the **color** of the datapoints as the **region** column.

- Assign the **country** column to the **hover_name** parameter.

- Set the **facet_col** parameter as the **region** column (this divides our plot into six columns, one for each region).

- Set the width as **1579** and the height as **400**.

- The x-axis must be logarithmic.

- Set the **size_max** parameter as **45**.

- Assign the range of the x-axis and the y-axis as **xmin**, **xmax** and **ymin**, **ymax**, respectively:

```
fig = px.scatter(data, x="gdp", y="co2", animation_frame="year",
animation_group="country", color="region", hover_name="country",
facet_col="region", width=1579, height=400, log_x=True, size_max=45,
range_x=[xmin,xmax], range_y=[ymin,ymax])
```

7. Display the figure:

```
fig.show()
```

The expected output is as follows:

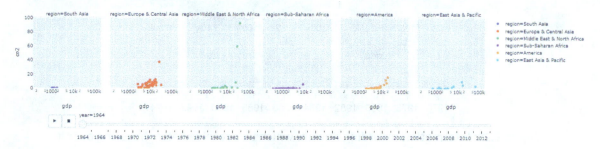

Figure 3.27: The landing plot

As you can see, we have a plot with six subplots; one for each region. Each region is color-coded. Each subplot has carbon dioxide emissions in tons per person as the y-axis and the income per person as the x-axis.

There is a slider at the bottom of the plot that allows us to compare the correlation between the carbon dioxide emissions and the income per year between regions and countries per year. Upon hitting the play button in the bottom-left corner, the plot automatically progresses from the year **1964** to **2013**, showing us how the datapoints vary with time.

We can also manually move the slider:

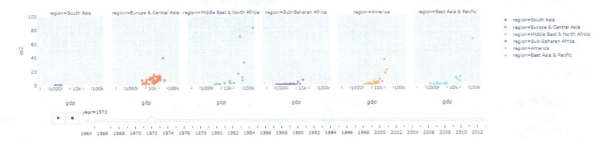

Figure 3.28: The plot in the year 1972

Additionally, we can hover over a datapoint to get more information about it:

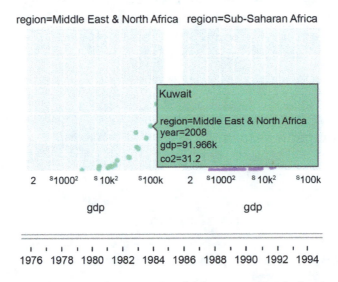

Figure 3.29: Information regarding Kuwait, which was received after hovering over it

Plotly Express also automatically generates a number of interactive features that can be found at the top-right corner of the plot. These include pan, zoom in and out, box select, and hover.

As you can see, creating an interactive data visualization with **Plotly Express** takes very few lines of code and the syntax is easy to learn and use. Besides scatter plots, the library has many other types of plots that you can use to interactively visualize different types of data. In the following activities, you will be a taking a closer look at them.

> **Note**
>
> Click on the following link to check out some more plots that are available with **Plotly Express**: https://plot.ly/python/plotly-express/.

Activity 3: Creating Different Interactive Visualizations Using Plotly Express

In this activity, you will be working on the same dataset that you worked on in exercises of this chapter. It is important that you try out several different types of visualization to determine the visualization that best conveys the message you are trying to put across with your data. Let's create a few interactive visualizations using the Plotly Express library to determine which is the best fit for our data.

High-Level Steps

1. Recreate the carbon dioxide emissions and GDP DataFrame.

2. Create a scatter plot with the x- and y-axes as **year** and **co2** respectively. Add a box plot for the **co2** values with the **marginaly_y** parameter.

3. Create a rug plot for the **gdp** values with the **marginal_x** parameter. Add the animation parameters on the **year** column

4. Create a scatter plot with the x- and y-axes as **gdp** and **co2** respectively.

5. Create a density contour with the x- and y-axes as **gdp** and **co2** respectively.

The outputs should be :

After Step 2:

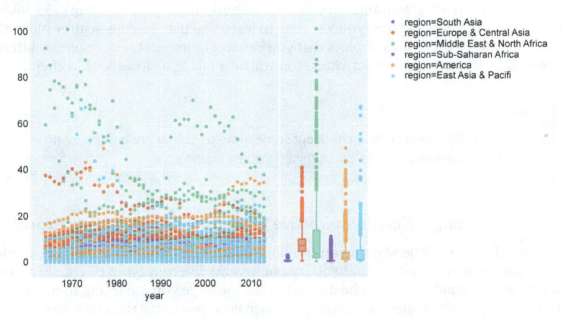

Figure 3.30: Scatter plot of CO2 emissions per year

After Step 3:

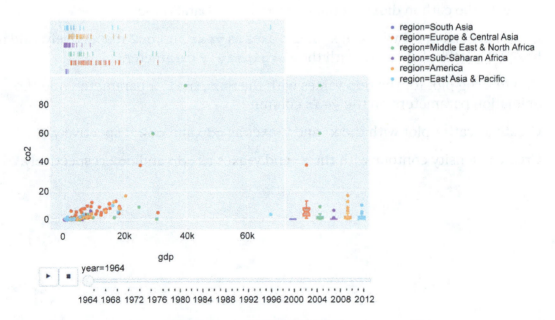

Figure 3.31: Scatter plot of CO2 emissions versus GDP

After Step 5:

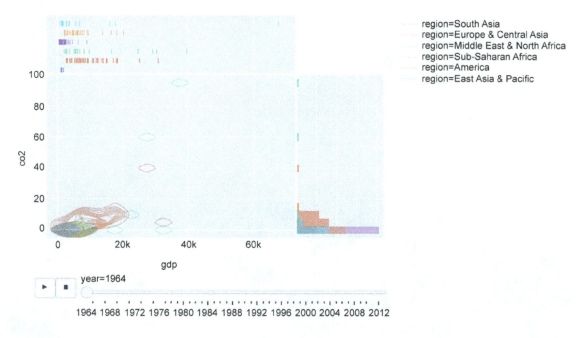

Figure 3.32: Density contour of CO2 emissions versus GDP

> **Note**
>
> The solution steps can be found on page 264.

Summary

In this chapter, we learned how interactive data visualizations are a step ahead of static data visualizations due to their ability to respond to human inputs in real time. The range of applications of interactive data visualizations is vast, and we can visualize almost any type of data interactively.

The human inputs that can be incorporated in interactive data visualizations include, but are not limited to, sliders, zoom features, hover tools, and clickable parameters. `Bokeh` and `Plotly Express` are two of the most popular and easy Python libraries that create interactive data visualizations. In the next chapter, we will look at how to create beautiful context-based interactive data visualizations.

Interactive Visualization of Data across Strata

Learning Objectives

By the end of this chapter, you will be able to:

- Create interactivity in scatter plots using altair

- Use zoom in and out, hover and tooltip, and select and highlight on scatter plots

- Create interactive bar plots and heatmaps

- Create dynamic links between different types of plots within a single rich interactive visualization

In this chapter, you will learn to create interactive visualizations for data stratified with respect to any categorical variable.

Introduction

In the previous chapters, we went through a variety of techniques for visualizing data effectively based on the type of features in the dataset and learned how to introduce interactivity in plots using the `plotly` library. The second section of this book, starting with this chapter, will guide you on building interactive visualizations with Python for a variety of contexts. An observation made in the previous chapter was that when it comes to introducing interactivity in certain types of Python plots, `plotly` can sometimes be verbose, and may involve a steep learning curve. Therefore, in this chapter, we'll introduce `altair`, a library designed especially for generating interactive plots. We will demonstrate how to create interactive visualizations with `altair` for data stratified with respect to any categorical variable. For illustration, we will use a publicly available dataset to generate scatter plots and bar plots with the features in the dataset and add a variety of interactive elements to the plots. We will also learn about some specific advantages of using `altair` over a more multi-purpose library such as `plotly`.

We will use the **Happy Planet Index** (**HPI**) http://happyplanetindex.org/ dataset throughout this chapter. The dataset shows *where in the world people are using ecological resources most efficiently to live long, happy lives.* It is not only an interesting resource for learning more about the ecological conditions as well as the socio-economic well-being in various parts of our planet but also has an interesting mix of features that help us demonstrate certain key concepts of interactive visualization. So, let's dive right in and explore interactive plots using `altair`.

> **Note**
>
> Some of the images in this chapter have colored notations, you can find high-quality color images used in this chapter at: https://github.com/TrainingByPackt/Interactive-Data-Visualization-with-Python/tree/master/Graphics/Lesson4.

Interactive Scatter Plots

As you know by now, scatter plots are one of the most essential types of plots for presenting global patterns within a dataset. Naturally, it is important to know how to introduce interactivity in these plots. We will first look at the zoom and reset actions on plots. Before that, though, let's have a look at the dataset.

We can view the **HPI** dataset using the following code:

```
import pandas as pd

#Download the data from Github repo
```

```
hpi_url = "https://raw.githubusercontent.com/TrainingByPackt/
Interactive-Data-Visualization-with-Python/master/datasets/hpi_data_
countries.tsv"

# Once downloaded, read it into a DataFrame using pandas

hpi_df = pd.read_csv(hpi_url, sep='\t')

hpi_df.head()
```

The output is as follows:

	HPI Rank	Country	Region	Life Expectancy (years)	Wellbeing (0-10)	Inequality of outcomes	Ecological Footprint (gha/capita)	Happy Planet Index
0	1	Costa Rica	Americas	79.1	7.3	15%	2.8	44.7
1	2	Mexico	Americas	76.4	7.3	19%	2.9	40.7
2	3	Colombia	Americas	73.7	6.4	24%	1.9	40.7
3	4	Vanuatu	Asia Pacific	71.3	6.5	22%	1.9	40.6
4	5	Vietnam	Asia Pacific	75.5	5.5	19%	1.7	40.3

Figure 4.1: HPI dataset

Note that there are **5** numerical/quantitative features in this dataset: `Life Expectancy (years)`, `Wellbeing (0-10)`, `Inequality of outcomes`, `Ecological Footprint (gha/capita)`, and `Happy Planet Index`. There are two categorical/nominal features: `Country` and `Region`. In `altair`, quantitative features are denoted as `Q`, and nominal features are denoted as `N`. We will soon see how to use this in our visualizations.

This is actually quite tricky. Generally, for the purpose of visualization, if a feature that denotes an attribute such as rank has a wide range (roughly more than **10** ranks), you can treat the feature as just another numerical or quantitative feature. But with fewer ranks, it almost acts like a label and resembles a nominal feature. However, there is one crucial difference in the way in which rank features differ from nominal features – the order is important in ordinal features. Rank **1** has a different meaning and priority level than rank **5**.

> **Note**
>
> Each datapoint in the **HPI** dataset corresponds to one country.

Let's generate and observe a static scatter plot, through an exercise, of the `Wellbeing (0-10)` and `Happy Planet Index` features for each country, using different colors to denote the region to which the country belongs and go ahead and add interactivity to it.

Exercise 27: Adding Zoom-In and Zoom-Out to a Static Scatter Plot

In this exercise, we'll generate a static scatter plot using **matplotlib**. We'll use the **hpi_data_countries** dataset here for the plot and we'll analyze the **Wellbeing** scores for each country represented by the legend on the plot. We'll go ahead and add a zoom feature to it. We will be using the **altair** library to do this. Let's break the simple code down into simpler components since this is our first interactive plot using **altair**. To do so, let's go through the following steps:

1. Load the **hpi** dataset and read from the dataset using **pandas**:

```
import pandas as pd
hpi_url = "https://raw.githubusercontent.com/TrainingByPackt/
Interactive-Data-Visualization-with-Python/master/datasets/hpi_data_
countries.tsv"
# Once downloaded, read it into a DataFrame using pandas
hpi_df = pd.read_csv(hpi_url, sep='\t')
```

2. Plot a static scatter plot using **matplotlib**:

```
import seaborn as sns
import matplotlib.pyplot as plt
fig = plt.figure()
ax = fig.add_subplot(111)
ax = sns.scatterplot(x='Wellbeing (0-10)', y='Happy Planet Index',
hue='Region', data=hpi_df)
plt.show()
```

The output is as follows:

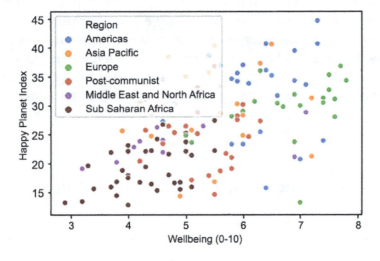

Figure 4.2: Static scatter plot

Each dot here represents a country from one of the **7** regions. **Wellbeing** and **Happy Planet Index** appear to be correlated. We see a trend in the **Happy Planet Index** scores and **Wellbeing** scores of different regions.

Now that we have a static scatter plot, let's explore the interactivity on this plot. We'll look into zoom in and out.

3. Import the **altair** module as **alt**:

```
import altair as alt
alt.renderers.enable('notebook')
```

The output is as follows:

```
RendererRegistry.enable('notebook')
```

4. Provide the DataFrame of choice (**hpi_df** in our case) to the **altair Chart** function.

5. Use the **mark_circle()** function to denote datapoints in the scatter plot using filled circles.

> **Note**
>
> You can also use the **mark_point()** function to use empty circles instead of filled ones. Try it.

6. Use the **encode** function to specify the features on the *x* and *y* axes. Although we also used the **color** parameter in this function to color-code the datapoints using the **region** feature, this is optional. Lastly, add the **interactive()** function to make the plot interactive for zooming! This does require *Jupyter Notebook version 5.3 or above*. Use the following code:

```
alt.Chart(hpi_df).mark_circle().encode(
    x='Wellbeing (0-10):Q',
    y='Happy Planet Index:Q',
    color='Region:N',
).interactive()
```

The output is as follows:

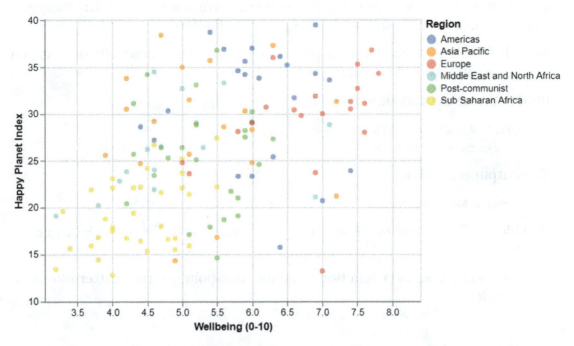

Figure 4.3a: The zoom-in feature on a static scatter plot

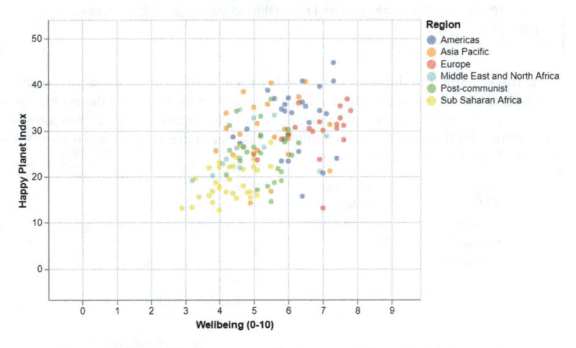

Figure 4.3b: The zoom-out feature on a static scatter plot

And that's it.

Play around a little with that plot to ensure that you can actually zoom in and out.

Did you notice that we added a :Q suffix next to our quantitative features and a :N suffix next to our nominal feature? Adding suffixes like this helps **altair** to know the type of feature beforehand, instead of having to infer it by itself. You can also try eliminating the suffixes in this plot and you'll find that the plot is still generated without error because **altair** can guess the type of features in this case. Therefore, it is good practice to include the suffixes since there are cases where **altair** fails to infer the feature type.

An important concept in **altair** plots is that of *encoding* and *channels*. The concept is really simple – **altair** tries to map/encode various aspects of data for better visualization. This is why you see that there is an **encode()** function in the code. The various parameters, such as **x**, **y**, and **color**, that we specify in the **encode** function are called *channels* in **altair**. Now that you are aware of these important terminologies, let's look at other interesting forms of interactivity in **altair**.

> **Note**
>
> Notice the three little dots next to your plot? You can use that to save your plot in a **.png** (static) or **.svg** (interactive) file, once you have set your interactive plot in the desired configuration. However, the interactivity feature in a **.svg** file will not work unless you open it in compatible software such as Adobe Animate.

Exercise 28: Adding Hover and Tooltip Functionality to a Scatter Plot

In this exercise, we'll add hover and tooltip functionality to a static scatter plot using **altair**. We will work with the same scatter plot but add the ability to hover over any **country** (datapoint) and display information regarding the **Region**, **Wellbeing (0-10)**, **Happy Planet Index**, and **Life Expectancy (years)** of that country:

1. Load the **hpi** dataset and read from the dataset using **pandas**:

    ```
    import pandas as pd
    hpi_url = "https://raw.githubusercontent.com/TrainingByPackt/
    Interactive-Data-Visualization-with-Python/master/datasets/hpi_data_
    countries.tsv"
    # Once downloaded, read it into a DataFrame using pandas
    hpi_df = pd.read_csv(hpi_url, sep='\t')
    ```

2. Import the **altair** module as **alt**:

```
import altair as alt
```

3. Provide the DataFrame of choice (**hpi_df** in our case) to the **altair Chart** function. Use the **mark_circle()** function to denote datapoints in the scatter plot using filled circles. Use the **encode** function to specify the features on the **x** and **y** axes. Although we used the **color** parameter in this function to color-code the datapoints using the **region** feature, this is optional. Specify the **tooltip** channel as shown here:

```
# hover and tooltip in altair
alt.Chart(hpi_df).mark_circle().encode(
    x='Wellbeing (0-10):Q',
    y='Happy Planet Index:Q',
    color='Region:N',
    tooltip=['Country', 'Region', 'Wellbeing (0-10)', 'Happy Planet
Index', 'Life Expectancy (years)'],
    )
```

The output is as follows:

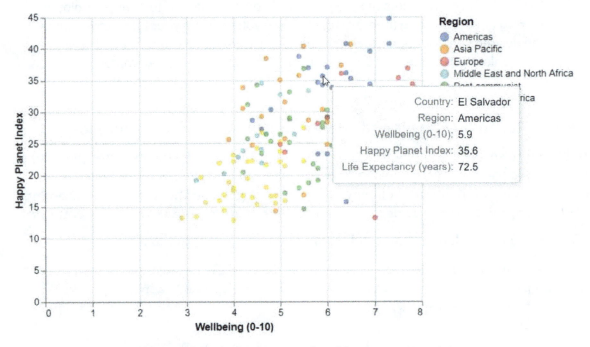

Figure 4.4: Exploring hover and tooltip on a scatter plot

In the preceding plot, you'll find that the features mentioned in the **tooltip** parameter in the **encode** function are all displayed when the cursor is taken near any datapoint. We can see here that when we hover over a datapoint, it displays information regarding the **Region**, **Wellbeing (0-10)**, **Happy Planet Index**, and **Life Expectancy (years)** of that country. In this case, **Country – El Salvador**, **Wellbeing -5.9**, **HPI-35.6**, **Life Expectancy-72.5**.

However, the zoom function is now lost. *How will you bring it back?* Simple – just add the **interactive()** function!

4. Add the **interactive()** function to bring back the zoom feature on the plot as shown here:

```
# zoom feature
import altair as alt
alt.Chart(hpi_df).mark_circle().encode(
    x='Wellbeing (0-10):Q',
    y='Happy Planet Index:Q',
    color='Region:N',
    tooltip=['Country', 'Region', 'Wellbeing (0-10)', 'Happy Planet
Index', 'Life Expectancy (years)'],
).interactive()
```

The output is as follows:

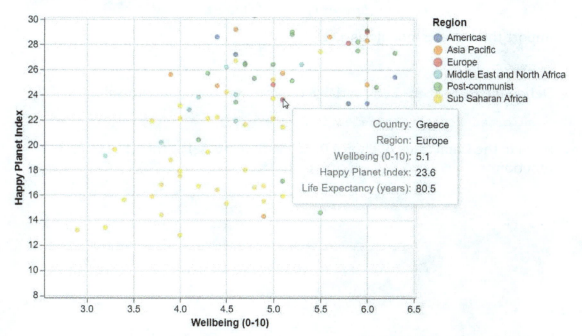

Figure 4.5: Exploring hover and tooltip on a zoomed-in scatter plot

We can see here, in the preceding zoomed-in plot, that when we hover over a datapoint, it displays information regarding the **Region,Wellbeing (0-10),Happy Planet Index**, and **Life Expectancy (years)** of that country. In this case, **Country – Greece, Wellbeing -5.1, HPI-23.6, Life Expectancy-80.5**.

Now, let's consider a more interesting scenario. Suppose we want to select an area on the plot to examine datapoints within it. Let's go through the following exercise for this scenario.

Exercise 29: Exploring Select and Highlight Functionality on a Scatter Plot

In this exercise, we will be using select and highlight functionality using **altair**. We can do this using a function called **add_selection**. We first need to define a variable that will store a *selection interval* and then generate the plot to which we want to add the *selection* function. In the resultant plot, we can click and then drag the cursor to create a selection area, which will be colored *gray*. Let's go through the following steps to do so:

1. Load the **hpi** dataset and read from the dataset using **pandas**:

   ```
   import pandas as pd
   hpi_url = "https://raw.githubusercontent.com/TrainingByPackt/
   Interactive-Data-Visualization-with-Python/master/datasets/hpi_data_
   countries.tsv"
   # Once downloaded, read it into a DataFrame using pandas
   hpi_df = pd.read_csv(hpi_url, sep='\t')
   ```

2. Import the **altair** module as **alt**:

   ```
   import altair as alt
   ```

3. Define the **selected_area** variable to store the selection interval:

   ```
   selected_area = alt.selection_interval()
   ```

4. Provide the DataFrame of choice (**hpi_df** in our case) to the **altair Chart** function.

5. Use the **mark_circle()** function to denote datapoints in the scatter plot using filled circles. Use the **encode** function to specify the features on the **x** and **y** axes. Although we used the **color** parameter in this function to color-code the datapoints using the **region** feature, this is optional. Use the **add_selection()** function to specify the selected area. Use the following code:

```
alt.Chart(hpi_df).mark_circle().encode(
    x='Wellbeing (0-10):Q',
    y='Happy Planet Index:Q',
    color='Region:N'
).add_selection(
    selected_area
)
```

The output is as follows:

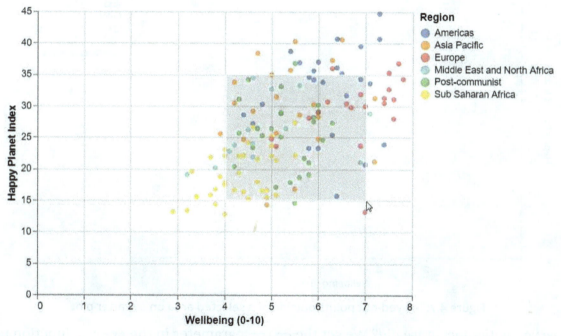

Figure 4.6: Exploring select and highlight on a scatter plot

Have you made sure you can click and drag to create a selection area? Now, let's make the plot respond to our selection by adding focus to our selection and graying out all the points outside of the selection.

6. Add **alt_value** as **lightgray** to gray out all the points outside of the selection:

```
selected_area = alt.selection_interval()
alt.Chart(hpi_df).mark_circle().encode(
    x='Wellbeing (0-10):Q',
    y='Happy Planet Index:Q',
    color=alt.condition(selected_area, 'Region:N', alt.
value('lightgray'))
).add_selection(
    selected_area
)
```

The output is as follows:

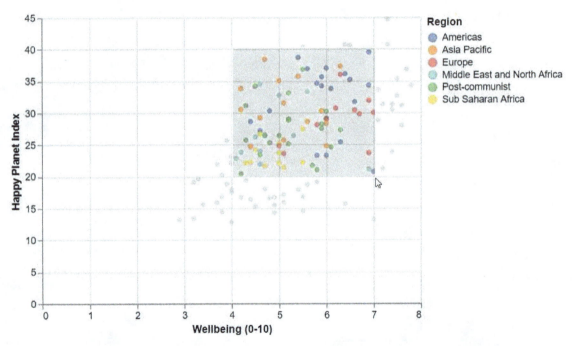

Figure 4.7: Grayed-out points outside of a selected area on a scatter plot

Have you noticed what we did? We set the **color** parameter in the **encode** function to an **altair** condition that retains the colors of only the points within the selected area. This can be useful when you want to get insights into a particular range of features on the axes of a scatter plot. Let's go through an exercise to illustrate this.

Exercise 30: Generating a Plot with Selection, Zoom, and Hover/Tooltip Functions

In this exercise, we will continue to work with the **happy planet index** dataset. The task is to create a scatter plot of **Well-being** versus **Happy Planet Index** and zoom into the area with high **Well-being** and a high **Happy Planet index**. You will need to determine which region is predominant in the selection area, then list the countries in the area. Let's go through the following steps:

1. Import the necessary modules and the dataset:

```
import altair as alt
import pandas as pd
# Download the data from "https://raw.githubusercontent.com/
TrainingByPackt/Interactive-Data-Visualization-with-Python/master/
datasets/hpi_data_countries.tsv"
# Once downloaded, read it into a DataFrame using pandas
hpi_df = pd.read_csv('hpi_data_countries.tsv', sep='\t')
```

2. Create an **altair** scatter plot of **Wellbeing** versus **Happy Planet Index**, along with the zoom feature, using the **interactive()** function, and zoom into the area including the set of datapoints at the top right:

```
alt.Chart(hpi_df).mark_circle().encode(
    x='Wellbeing (0-10):Q',
    y='Happy Planet Index:Q',
    color='Region:N',
).interactive()
```

The output is as follows:

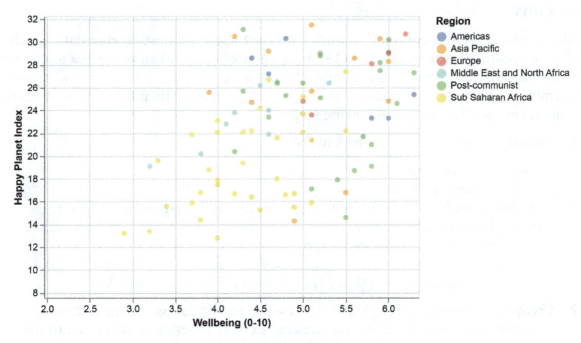

Figure 4.8: Scatter plot with a zoom feature

3. Now add the *selection* feature by changing the **color** parameter to include the **altair** selection condition:

```
selected_area = alt.selection_interval()
alt.Chart(hpi_df).mark_circle().encode(
    x='Wellbeing (0-10):Q',
    y='Happy Planet Index:Q',
    color=alt.condition(selected_area, 'Region:N', alt.
value('lightgray'))
).interactive().add_selection(
    selected_area
)
```

The output is as follows:

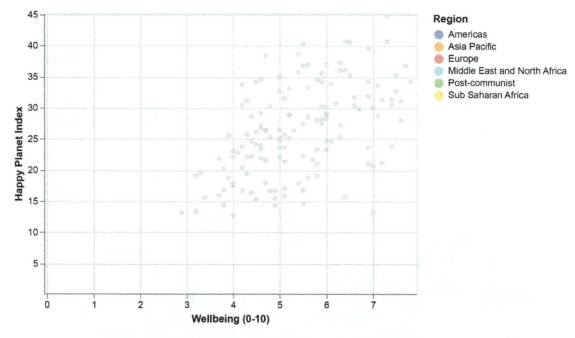

Figure 4.9: Scatter plot with a selection feature

Notice that most countries in the selection area (top right) belong to the Americas (colored blue). Did you expect this based on your general knowledge? Let's add the **tooltip** function to find out which countries appear in our area of interest.

4. Add the **tooltip** function to locate the area of interest:

```
selected_area = alt.selection_interval()
alt.Chart(hpi_df).mark_circle().encode(
    x='Wellbeing (0-10):Q',
    y='Happy Planet Index:Q',
    color=alt.condition(selected_area, 'Region:N', alt.
value('lightgray')),
    tooltip= ['Country', 'Region', 'Wellbeing (0-10)', 'Happy Planet
Index', 'Life Expectancy (years)']
).interactive().add_selection(
    selected_area
)
```

The output is as follows:

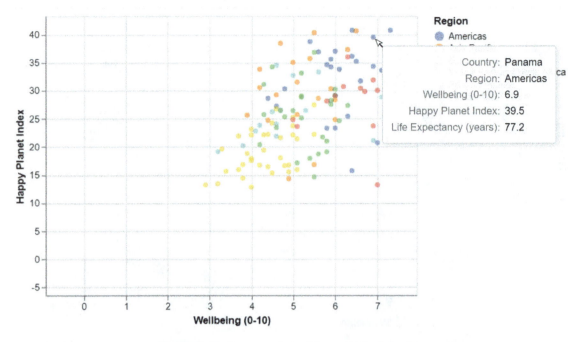

Figure 4.10: Scatter plot with a tooltip function

If you hover over the area of interest, you will see that the top countries are *Costa Rica*, *Mexico*, *Panama*, and *Colombia*.

Now, let's jump to the next section to observe how the *selection* feature could be used across multiple plots.

Selection across Multiple Plots

The selection feature can be much more powerful when linked across multiple plots. We will consider the example of two scatter plots:

- **wellbeing** versus **happy planet index**
- **life expectancy** versus **happy planet index**

Let's go through the following exercise to create selection feature across multiple plots.

Exercise 31: Selection across Multiple Plots

In this exercise, let's go step by step to generate an interactive plot. For our first scatter plot, since we want the y axis to be common across both plots, we will specify only the y axis feature in the **encode** function of our **altair** chart, and then add the x axis features separately on the **Chart** object. Further, to put the two plots one after the other and enable selection across them, we will use the **altair vconcat** function. See the following code for details:

1. Open a Jupyter notebook and import the necessary Python modules:

    ```
    import altair as alt
    import pandas as pd
    ```

2. Read from the dataset:

    ```
    hpi_url = "https://raw.githubusercontent.com/TrainingByPackt/
    Interactive-Data-Visualization-with-Python/master/datasets/hpi_data_
    countries.tsv"
    #read it into a DataFrame using pandas
    hpi_df = pd.read_csv(hpi_url, sep='\t')
    ```

3. Plot the scatter plot with the **Chart altair vconcat** function to place two plots *vertically* one after the other:

    ```
    # multiple altair charts placed one after the other
    chart = alt.Chart(hpi_df).mark_circle().encode(
        y='Happy Planet Index',
        color='Region:N'
    )
    chart1 = chart.encode(x='Wellbeing (0-10)')
    chart2 = chart.encode(x='Life Expectancy (years)')
    alt.vconcat(chart1, chart2)
    ```

The output is as follows:

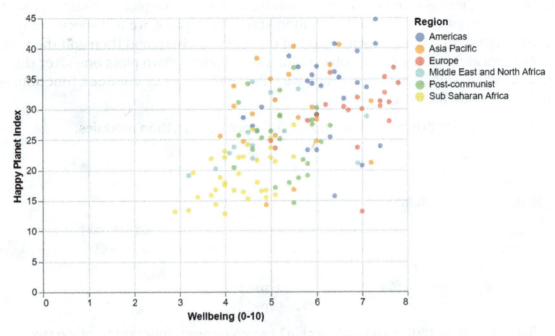

Figure 4.11: Scatter plot for HPI versus Well-Being (0-10)

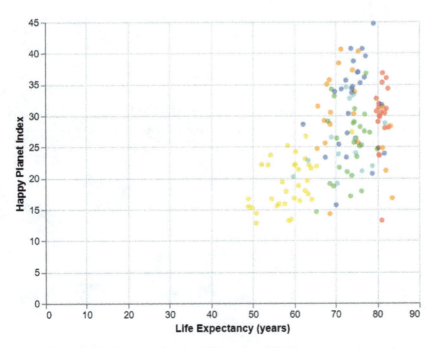

Figure 4.12: Scatter plot for HPI versus Life Expectancy (years)

4. We can also place the two plots *horizontally* next to each other with the **hconcat** function. Here's how:

```
# multiple altair charts placed horizontally next to each other
chart = alt.Chart(hpi_df).mark_circle().encode(
    y='Happy Planet Index',
    color='Region:N'
)
chart1 = chart.encode(x='Wellbeing (0-10)')
chart2 = chart.encode(x='Life Expectancy (years)')
alt.hconcat(chart1, chart2)
```

The output is as follows:

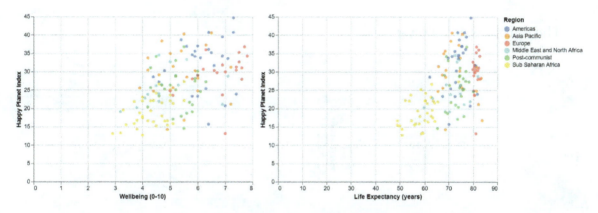

Figure 4.13:Scatter plots placed horizontally

By the way, there are shortcuts for the **hconcat** and **vconcat** functions. We can substitute **alt.hconcat(chart1, chart2)** with **chart1 | chart2** and **alt. vconcat(chart1, chart2)** with **chart1 & chart2**.

5. Add the hover and tooltip functions linking the two plots using the following code:

```
# hover and tooltip across multiple charts
selected_area = alt.selection_interval()
chart = alt.Chart(hpi_df).mark_circle().encode(
    y='Happy Planet Index',
    color=alt.condition(selected_area, 'Region', alt.
value('lightgray'))
).add_selection(
    selected_area
)
chart1 = chart.encode(x='Wellbeing (0-10)')
chart2 = chart.encode(x='Life Expectancy (years)')
chart1 | chart2
```

The output is as follows:

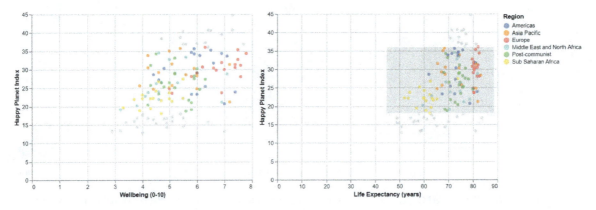

Figure 4.14: Hover and tooltip functionality on the linked scatter plots

Try selecting an area on either of the plots. You will notice that selection on one plot automatically leads to highlighting the same datapoints on the other plot. Isn't that cool?

Selection Based on the Values of a Feature

So far, we have used user input to create a rectangular area of selection using the **selection_interval()** function. Now, let's look at how to create a selection based on the values of a feature.

We'll look at an exercise here. Suppose that we want to select all countries belonging to a region of our choice – *Americas/Asia Pacific/Europe/Middle East and North Africa/ Post-communist/Sub-Saharan Africa*. We can do this using a **selection** function called **selection_single()** instead of **selection_interval()**.Refer to the following exercise to see how this is done.

Exercise 32: Selection Based on the Values of a Feature

In this exercise, we'll create an interactive plot where we'll be able to see the datapoints based on a particular **Region**. We'll use the **selection_single()** function to get a selected set of datapoints. If you study the code carefully, you will find that the parameters for this function are self-explanatory. For any clarifications, please read about them in the official documentation at https://altair-viz.github.io/user_guide/generated/api/altair.selection_single.html. Let's go through the following steps to do this:

1. Import the necessary Python modules:

    ```
    import altair as alt
    import pandas as pd
    ```

2. Read from the dataset:

    ```
    hpi_url = "https://raw.githubusercontent.com/TrainingByPackt/
    Interactive-Data-Visualization-with-Python/master/datasets/hpi_data_
    countries.tsv"
    #read it into a DataFrame using pandas
    hpi_df = pd.read_csv(hpi_url, sep='\t')
    ```

3. Create an **input_dropdown** variable using the **binding_select()** function and set the **options** parameter to the list of regions in our dataset. Use the **selection_single()** function to select a set of datapoints. Use the **color** variable to store the condition under which datapoints will be selected – the colors assigned to datapoints within and outside of the selection:

    ```
    input_dropdown = alt.binding_select(options=list(set(hpi_
    df.Region)))
    selected_points = alt.selection_single(fields=['Region'], bind=input_
    dropdown, name='Select')
    color = alt.condition(selected_points,
                          alt.Color('Region:N'),
                          alt.value('lightgray'))
    alt.Chart(hpi_df).mark_circle().encode(
        x='Wellbeing (0-10):Q',
        y='Happy Planet Index:Q',
        color=color,
        tooltip='Region:N'
    ).add_selection(
        selected_points
    )
    ```

The output is as follows:

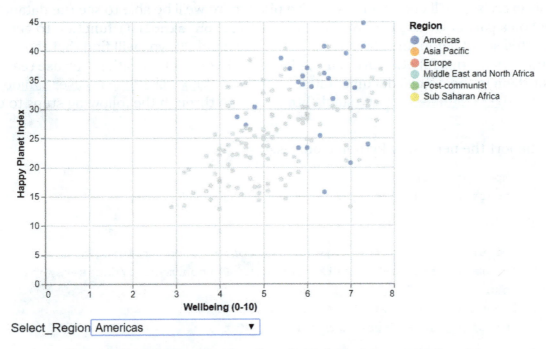

Select_Region [Americas ▼]

Figure 4.15a: Selection based on the values of a feature on a scatter plot

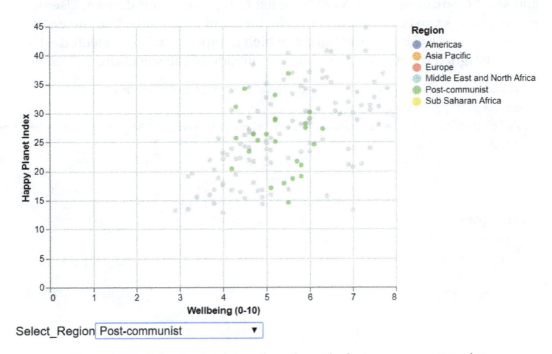

Select_Region [Post-communist ▼]

Figure 4.15b: Selection based on the values of a feature on a scatter plot

The preceding plot initially has all its datapoints in color. However, as you select a value for the **Region** feature from the input dropdown, you'll notice that the corresponding countries are highlighted in color, while all the other countries are grayed out. In the preceding two plots, the first plot shows datapoints for the **Americas** region and the second plot shows datapoints for the **Post-communist** region.

That is quite nice!

> **Note**
>
> There are a variety of ways to perform selection and highlighting in **altair** interactive plots. You can learn more about them at https://altair-viz.github.io/user_guide/interactions.html.

In this preceding section, we presented an overview of the important ways in which you can harness the capabilities of **altair** to make interactive scatter plots. Specifically, we learned:

- How to generate a scatter plot using the **altair Chart()** function, to which interactive components can be added

- How to add interactivity to a scatter plot in the form of zooming in and out with the **interactive()** function

- How to add interactivity to a scatter plot in the form of hovering and displaying information regarding datapoints based on cursor movement with the tooltip parameter

- How to add interactivity to a scatter plot in the form of selections and highlighting with the **selection_interval()** and **selection_single()** functions, and also how to link selections across multiple scatter plots

In the next section, we'll explore how to use **altair** to add interactivity to various other plots.

Other Interactive Plots in altair

Now that we know how to add interactivity to scatter plots, let's learn how to introduce interactivity to two other important visualization types – *bar plots* and *heatmaps*. We also encourage you to read the official documentation and look at the official example gallery at https://altair-viz.github.io/gallery/index.html to explore **altair** so as to be aware of the wide variety of visualization types possible in it.

Exercise 33: Adding a Zoom-In and Zoom-Out Feature and Calculating the Mean on a Static Bar Plot

In this exercise, first, we will generate a *simple (static)* *bar plot* and then explore interactivity such as zooming in and out. Then, we'll use the same bar plot and find out the mean of the **Happy Planet Index** of each region. We'll use the **altair** library here and the **Happy Planet Index** dataset:

1. Import the **altair** module as **alt**:

   ```
   import altair as alt
   ```

2. Read from the dataset:

   ```
   hpi_url = "https://raw.githubusercontent.com/TrainingByPackt/
   Interactive-Data-Visualization-with-Python/master/datasets/hpi_data_
   countries.tsv"
   #read it into a DataFrame using pandas
   hpi_df = pd.read_csv(hpi_url, sep='\t')
   ```

3. Provide the DataFrame of choice (**hpi_df** in our case) to the **altair Chart** function.

4. Use the **mark_bar()** function to denote datapoints on the bar plot. Use the **encode** function to specify the features on the **x** and **y** axes:

   ```
   alt.Chart(hpi_df).mark_bar().encode(
       x='Region:N',
       y='mean(Happy Planet Index):Q',
   )
   ```

The output is as follows:

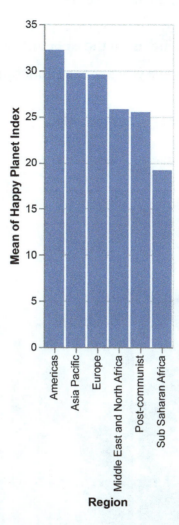

Figure 4.16: Static bar plot

That was easy! *Did you notice that we simply had to set the y parameter to 'mean (Happy Planet Index)' to get the mean per region?*

The above plot looks a bit too narrow, though. We can easily fix this by setting the plot width to a different value using the **properties** function.

5. Set the width to **400** using the **properties** function to increase the width of the bar plot:

```
alt.Chart(hpi_df).mark_bar().encode(
    x='Region:N',
    y='mean(Happy Planet Index):Q',
).properties(width=400)
```

The output is as follows:

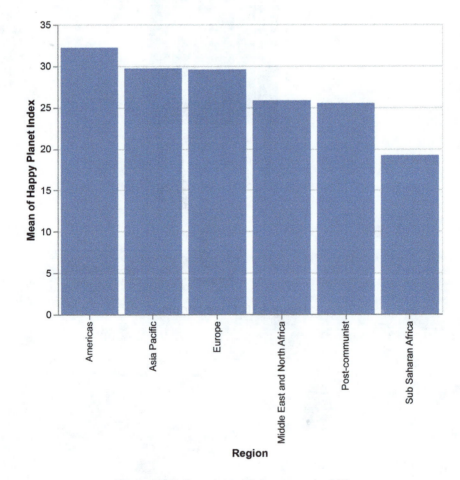

Figure 4.17: Bar plot with increased width

Are you wondering whether you can make the plot zoom in and out? Let's give it a try by adding the **interactive()** *function.*

6. Use the **interactive** function to zoom in and out:

```
import altair as alt
alt.Chart(hpi_df).mark_bar().encode(
    x='Region:N',
    y='mean(Happy Planet Index):Q',
).properties(width=400).interactive()
```

The output is as follows:

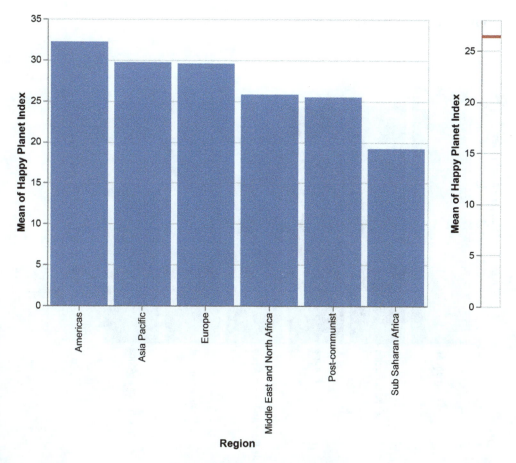

Figure 4.18: Zoomed-in bar plot

And it works! Try zooming in and out of the preceding plot if you don't believe it.

Now let's add a line to show the *mean* of **Happy Planet Index** across all regions. *Any ideas on how to do this?*

7. Use the | operator to show the mean of **HPI** across all regions:

```
import altair as alt
bars = alt.Chart(hpi_df).mark_bar().encode(
    x='Region:N',
    y='mean(Happy Planet Index):Q',
).properties(width=400)
line = alt.Chart(hpi_df).mark_rule(color='firebrick').encode(
    y='mean(Happy Planet Index):Q',
    size=alt.SizeValue(3)
)
bars | line
```

The output is as follows:

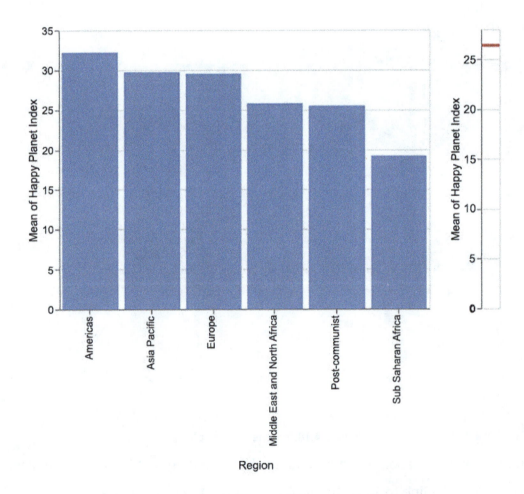

Figure 4.19: Bar plot with the line on the map

Nah, that's not what we wanted. We don't want the line to be placed next to our bar plot. We want it *on* the plot. So, *how do we do that?* For this, we need to use the layer concept in **altair**. The idea is to create variables to store the bar plot and line plot, and then *layer* them one on top of the other. Check out the code in the next step.

8. Add the **layer** function from the **altair** library:

```
import altair as alt
bars = alt.Chart().mark_bar().encode(
    x='Region:N',
    y='mean(Happy Planet Index):Q',
).properties(width=400)

line = alt.Chart().mark_rule(color='firebrick').encode(
    y='mean(Happy Planet Index):Q',
    size=alt.SizeValue(3)
)
alt.layer(bars, line, data=hpi_df)
```

The output is as follows:

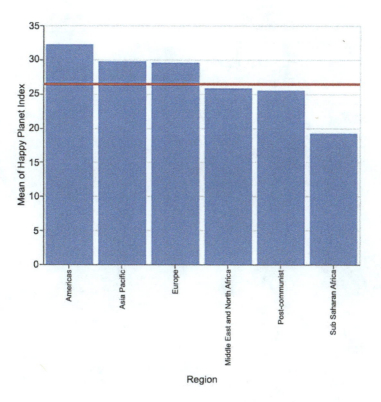

Figure 4.20: Showing the mean on the bar plot

So, now we know that the mean Happy Planet Index across all regions is around **26**. Looks like there's a lot more happiness that our planet could take. Interesting!

By the way, you should also note that we didn't specify the dataset until we used the **layer** function. That is, we did not provide the **hpi_df** dataset in the **Chart()** function as we would usually do. Instead, we mentioned it in the **layer** function with the **data=hpi_df** parameter.

Now that you know about the concept of layering in **altair**, you can be trusted with a shortcut for it. Just write code independently for different plots, as you would usually write it, then use the **+** operator, as shown in the following example!

Exercise 34: An Alternative Shortcut for Representing the Mean on a Bar Plot

In this exercise, we'll calculate the mean of the HPI index on a bar plot using a shortcut to the code used in *Exercise 33, Adding a Zoom-In and Zoom-Out Feature and Calculating the Mean on a Static Bar Plot*. To do so, let's go through the following steps:

1. Calculate the mean of the **HPI** index on a bar plot using the following code:

```
import altair as alt
bars = alt.Chart(hpi_df).mark_bar().encode(
    x='Region:N',
    y='mean(Happy Planet Index):Q',
).properties(width=400)
line = alt.Chart(hpi_df).mark_rule(color='firebrick').encode(
    y='mean(Happy Planet Index):Q',
    size=alt.SizeValue(3)
).interactive()
bars + line
```

The output is as follows:

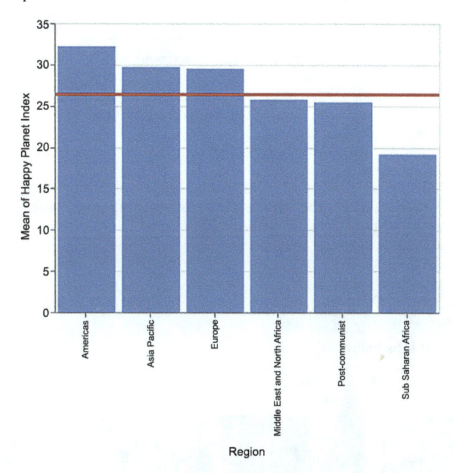

Figure 4.21: Mean of the HPI index on a bar plot

Now let's add some interactivity to our plot. Say we want to be able to see the mean **Happy Planet Index** of any set of bars that we select using the click – and – drag mechanism.

2. Use the click-and-drag mechanism using the following code in **altair**:

```
import altair as alt
selected_bars = alt.selection(type='interval', encodings=['x'])
bars = alt.Chart(hpi_df).mark_bar().encode(
    x='Region:N',
    y='mean(Happy Planet Index):Q',
    opacity=alt.condition(selected_bars, alt.OpacityValue(1), alt.
OpacityValue(0.7)),
).properties(width=400).add_selection(
    selected_bars
)
line = alt.Chart(hpi_df).mark_rule(color='firebrick').encode(
    y='mean(Happy Planet Index):Q',
    size=alt.SizeValue(3)
).transform_filter(
    selected_bars
)
bars + line
```

The output is as follows:

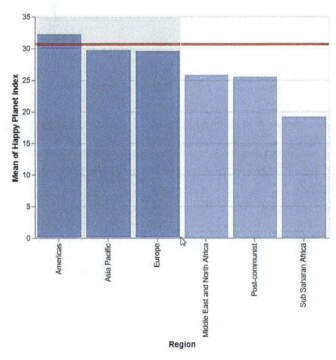

Figure 4.22a: HPI=31 for the Americas, Asia Pacific, and Europe regions on a bar plot

Did you play around with the preceding plot? You can use the click - drag mechanism to select any set of bars and see how the line indicating the mean Happy Planet Index shifts accordingly. For example, if you select the three bars on the left (**Americas**, **Asia Pacific**, and **Europe**), you will notice that the mean **HPI** is around **31**:

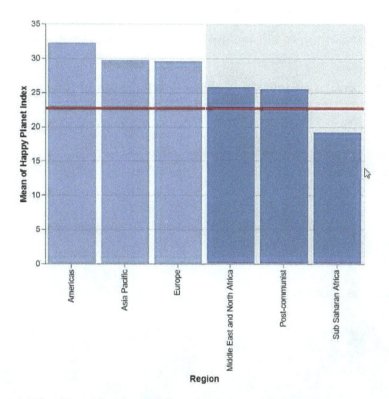

Figure 4.22b: HPI=24 for the Middle East and North Africa, Post-communist, and Sub-Saharan Africa regions on a bar plot

If you select the three bars on the right (**Middle East and North Africa**, **Post-communist**, and **Sub Saharan Africa**), the mean **HPI** will be shown as around **24**.

Exercise 35: Adding a Zoom Feature on a Static Heatmap

In this exercise, we'll use **altair** to create a *heatmap* indicating the number of countries with **HPI** and **Wellbeing** in various ranges. Next, we'll add zoom functionality to the map. We'll move on to also add circles on the heatmap to show different countries. We'll continue using the **HPI** dataset. To do so, let's go through the following steps:

1. Import the **altair** module as **alt**:

    ```
    import altair as alt
    ```

2. Read from the dataset:

```
hpi_url = "https://raw.githubusercontent.com/TrainingByPackt/
Interactive-Data-Visualization-with-Python/master/datasets/hpi_data_
countries.tsv"
#read it into a DataFrame using pandas
hpi_df = pd.read_csv(hpi_url, sep='\t')
```

3. Provide the DataFrame of choice (**hpi_df** in our case) to the **altair Chart** function.

4. Use the **mark_rect()** function to denote datapoints in the bar plot. Use the **encode** function to specify the features on the **x** and **y** axes:

```
alt.Chart(hpi_df).mark_rect().encode(
    alt.X('Happy Planet Index:Q', bin=True),
    alt.Y('Wellbeing (0-10):Q', bin=True),
    alt.Color('count()',
        scale=alt.Scale(scheme='greenblue'),
        legend=alt.Legend(title='Total Countries')
    )
)
```

The output is as follows:

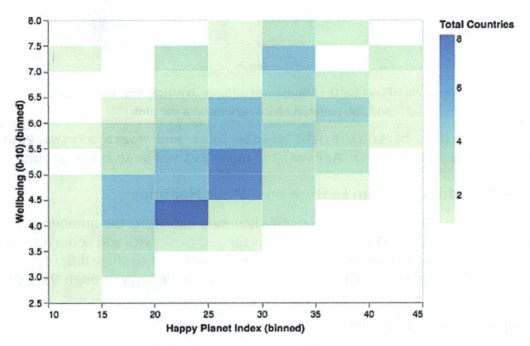

Figure 4.23: Static heatmap

Did you notice how easy it was to *bin* the **Happy Planet Index** and **Wellbeing** features? We simply had to set the **bin** parameter to **True**. **altair** is lovely!

5. Use the **interactive** function and add zoom capability. Use the following code:

```
alt.Chart(hpi_df).mark_rect().encode(
    alt.X('Happy Planet Index:Q', bin=True),
    alt.Y('Wellbeing (0-10):Q', bin=True),
    alt.Color('count()',
        scale=alt.Scale(scheme='greenblue'),
        legend=alt.Legend(title='Total Countries')
    )
).interactive()
```

The output is as follows:

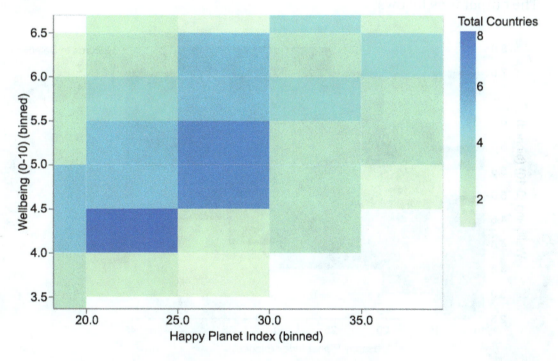

Figure 4.24: Heatmap with a zoom feature

Just as we can use a color palette to indicate the number of countries in each cell of the heatmap, we can also draw circles of varying sizes on a heatmap to indicate the number of countries.

6. Draw circles on the heatmap using the **heatmap+circles** function:

```
heatmap = alt.Chart(hpi_df).mark_rect().encode(
    alt.X('Happy Planet Index:Q', bin=True),
    alt.Y('Wellbeing (0-10):Q', bin=True)
)

circles = heatmap.mark_point().encode(
    alt.ColorValue('lightgray'),
    alt.Size('count()',
        legend=alt.Legend(title='Records in Selection')
    )
)
heatmap + circles
```

The output is as follows:

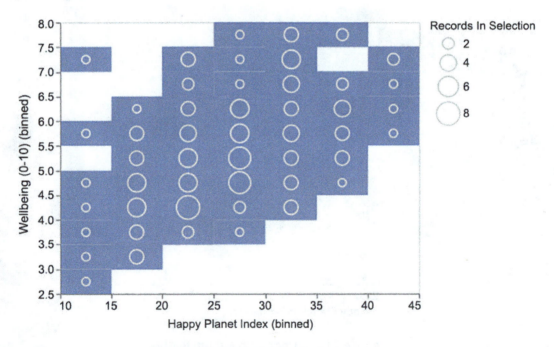

Figure 4.25: Circles on the heatmap

Varying circle sizes indicate the number of countries with a varying **Wellbeing** range. Exciting, isn't it? In the following exercise, we'll generate a bar plot and a heatmap to draw a comparison between the two.

Exercise 36: Creating a Bar Plot and a Heatmap Next to Each Other

In this exercise, we will continue to work with the **HPI** dataset. The objective is to draw a bar plot depicting the number of countries in each region and a heatmap next to it, indicating the number of countries in various ranges of **wellbeing** and **life-expectancy**. Let's see the following code:

1. Import the necessary modules and dataset:

```
import altair as alt
import pandas as pd
```

2. Read from the dataset:

```
import pandas as pd
hpi_url = "https://raw.githubusercontent.com/TrainingByPackt/
Interactive-Data-Visualization-with-Python/master/datasets/hpi_data_
countries.tsv"
# Once downloaded, read it into a DataFrame using pandas
hpi_df = pd.read_csv(hpi_url, sep='\t')
```

3. Generate the required bar chart using the **mark_bar()** function:

```
alt.Chart(hpi_df).mark_bar().encode(
    x='Region:N',
    y='count():Q',
).properties(width=350)
```

The output is as follows:

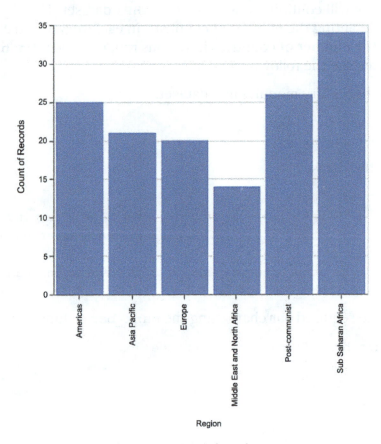

Figure 4.26: Static bar plot

4. Generate the required heatmap using the **mark_rect()** function:

```
alt.Chart(hpi_df).mark_rect().encode(
    alt.X('Wellbeing (0-10):Q', bin=True),
    alt.Y('Life Expectancy (years):Q', bin=True),
    alt.Color('count()',
        scale=alt.Scale(scheme='greenblue'),
        legend=alt.Legend(title='Total Countries')
    )
).properties(width=350)
```

The output is as follows:

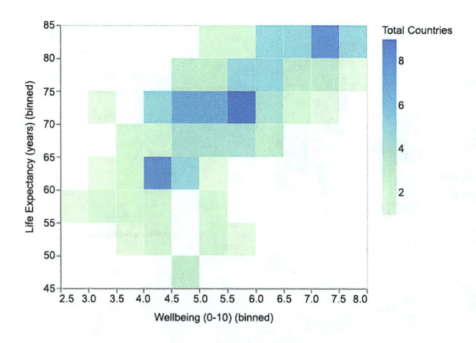

Figure 4.27: Static heatmap

5. Merge the code to place the bar chart and heatmap next to each other using the **bars | heatmap** function:

```
bars = alt.Chart(hpi_df).mark_bar().encode(
    x='Region:N',
    y='count():Q',
).properties(width=350)
heatmap = alt.Chart(hpi_df).mark_rect().encode(
    alt.X('Wellbeing (0-10):Q', bin=True),
    alt.Y('Life Expectancy (years):Q', bin=True),
    alt.Color('count()',
        scale=alt.Scale(scheme='greenblue'),
        legend=alt.Legend(title='Total Countries')
    )
).properties(width=350)
bars | heatmap
```

The output is as follows:

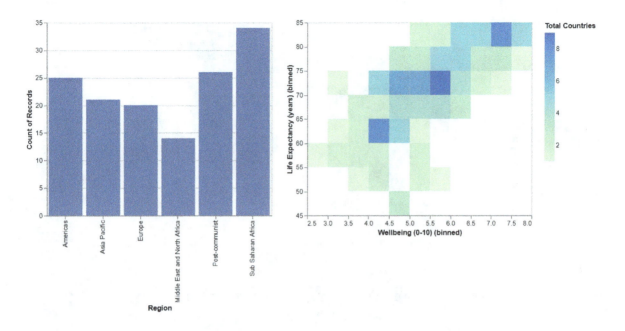

Figure 4.28: Horizontally placing a bar plot and a heatmap

Well done!

Now onto a much more interesting exercise – linking a bar chart with the heatmap we generated in the previous exercise.

Exercise 37: Dynamically Linking a Bar Plot and a Heatmap

In this exercise, we will link a bar plot and a heat map dynamically. Consider a scenario where you want to be able to click on any of the bars in a bar chart and have an updated heatmap corresponding to the region represented by the bar. So, for instance, you want to update the **Life Expectancy** versus **Well Being** heatmap only for the countries in a particular region. We can make this work with the following code:

1. Import the necessary modules and dataset:

```
import altair as alt
import pandas as pd
# Download the data from "https://raw.githubusercontent.com/
TrainingByPackt/Interactive-Data-Visualization-with-Python/master/
datasets/hpi_data_countries.tsv"
# Once downloaded, read it into a DataFrame using pandas
hpi_df = pd.read_csv('hpi_data_countries.tsv', sep='\t')
hpi_df.head()
```

2. Select the region using the **selection** method:

```
selected_region = alt.selection(type="single", encodings=['x'])
heatmap = alt.Chart(hpi_df).mark_rect().encode(
    alt.X('Wellbeing (0-10):Q', bin=True),
    alt.Y('Life Expectancy (years):Q', bin=True),
    alt.Color('count()',
        scale=alt.Scale(scheme='greenblue'),
        legend=alt.Legend(title='Total Countries')
    )
).properties(
    width=350
)
```

3. Place the circles on a heatmap:

```
circles = heatmap.mark_point().encode(
    alt.ColorValue('grey'),
    alt.Size('count()',
        legend=alt.Legend(title='Records in Selection')
    )
).transform_filter(
    selected_region
)
```

4. Use the **heatmap+circles | bars** function to dynamically link the bar plot and the heatmap:

```
bars = alt.Chart(hpi_df).mark_bar().encode(
    x='Region:N',
    y='count()',
    color=alt.condition(selected_region, alt.
ColorValue("steelblue"), alt.ColorValue("grey"))
).properties(
    width=350
).add_selection(selected_region)
heatmap + circles | bars
```

The output is as follows:

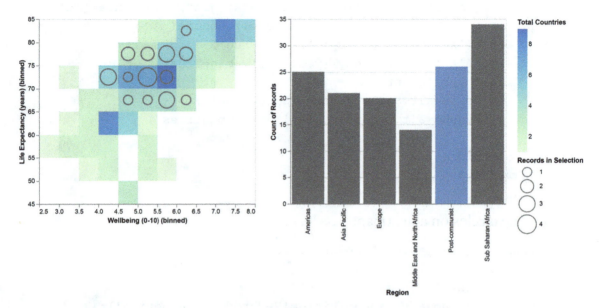

Figure 4.29: A dynamically linked bar plot and heatmap

Spend some time playing around with the visualization and studying the code. *Did you notice how we used both the color palette and circles on the heatmap?* As you click on each bar chart, you will find that the color palette indicating the total countries in a certain range of **well-being** and **life-expectancy** remains constant, whereas the circles get updated to reflect the number of countries in the corresponding range for the selected region. Making intelligent design choices such as these will not only increase your audience's understanding of your dataset but will also help you present your data with confidence and ease.

> **Note**
>
> **altair** is a rich library designed to build both simple and complex interactive visualizations with ease. Due to time and space limitations, it is impossible to cover them comprehensively in any chapter. Therefore, we encourage you to build on the foundations laid in this chapter and study the examples on the **altair** official Example Gallery at https://altair-viz.github.io/gallery/index.html. This will equip you with a deeper understanding of the visualization possibilities in **altair**.

In the preceding section, we presented an overview of some important ways to add interactivity to bar plots and heatmaps. Specifically, we learned:

- How to generate a bar plot using the `altair mark_bar()` function

- How to generate a heatmap using the `altair mark_rect()` function, and how to use color palettes and circles to visually represent heatmap data

- How to add zoom capabilities to bar plots and heatmaps using the `interactive()` function

- How to use the layering capability in `altair` to present plots on top of each other using the `layer()` function or the + operator

- How to dynamically link bar plots and heatmaps to create a single compelling visualization

Activity 4: Generate a Bar Plot and a Heatmap to Represent Content Rating Types in the Google Play Store Apps Dataset

We will be working with the `Google Play Store Apps` dataset hosted on the book repository. Your task is to create a visualization with:

(a) A bar plot of a number of apps stratified by each *Content Rating* category (rated by `Everyone/Teen`).

(b) A heatmap indicating the number of apps stratified by app *Category* and binned ranges of *Rating*. The user should be able to interact with the plot by selecting any of the `Content Rating` types and the corresponding change should reflect in the heatmap to only include the number of apps in that *Content Rating* category.

High-Level Steps

1. Download the dataset hosted in the book GitHub repository and format it as a `pandas` DataFrame.

2. Remove the entries in the DataFrame that have feature values of `NA`.

3. Create the required bar plot of the number of apps in each `Content Rating` category.

4. Create the required heatmap indicating the number of apps across the app `Category` and `Rating` ranges.

5. Merge the code for the bar chart and the heatmap and create a visualization with both plots linked dynamically to each other.

The expected output:

After step 3:

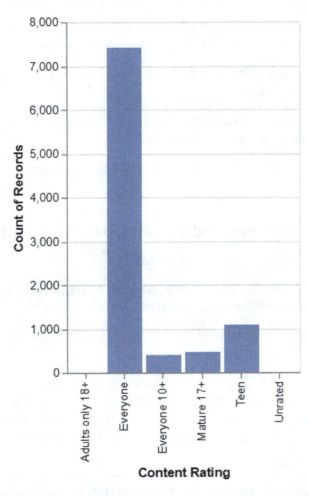

Figure 4.30: Bar plot

After step 4:

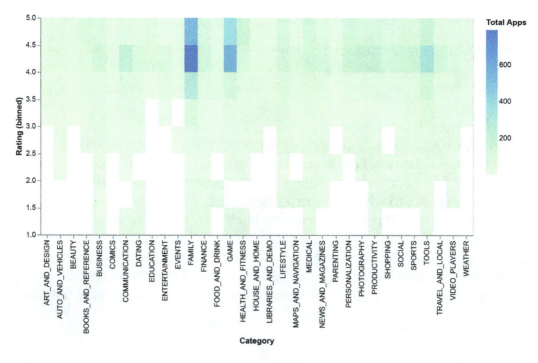

Figure 4.31: Heatmap

After step 5:

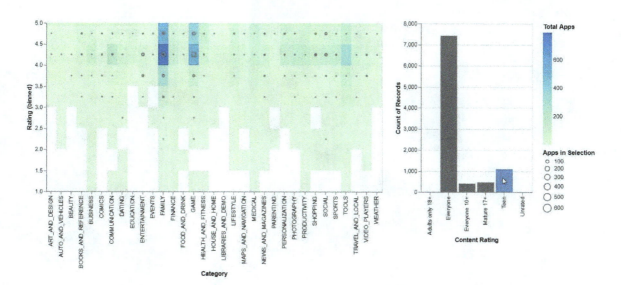

Figure 4.32: Linked bar plot and heatmap

And that's it. Congratulations!

> **Note**
>
> The solution steps can be found on page 268.

Summary

In this chapter, we learned how to create visualizations that respond to the selection of specific strata in a dataset. For illustration purposes, we used the `Happy Planet Index` dataset of `140` countries, creating a variety of plots with stratification based on the different regions to which countries belonged. We generated scatter plots, bar plots, and heatmaps with interactive features such as zooming in and out, tool tipping, the selection of datapoints in a user-specified interval, and the selection of datapoints belonging to specific strata. We also generated more complex visualizations with multiple plots interlinked with each other that dynamically respond to user inputs. In the next chapter, we will learn how to create interactive visualizations of data across time.

Interactive Visualization of Data across Time

Learning Objectives

By the end of this chapter, you will be able to:

- Explain temporal data and how it is used in the real world

- Use pandas to manipulate time-series data

- Build basic interactive plots by adding custom buttons and a range slider to better represent time-series data with the Bokeh library

- Use custom aggregators on time-series plots to explain the behavior of data

In this chapter, we will explore the interactive visualization of data across time.

Introduction

In the previous chapters, we learned how to create interactive visualizations to represent data in different contexts, such as creating bar plots for stratified data. In this chapter, we will learn how to create interactive visualizations to present data over a period of time. Plotting data against time gives us insights into trends, seasonality, outliers, and important events present in a dataset. Adding a time dimension on a static plot means that one of the axes of the plot will represent time. Adding interactivity on top of that gives us the freedom to explore and analyze the data. In an interactive visualization, we can manipulate the graph according to the user requirements on the fly.

We'll see how to manipulate and plot temporal data in Python. To plot timed data, we will first preprocess the time. Time is composed of units such as seconds, minutes, days, and weeks. So, we first parse the time into the required unit in order to visualize it. **Pandas** library provides utilities to parse different time formats, such as **dd/mm/yy** and **mm/dd/yyyy**. Then, by using the **datetime** object, we can segregate these formats.

To add interactivity, we will use the **Bokeh** library, which fits easily into the **pandas** and **matplotlib** ecosystem. By default, **Bokeh** provides many interactive tools, such as zoom-in and zoom-out, hover, and more. It can easily be integrated into Jupyter Notebook in a browser, you can run plots on a **Bokeh** server, or you can integrate them as a service with web frameworks such as Flask.

This chapter is designed to explain concepts by using practical examples. The first thing we will do is learn about temporal data. Then, we'll look at a few use cases of temporal visualization. Then, we will work on the manipulation of data. Finally, we'll use these concepts and apply them to create interactive plots using **Bokeh**. Let's explore the concept of temporal data.

> **Note**
>
> Some of the images in this chapter have colored notations, you can find high-quality color images used in this chapter at: https://github.com/TrainingByPackt/Interactive-Data-Visualization-with-Python/tree/master/Graphics/Lesson5.

Temporal Data

Data that depends on time and where time is recorded explicitly is referred as **temporal data**. For this kind of data, time is an inherent dimension and is always attached to the data. For example, suppose we have a dataset that has records of the rate of ice melting over the last five years in Greenland.

Let's look at the following dataset:

	Year	TemperatureChange
0	1880	-0.07
1	1881	-0.06
2	1882	-0.08
3	1883	-0.12
4	1884	-0.29

Figure 5.1: Rate of temperature change between 1880 and 1884 in Greenland

As we can see, time is an inherent component of this kind of data.

Types of Temporal Data

Temporal data can contain information about the following:

- Events: An event is a change in the state of an object at a given time. Event = Time + Object State. Examples of events are posting a tweet, sending an email, or sending a message.

  Temporal information in tweets helps us understand trending topics, get the latest news updates, and analyze the sentiment of topics over time.

- Measurements: Measurements records values across time. Measurement = Time + Measures. Examples of measurements are sensor data, revenue, and stock values.

  Temporal measurement information is the key feature of time-series forecasting. Also, it helps us find patterns and anomalies in a dataset with sensor data.

Another view of time can be based on how it progresses:

- Sequential: We consider time as continuous linear values here. An example of this type is a Unix timestamp.

- Cyclical: Time can be viewed as a recurrent event, where it is understood as fixed periods, such as weeks or months. The cyclical interpretation of time is used to compare values for the same period, such as sales values per month or yearly temperature change.

- Hierarchical: Another way to understand temporal information is through an hierarchical pattern. A hierarchical time structure helps us to visualize data at different levels. Suppose you are plotting sales data for each month. To understand the pattern for each week for a given month, we are hierarchically breaking the time from a larger periods (months) into smaller periods (weeks).

Why Study Temporal Visualization?

Visualization reveals hidden structures and insights. It helps us understand how values change. For example, with a product sales count dataset, we can plot a comparative view of month-on-month or year-on-year changes and understand trends of sales behavior.

In visualizations with temporal data, time is plotted on the x axis, and the other features of the dataset are plotted on the y axis.

Understanding and using temporal features of data play a crucial role in time-series forecasting, recommendations, rankings, and more.

A static plot shows how a feature on a temporal dataset changes over a period of time. In contrast to that, interactive plots can be visualized with user input/interactivity in mind. Also, interactive plots can ingest stream data to show the behavior of online data.

Let's look at example bar plots.

Here is the first plot:

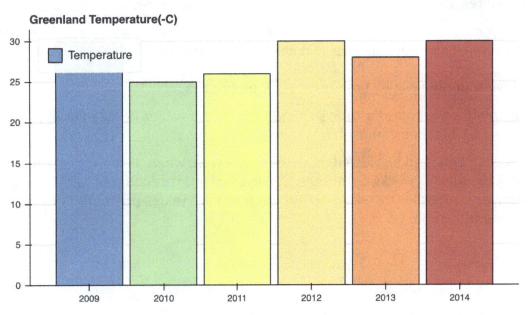

Figure 5.2a: Static bar plot showing the change in temperature in Greenland

Here is the second plot:

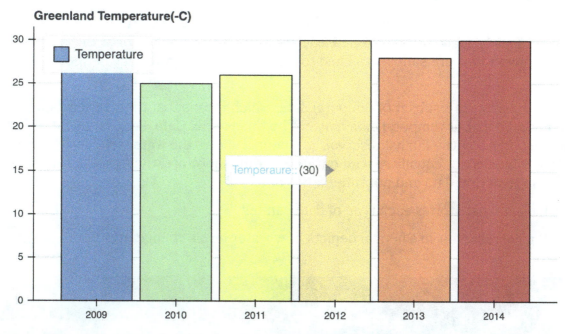

Figure 5.2b: Interactive plot of Greenland's temperature shown by the hover tooltip

In the preceding plots, we can see the change in temperature in Greenland over the last 10 years in Figure 5.2a, which is essentially a static plot. Now, when we add interactivity on this plot and use the hover functionality, we will be able to see the exact value of temperature for a particular year. We can see in Figure 5.2b that it's `-30 degrees C` in `2012`.

The plots allow the reader to get a deeper understanding of the data because we can play with the plot. Interactive visualizations allow multiple perspectives of the same data; the problem with static visualizations is that they have been drawn to keep one view in mind.

We will be using temporal data and time-series data interchangeably throughout the chapter. Although these terms might not be very similar, they are in fact correlated. Let's first learn how they are related.

Understanding the Relation between Temporal Data and Time-Series Data

Time-series data is a more refined version of temporal data where observations are taken at equally spaced points in time successively. With temporal data, on the other hand, observations are simply attached to time, and the intervals may not be equally spaced.

Time-series data is a subset of temporal data, which means that time-series data is temporal data but temporal data may not be time-series data. For example, the following figure of the Puzhal reservoir in Chennai shows the water level over a period of time, which is not equally spaced out necessarily; therefore, the figure is plotted based on temporal data and not time-series data.

Let's look at what stories each type of data can tell:

- Puzhal reservoir in Chennai depicts how water levels change over time:

Figure 5.3: June 15, 2018 (L) and April 6, 2019 (R)

This picture is courtesy of https://time.com/5611385/india-chennai-water-crisis/.

Effect of draught: The photos of the *Puzhal reservoir in Chennai* depict the change in water level over time. Here, we can study the effect of drought and can conclude that how water has depleted from 2018 to 2019.

- Comparative study of GDP growth depicts the **growth_rate** of US and India:

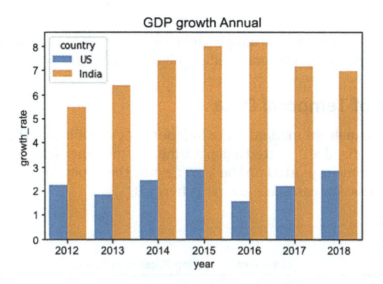

Figure 5.4: Annual GDP growth of US and India

An interesting thing to note here is how the GDP of India has started going down in recent years compared to the US, which started going up from 2016. This is an example of a time-series dataset; we can see that data has been recorded at equal intervals of time.

Examples of Domains That Use Temporal Data

Easily accessible, yet information-dense, temporal visualizations are the result of accurate interpretations of data. There are different domains that use temporal and time-series data for interactive visualizations:

- Finance: Examples include the study of a country's GDP growth and the study of the revenue growth of a country. In these cases, we use a time-series dataset.

- Meteorological: Forecasting the surface temperature change of a geographical region over time, for example, CO_2 emissions by countries per year, again uses time-series data.

- Traffic/mobility: Routing of vehicles/cabs for efficient operations and solving supply and demand problems pertaining to mobility could use time-series traffic data.

- Medical/healthcare: Some examples include studies of life expectancy over time, patients' temporal reports, and medical history analysis.

Visualization of Temporal Data

In temporal data visualization, time is the independent variable and the other features that are being visualized are plotted against time. So, the other features are dependent variables. Usually, time is plotted on the x axis, while the dependent variables are plotted on the y axis. We can see a few plots here:

- *Line graph:*

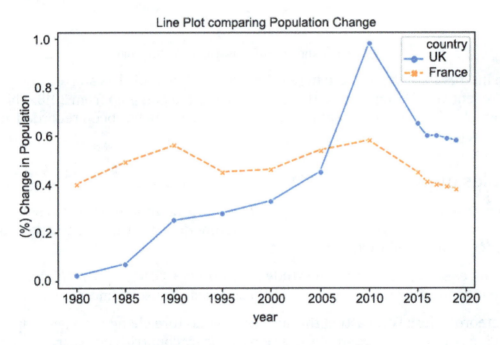

Figure 5.5: Line plot representing temporal data

This line graph shows the percentage change in the population of a country for each year. If multiple lines are plotted on the same graph, then it gives us a comparative study of the features. Lines plots are easy to interpret and also simple to plot.

- *Grouped bar chart:*

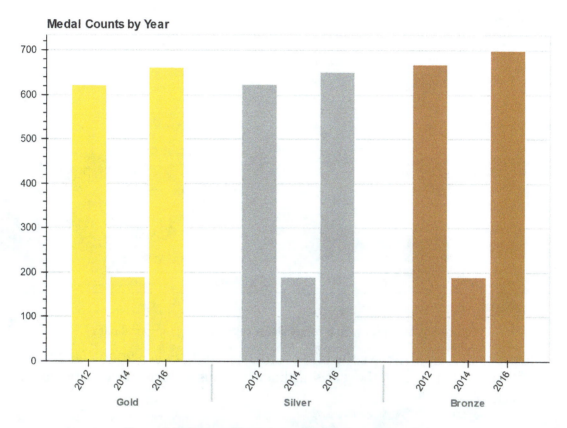

Figure 5.6: Grouped bar plot representing temporal data

This grouped bar chart shows the counts of medals (shown on the y axis) received in 2012, 2014, and 2016. Having many lines on the same line graph plot makes visibility and comparability poor. In this case, a grouped bar chart is a neat option.

- *Line plot with a range slider:*

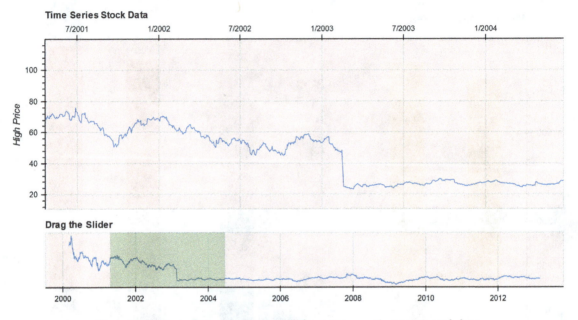

Figure 5.7: Line plot with a range slider representing temporal data

The preceding graph shows the plot of stock prices between 2000 and 2013. If we have a wide range on the x axis, a slider helps us to focus on a particular year range.

- *Timed pie charts:*

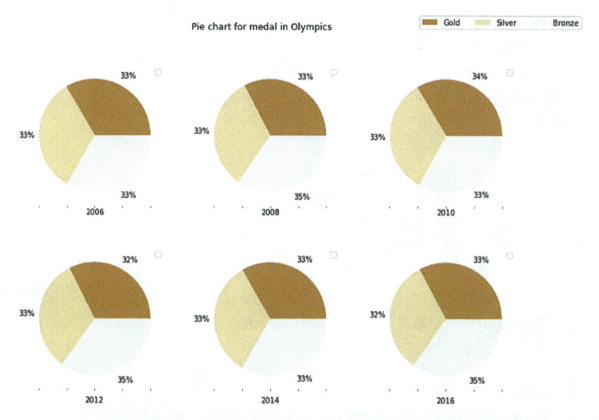

Figure 5.8: Timed pie charts representing medal counts in Olympics

The series of pie-charts show the distribution of medal count in the Olympics for each year. Pie charts provide a ratio of the values being visualized. Pie charts are recommended when there are not many types of values shown on the chart.

How Time-Series Data Is Manipulated and Visualized

Pandas is the most common library for importing, wrangling, and analyzing data. For time- series data, it has built-in **datetime** function that makes time-series analysis and visualization easy. When we plot time-series data, we want to perform operations such as resampling, upsampling, or parsing dates for a month or a day to customize the visualization according to the requirements. Resampling and upsampling are ways to aggregate time periods. We will get a better understanding of resampling in the next section with some hands-on exercises.

For now, let's look at a parsing example using **pandas** and the **Airpassengers.csv** dataset:

```
import pandas as pd

from pathlib import Path

DATA_PATH = Path("datasets/chap5_data")

passenger_df = pd.read_csv(DATA_PATH /"AirPassengers.csv")

print(passenger_df.info())
```

Here is the output:

```
<class 'pandas.core.frame.DataFrame'>

RangeIndex: 144 entries, 0 to 143

Data columns (total 2 columns):

Month           144 non-null object

#Passengers     144 non-null int64

dtypes: int64(1), object(1)

memory usage: 2.3+ KB

None
```

> **Note**
>
> The datasets used in this chapter can be found here https://github.com/
> TrainingByPackt/Interactive-Data-Visualization-with-Python/tree/master/datasets/
> chap5_data.

We can see the **Month** column contains data of the **object** type. Now, let's convert it to **datetime** using the following code:

```
passenger_df["Month"] = pd.to_datetime(passenger_df["Month"])

# converts into datetime object

print(passenger_df.info())
```

Here is the output:

```
<class 'pandas.core.frame.DataFrame'>

RangeIndex: 144 entries, 0 to 143

Data columns (total 2 columns):
```

```
Month              144 non-null datetime64[ns]

#Passengers        144 non-null int64

dtypes: datetime64[ns](1), int64(1)

memory usage: 2.3 KB

None
```

Before playing with time-series data, let's introduce you to the main concepts of time and date manipulation in **pandas**.

Date/Time Manipulation in pandas

Here are the common date/time manipulation techniques or functions in pandas that are used during analysis and visualization:

- **Datetime**: A specific date and time with time zone support. **Datetime** is used to convert a **str** object to a **datetime** object. Generally, it is applied to a column to do temporal analysis. It supports various types of **date/time** formats:

  ```
  pd.to_datetime(['2019/09/20', '2019.10.31'])
  ```

  Here is the output:

  ```
  DatetimeIndex(['2019-09-09', '2019-09-10'], dtype='datetime64[ns]',
  freq=None)
  ```

- **timedelta**: **timedelta** is used for calculating an absolute time duration. **timedelta** can be used to add or subtract specific time values from a **datetime** column. Let's see an example of adding a day to a date:

  ```
  import numpy as np
  #week_delta arranged over week period, we can add these dates.
  week_delta = pd.to_timedelta(np.arange(5), unit='w')
  dates = pd.to_datetime(['9/9/2019', '9/9/2019', '9/9/2019',
  '9/9/2019', '9/9/2019'])
  print(dates + week_delta)
  ```

  Here is the output:

  ```
  DatetimeIndex(['2019-09-09', '2019-09-16', '2019-09-23', '2019-09-
  30', '2019-10-07'],
  dtype='datetime64[ns]', freq='W-MON')
  #freq='W-MON' implies weekday starting from Monday
  ```

- **Time spans**: A span of time defined by a point in time and its associated frequency. Both timestamp and time span can be indexed to a DataFrame:

```
pd.Period('2019-09')
```

Here is the output:

```
Period('2019-09', 'M')
```

- **Date offsets**: Date offsets are relative time durations with respect to calendar arithmetic:

```
## Day-light saving in US (2019)
timestamp = pd.Timestamp('2019-03-10 00:00:00', tz='US/Pacific')
# Timedelta with respect to absolute time
print(timestamp + pd.Timedelta(days=1))
```

Here is the output:

```
2019-03-11 01:00:00-07:00
```

Here's another example:

```
# DateOffset with respect to calendar time
print(timestamp + pd.DateOffset(days=1))
```

Here is the output:

```
2019-03-11 00:00:00-07:00
```

Building a DateTime Index

`Pandas` DataFrames are indexed by an ordered sliceable set. If we assign `DatetimeIndex` as the index of a DataFrame, then we can slice and filter based on date, months, and so on.

Here is one way to make a `datetime` index:

```
passenger_df = passenger_df.set_index(pd.DatetimeIndex(passenger_
df['Month']))
```

Or, we can do it this way:

```
passenger_df.index = passenger_df['Month']
```

Here is the output:

```
DatetimeIndex(['1949-01-01', '1949-02-01', '1949-03-01', '1949-04-01',
               '1949-05-01', '1949-06-01', '1949-07-01', '1949-08-01',
               '1949-09-01', '1949-10-01',
```

```
...
    '1960-03-01', '1960-04-01', '1960-05-01', '1960-06-01',
    '1960-07-01', '1960-08-01', '1960-09-01', '1960-10-01',
    '1960-11-01', '1960-12-01'],
    dtype='datetime64[ns]', name='Month', length=144,
freq=None)
```

We can also set the **date** index while reading the data in the DataFrame:

```
athelete_df = pd.read_csv(DATA_PATH / "athletes.csv",
parse_dates=['date_of_birth'],index_col='date_of_birth')
```

Choosing the Right Aggregation Level for Temporal Data

We will now introduce how time is handled and how to extract time components from a **datetime** object. Choosing the right aggregation level can be tricky and is worth exploring. A natural time aggregation, such as day or hour, may not be representative of the pattern. For example, an e-commerce website might have cyclical patterns on active users based on morning, afternoon, and evening. The aggregation level might not be present in the data and will need to be feature engineered in order to create new features. This is a common practice in the **Machine Learning(ML)** domain.

Now, let's do some hands-on exercises pertaining to date handling. We will use the **AirPassengerDates.csv** dataset.

Example 1: Converting Date Columns to pandas DateTime Objects

We'll start by importing the necessary Python modules and read from the **AirpassengersDates.csv** dataset using the following code:

```
#Import pandas library and read DataFrame from DATA_PATH
import pandas as pd
import numpy as np
from pathlib import Path
DATA_PATH = Path("../datasets/chap5_data/")
passenger_df = pd.read_csv(DATA_PATH/"AirPassengersDates.csv")
passenger_df.head()
```

Here is the output:

	Date	#Passengers
0	1949-01-12	112
1	1949-02-24	118
2	1949-03-22	132
3	1949-04-05	129
4	1949-05-24	121

Figure 5.9: The airpassengersdates dataset

We'll now convert the **Date** column to **datetime** by setting the index to **Date**:

```
passenger_df["Date"] = pd.to_datetime(passenger_df["Date"])
passenger_df.head()
```

Here is the output:

	Date	#Passengers
0	1949-01-12	112
1	1949-02-24	118
2	1949-03-22	132
3	1949-04-05	129
4	1949-05-24	121

Figure 5.10: Converting the date to datetime in the dataset

Example 2: Creating month, day, and day_name Columns from the Date Column

In this example, we'll create **month** and **day** columns in the **passenger_df** DataFrame using the following code:

```
passenger_df["month"] = passenger_df["Date"].dt.month
passenger_df["day"] = passenger_df["Date"].dt.day
```

Now, we'll create a **day_name** column in the **passenger_df** DataFrame by accessing the **day_name** method:

```
passenger_df["day_name"] = passenger_df["Date"].dt.day_name()
```

Let's print **passenger_df**:

```
passenger_df.head()
```

Here is the output:

	Date	#Passengers	month	day	day_name
0	1949-01-12	112	1	12	Wednesday
1	1949-02-24	118	2	24	Thursday
2	1949-03-22	132	3	22	Tuesday
3	1949-04-05	129	4	5	Tuesday
4	1949-05-24	121	5	24	Tuesday

Figure 5.11: Creating day, month, and day_name columns from the Date column

Now we will analyze the **#Passenger** column against **time** in the following exercise.

Exercise 38: Creating a Static Bar Plot and Calculating the Mean and Standard Deviation in Temporal Data

In this exercise, we'll count all passengers by month using the **AirPassengerDates. csv** dataset, available on Packt's GitHub repository, and we will create a bar plot to visualize the data and calculate the mean and standard deviation in the dataset. To do so, we'll use the following code:

1. Import the **pandas** library and read the DataFrame using **DATA_PATH**:

```
%matplotlib inline
import pandas as pd
import numpy as np
from pathlib import Path
DATA_PATH = Path("../datasets/chap5_data/")
```

2. Read the data and parse the **Date** column:

```
passenger_df = pd.read_csv(DATA_PATH/"AirPassengersDates.csv")
passenger_df["Date"] = pd.to_datetime(passenger_df["Date"])
passenger_df.head()
```

Here is the output:

	Date	#Passengers
0	1949-01-12	112
1	1949-02-24	118
2	1949-03-22	132
3	1949-04-05	129
4	1949-05-24	121

Figure 5.12: The AirpassengersDates dataset

Let's try to visualize the data using **Seaborn**. **Seaborn** handles categorical data well. We will get a better understanding by plotting this dataset. Also, a visualization or a graphical representation is more appealing to look at than tables.

3. Create **month**, **day**, and **day-name** columns from the **Date** column:

```
passenger_df["month"] = passenger_df["Date"].dt.month passenger_
df["day"] = passenger_df["Date"].dt.day passenger_df["day_name"] =
passenger_df["Date"].dt.day_name()
```

4. Aggregate the #Passengers column by the month column:

```
passenger_per_month = passenger_df.groupby(["month"])
[["#Passengers"]].agg("sum")
passenger_per_month = passenger_per_month.reset_index()
passenger_per_month.head()
```

The output is as follows:

	month	#Passengers
0	1	2901
1	2	2820
2	3	3242
3	4	3205
4	5	3262

Figure 5.13: Aggregated passengers by the month column

5. Import the required libraries and set the figure size to create the bar plot:

```
import seaborn as sns
import matplotlib.pyplot as plt
plt.figure(figsize=(16,8))
```

6. Create a bar plot using **sns** and pass the column names to the x axis and y axis. Now we will use the **passenger_per_month** DataFrame because it has been processed:

```
ax = sns.barplot(x="month",y="#Passengers", data=passenger_per_
month)
ax.set_title("Bar Plot - Passengers per month")

#Annotate the bars with value to have better idea
for p, v in zip(ax.patches, passenger_per_month['#Passengers']):
    height = p.get_height()
    ax.text(p.get_x() + p.get_width() / 2, height + 5, v,
            ha='center', va='bottom')
plt.show()
```

The output is as follows:

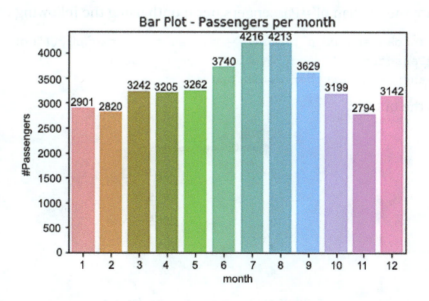

Figure 5.14: Static bar plot

As we can see, the number of passengers for each month is displayed at the top of each bar. Now, suppose we also want to calculate the mean of **#Passengers** per month.

7. Calculate the mean of **#Passengers** per month using the following code:

```
mean_passengers_per_month = passenger_df.groupby(["month"])
[["#Passengers"]].agg("mean").reset_index()
mean_passengers_per_month.head()
```

Here is the output:

	month	#Passengers
0	1	241.750000
1	2	235.000000
2	3	270.166667
3	4	267.083333
4	5	271.833333

Figure 5.15: The mean of the dataset

8. Calculate the median of #Passengers per month using the following code:

```
median_passengers_per_month = passenger_df.groupby(["month"])
[["#Passengers"]].agg("median").reset_index()
median_passengers_per_month.head()
```

Here is the output:

	month	#Passengers
0	1	223.0
1	2	214.5
2	3	251.5
3	4	252.0
4	5	252.0

Figure 5.16: The median of the dataset

Now, suppose we want to plot the number of passengers with the standard deviation and cover 80% of the standard deviation.

9. Import the libraries and set up the figure:

```
import seaborn as sns
import matplotlib.pyplot as plt
plt.figure(figsize=(12,8))
```

10. Use the lineplot function from seaborn and set ci to 80 to cover 80% of the standard deviation:

```
ax = sns.lineplot(x="month",y="#Passengers", data=passenger_df,
ci=80)
ax.set_title("Bar Plot Mean and Standard Deviation per Month")
plt.show()
```

The output is as follows:

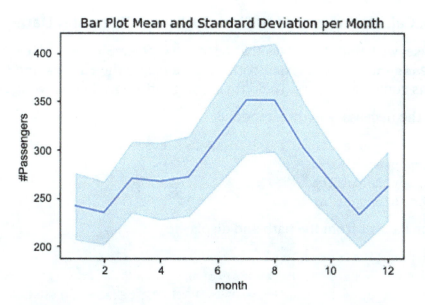

Figure 5.17: Bar plot showing the mean and the standard deviation

From the plot, we can see that the mean is **~230** and the standard deviation is **~80** for the second month.

Now, let's understand the **zscore** concept and why we use it.

The **zscore** of value x is a measure of how many standard deviations x is away from the mean. **zscore** is a normalization technique used in the preprocessing of features. It helps the ML model to learn better from data. High **zscore** values in a sample indicate that the sample value is far away from the mean and could be an outlier. Here's how we calculate **zscore** mathematically:

$$zscore = \frac{x - \bar{x}}{\sigma(x)}$$

$\bar{x}$ = mean

$\sigma(x)$ = standard deviation

Figure 5.18: Mathematical calcuation of zscore

We'll be using this concept of **zscore** to find outliers or anomalies in a dataset and visualize them using a line plot.

Exercise 39: Calculating zscore to Find Outliers in Temporal Data

In this exercise, we'll find the 5 days that have the highest **zscore** values. Next, we will use the **AirPassengersDates.csv** dataset to calculate the **zscore** and try to find which months could be outliers. To do this, let's go through the following steps:

1. Import the necessary Python modules:

    ```
    #Import pandas library and read DataFrame from DATA_PATH
    import pandas as pd
    %matplotlib inline
    import numpy as np
    ```

2. Read the dataset from the path and display it:

    ```
    from pathlib import Path
    DATA_PATH = Path("..datasets//chap5_data/")
    passenger_df = pd.read_csv(DATA_PATH/"AirPassengersDates.csv")
    ```

3. Parse the **Date** column:

    ```
    passenger_df["Date"] = pd.to_datetime(passenger_df["Date"])
    ```

4. Calculate the mean and standard deviation of the **#Passengers** column and assign them to new columns in **passenger_df**:

```
passenger_df['mean'] = passenger_df["#Passengers"].mean()
passenger_df['std'] = passenger_df["#Passengers"].std()
```

5. Calculate the **zscore** using the formula we introduced earlier by using the **mean** and **std** columns. Assign the result to a new column called **zscore**:

```
passenger_df['zscore'] = (passenger_df["#Passengers"] - passenger_
df['mean'])/passenger_df['std']
```

6. Now apply the **abs** function to calculate the absolute value of **zscore**:

```
passenger_df['zscore_abs'] = abs(passenger_df['zscore'])
```

7. Sort the DataFrame by **zscore_abs**:

```
passenger_df.sort_values(by="zscore_abs", ascending=False).head(100)
```

Here is the output:

	Date	#Passengers	mean	std	zscore	zscore_abs
138	1960-07-02	622	280.298611	119.966317	2.848311	2.848311
139	1960-08-16	606	280.298611	119.966317	2.714940	2.714940
127	1959-08-01	559	280.298611	119.966317	2.323164	2.323164
126	1959-07-29	548	280.298611	119.966317	2.231471	2.231471
137	1960-06-02	535	280.298611	119.966317	2.123108	2.123108
140	1960-09-14	508	280.298611	119.966317	1.898044	1.898044
115	1958-08-18	505	280.298611	119.966317	1.873037	1.873037
114	1958-07-13	491	280.298611	119.966317	1.756338	1.756338
136	1960-05-27	472	280.298611	119.966317	1.597960	1.597960
125	1959-06-24	472	280.298611	119.966317	1.597960	1.597960

Figure 5.19: zscore in AirpassengersDates

Let's try to visualize these outliers in **passenger_df**.

8. First, filter the high and low values using the zscore:

```
anamlous_df_high = passenger_df.sort_values(by="zscore",
ascending=False).head(10)
anamlous_df_high["Date"] = pd.to_datetime(anamlous_df_high["Date"])
anamlous_df_low = passenger_df.sort_values(by="zscore",
ascending=True).head(10)
anamlous_df_low["Date"] = pd.to_datetime(anamlous_df_low["Date"])
```

9. Import the seaborn and matplotlib libraries, which are required for visualization, and plot the outliers using the following code:

```
import seaborn as sns
import matplotlib.pyplot as plt
plt.figure(figsize=(15,8))
plt.grid=True
plt.title("Top 10 high traffic passenger count")
ax = sns.lineplot(x="Date", y="#Passengers", data=passenger_df)
ax = sns.scatterplot(x="Date",y="#Passengers", data=anamlous_df_
high, size="#Passengers")
ax = sns.lineplot(x="Date", y="mean", data=passenger_df)
ax.text(pd.to_datetime("1950"), 290, "Mean Line",
horizontalalignment='left', size='large', color='Blue')
ax = sns.scatterplot(x="Date",y="#Passengers", data=anamlous_df_low,
size="#Passengers")
ax.grid()
```

The output is as follows:

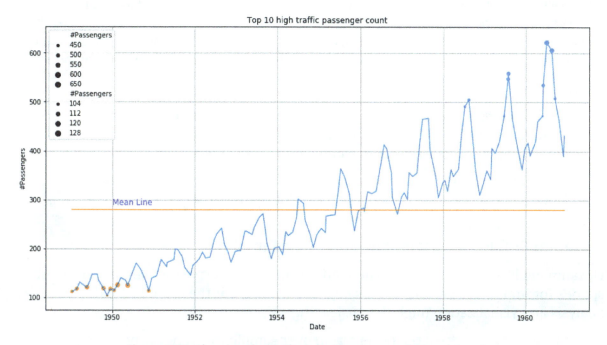

Figure 5.20: Showing the outliers in AirpassengerDates dataset

As we can see, the outliers in the dataset are represented by the orange dots and the blue dots.

We have learned so far that visualization of temporal data requires the DataFrame to be processed so that the required pattern can be represented on the plot. Here is a summary of what we have learned:

- We have learned three ways to make **datetime** as the index for plotting time-series data, while reading data and setting using **index_col**, while explicitly setting the index with **df.index = df['date']**, and while using **set_index()**.

- We saw how to convert a parsable string column to a datetime column using **pd.to_datetime()**.

- **datetime** arithmetics, for example, adding and subtracting **timedelta**.

- We saw how to aggregate data across different time values, for example, day, month, and week.

- We saw how to do analysis using **mean**, **median**, and zscore on the **time** axis.

Let's move on to the next section and delve into the concept of resampling in temporal data.

Resampling in Temporal Data

Resampling involves changing the frequency of the time values in a dataset. If data observed over time has been collected over different frequencies, for example, over weeks or months, resampling can be used to normalize datasets for a given frequency. During predictive modeling, resampling is widely used to perform feature engineering.

There are two types of resampling:

- **Upsampling**: Changing the time from, for example, minutes to seconds. Upsampling helps us to visualize and analyze data in more detail, and these fine-grained observations are calculated using interpolation.

- **Downsampling**: Changing the time from, for example, months to years. Downsampling helps to summarize and get a general sense of trends in data.

Common Pitfalls of Upsampling and Downsampling

Upsampling leads to **NaN** values. The methods used in interpolation are linear or cubic splines for imputing **NaN** values. This might not represent the original data, so the analysis and visualization might be misleading.

Downsampling aggregates the observation over sample frequency, where we provide a frequency to function as an argument, so we might lose some information.

Exercise 40: Upsampling and Downsampling in Temporal Data

In this exercise, we will perform upsampling and downsampling on the **walmart store** dataset. We'll first drop the **NaN** values, and then we'll merge the dataset. Then, we'll upsample the dataset to visualize the data in more detail. Next, we'll downsample and smoothen out the line plot. To do so, let's go through the following steps:

1. Import the necessary Python modules and set the data path:

```
%matplotlib inline
from datetime import datetime
import pandas as pd
from datetime import datetime
from pathlib import Path
DATA_PATH = Path('../datasets/chap5_data/')
```

2. Read the dataset using **pandas** and drop the **NA** values:

```
walmart_stores = pd.read_csv(DATA_PATH/'1962_2006_walmart_store_
openings.csv',
parse_dates=['date_super']).dropna()
```

3. Count the number of stores opened per year. We will use the **walmart_store_count** dataset as time-series data:

```
walmart_store_count = walmart_stores.groupby("YEAR")[["storenum"]].
agg("count") \
.rename(columns={"storenum": "store_count"})
```

4. Merge **walmart_store_count** with **walmart_stores**:

```
walmart_store_count = pd.merge(walmart_stores, walmart_store_count,
on="YEAR")
```

5. Set the index with **date_super**:

```
walmart_store_count= walmart_store_count.set_index(pd.
DatetimeIndex(walmart_store_count.date_super))
```

6. Filter out the required columns:

```
walmart_store_count = walmart_store_count[["date_super", "store_
count"]] walmart_store_count.drop_duplicates(subset="date_super",
inplace=True)
```

7. Print the DataFrame:

```
walmart_store_count.head(8)
```

The output is as follows:

date_super	date_super	store_count
1997-03-01	1997-03-01	1
1996-03-01	1996-03-01	1
2002-03-01	2002-03-01	1
1993-03-01	1993-03-01	1
1998-03-01	1998-03-01	5
1994-03-01	1994-03-01	5
2002-02-20	2002-02-20	5
2000-03-01	2000-03-01	5

Figure 5.21: The dataset showing the number of stores opened in a certain year

Upsampling helps us to visualize and analyze the data in more detail.

8. Convert the frequency of **walmart_store_count_series** to 2 days:

```
walmart_store_count_series = walmart_store_count.store_count
walmart_store_count_series = walmart_store_count_series.asfreq('2D')
walmart_store_count_series.head()
```

The output is as follows:

```
date_super
1997-03-01    1.0
1997-03-03    NaN
1997-03-05    NaN
1997-03-07    NaN
1997-03-09    NaN
Freq: 2D, Name: store_count, dtype: float64
```

Figure 5.22: Showing the frequency of walmart_store_count_series

9. Interpolate the missing values using linear interpolation:

```
walmart_store_count_series = walmart_store_count_series.
interpolate(method="spline", order=2) walmart_store_count_series.
plot(style=":")
```

The output is as follows:

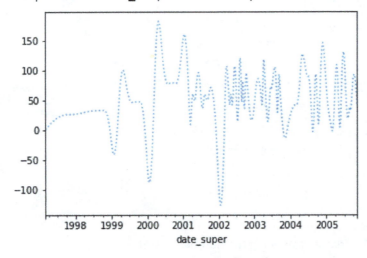

Figure 5.23: The line plot

Downsampling to a larger unit of time, for example, from day to week, will introduce smoothing. This is an aggregation method for the given frequency level.

10. Smooth out the plot using downsampling with a frequency of **BA** (business year) using the following code:

```
plt.figure(figsize=(12,8))
plt.ylabel("Interpolated Values")
plt.plot(walmart_store_count_series)
walmart_store_count_series.resample('BA').mean().plot(style=':',
title="Values Smoothen by Business Year Frequency") #BA stands for
Business Year
```

The output is as follows:

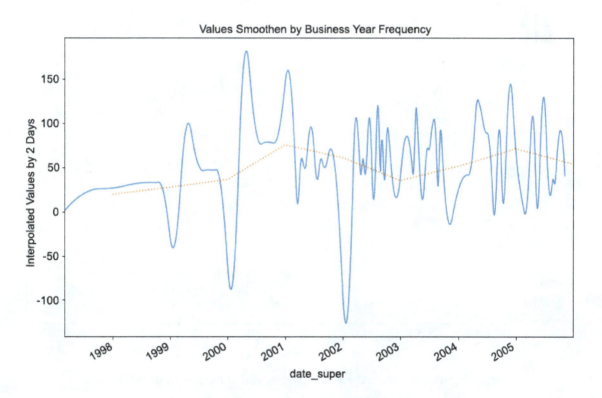

Figure 5.24: Smoothened-out line plot

11. Downsample with a frequency of **BQ** (business quarter) to observe higher granularity:

```
plt.figure(figsize=(12,8))
plt.ylabel("Interpolated Values")
walmart_store_count_series.plot(alpha=0.5, style='-')
walmart_store_count_series.resample('BQ').mean().plot(style=':',
title="Values Smoothen by Business Quarter Frequency")#BQ stands for
Business quarter
```

The output is as follows:

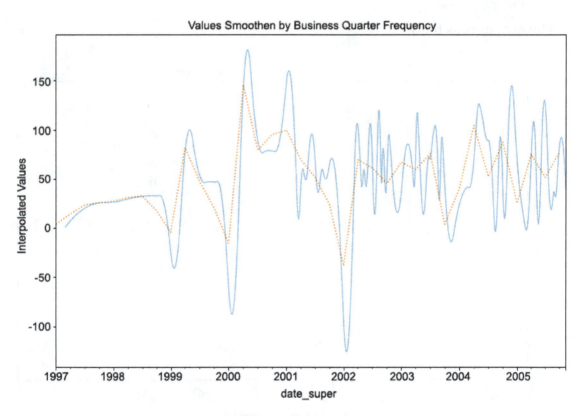

Figure 5.25: Smoothed-out line plot with a frequency of BQ

As we can see, upsampling and downsampling have been used to view the data with different levels of detail. We'll now see the lag in time-series data using the shift and tshift functions.

Using shift and tshift to Introduce a Lag in Time-Series Data

- **tshift**: Shifts the **datetime** index of the DataFrame by a given period. The period is unit count of frequency; frequency could be week, month, hour, and so on. It changes the value of **DateTimeIndex** within the DataFrame.

- **shift**: Shifts the DataFrame index by a given period. In the process, new rows or columns will be introduced in the DataFrame with **NaN** values.

Exercise 41: Using shift and tshift to Shift Time in Data

In this exercise, we will use shift and tshift to shift time in a dataset. We'll be using the 1962_2006_walmart_store_openings.csv dataset. We'll process the dataset, drop the NaN values, and merge the dataset with walmart_stores, and then we'll go ahead and create a line plot to visualize the data. To do this, let's go through the following steps:

1. Import the necessary Python modules and preprocess the data:

```
from datetime import datetime
%matplotlib inline
import pandas as pd
import matplotlib.pyplot as plt
from pathlib import Path
DATA_PATH = Path('../datasets/ chap5_data/')
walmart_stores = pd.read_csv(DATA_PATH / '1962_2006_walmart_store_
openings.csv',
parse_dates=['date_super']).dropna()
walmart_store_count = walmart_stores.groupby("YEAR")[["storenum"]].
agg("count").rename(columns={"storenum": "store_count"})
walmart_store_count = pd.merge(walmart_stores, walmart_store_count,
on="YEAR")
walmart_store_count= walmart_store_count.set_index(pd.
DatetimeIndex(walmart_store_count.date_super))
walmart_store_count = walmart_store_count[["date_super", "store_
count"]]
walmart_store_count.drop_duplicates(subset="date_super",
inplace=True)
walmart_store_count_series = walmart_store_count.store_count
walmart_store_count_series = walmart_store_count_series.asfreq('2D')
walmart_store_count_series = walmart_store_count_series.
interpolate(method="spline", order=2)
```

2. Create three plots: one normal, one shifted with index, and one shifted with **time**:

```
walmart_store_count_series = walmart_store_count_series.asfreq('D',
method='pad')
```

3. Set up the plot and **shift_val**. **shift_val** is the value of the lag we want to plot on **graphax[0].legend(['input'], loc=2)**:

```
fig, ax = plt.subplots(3, figsize=(14,9))
shift_val = 400
#create 3 plots, one normal, one shifted with index, and other
shifted with time
walmart_store_count_series.plot(ax=ax[0])
#shift the date by shift_val
walmart_store_count_series.shift(shift_val).plot(ax=ax[1])
#shift the time index using tshift
walmart_store_count_series.tshift(shift_val).plot(ax=ax[2])
#select a date to draw line on plot
date_max = pd.to_datetime('2002-01-01')
delta = pd.Timedelta(shift_val, 'D')
#Put marker on three plot to undestand how thsift shifting the index
and shift is changing the data.
ax[0].legend(['input'], loc=2)
ax[0].set_ylabel("Interpolated Store Count")
ax[0].get_xticklabels()[2].set(weight='heavy', color='green')
ax[0].axvline(date_max, alpha=0.3, color='red')
ax[1].legend(['shift({})'.format(shift_val)], loc=2)
ax[1].set_ylabel("Interpolated Store Count")
ax[1].get_xticklabels()[2].set(weight='heavy', color='green')
ax[1].axvline(date_max + delta, alpha=0.2, color='green')
ax[2].legend(['tshift({})'.format(shift_val)], loc=2)
ax[2].set_ylabel("Interpolated Store Count")
ax[2].get_xticklabels()[1].set(weight='heavy', color='black')
ax[2].axvline(date_max + delta, alpha=0.2, color='black');
```

The output is as follows:

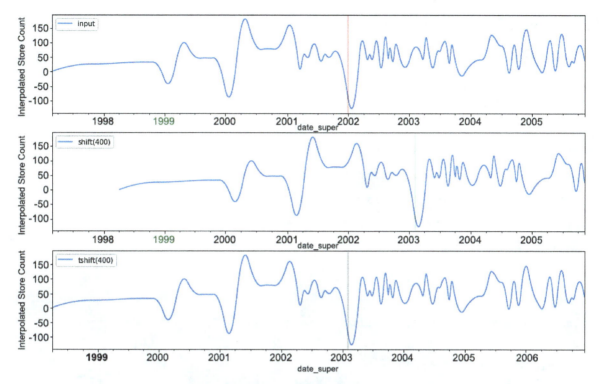

Figure 5.26: Line plots representing tshift and shift

Let's try to understand the **shift()** and **tshift()** functions using the preceding plots.

shift shifts the data to a given unit. Here, **shift(shift_val)** shifts by **400** days, since we have set the frequency to **D in the Timedelta function of pandas.**

Autocorrelation in Time Series

Calculating the correlation between time-series values with lagged/shifted values of the same time-series dataset is called **autocorrelation**.

A plot of autocorrelation is called an **Autocorrelation Function(ACF)**.

To understand how time-series values are correlated with past values, we need to find a value of **p** that gives the highest correlation value. **p** is also known as an auto-regressive value.

For example, if `p=6`, then the value of time-series data at time `t` will be determined by `x(t-1)...x(t-6)`.

Let's go through the following example:

```
#Drawing the autocorrelation function
from statsmodels.graphics.tsaplots import plot_acf
import numpy as np
import pandas as pd
from statsmodels.tsa.stattools import acf
from pandas_datareader.data import DataReader
from datetime import datetime
import matplotlib.pyplot as plt
%matplotlib inline


ibm = DataReader('IBM', 'yahoo', datetime(2010, 2, 1), datetime(2018, 2, 1))
ibm_close = ibm['Close']
ibm_close_month = ibm_close.resample("M").mean()
#plot_acf(ibm_close, lags=50)
lag_acf = acf(ibm_close_month, nlags=72)
#Plot ACF:
plt.figure(figsize=(10, 4))
plt.subplot(121)


plt.plot(lag_acf)
plt.axhline(y=0,linestyle='--',color='gray')
plt.axhline(y=-1.96/np.sqrt(len(ibm_close)),linestyle='--',color='gray')
plt.axhline(y=1.96/np.sqrt(len(ibm_close)),linestyle='--',color='gray')
plt.title('Autocorrelation Function')
```

The output is as follows:

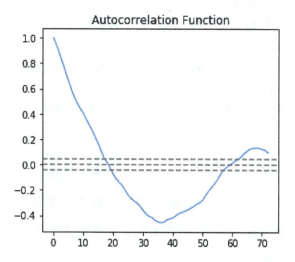

Figure 5.27: Autocorrelation represented through a line plot

As we can see, the graph touches the first confidence interval (represented by the `--` line in the plot) at **18**, hence `p = 18`.

In this section, we have learned about time-series manipulation and visualization. Here are the specific concepts that we have practiced:

- Understanding upsampling and downsampling
- Plotting upsampling and downsampling and the advantages and disadvantages of each technique
- Understanding `shift` and `tshift` understanding using visualization

Interactive Temporal Visualization

We have so far seen how to manipulate temporal data and create static plots. Now, we need a visualization that can be rendered at runtime based on events and information details – an interactive plot in which the events could be zoom, hover, change of axis, 3D rotations, and more. Information details could be changing the aggregation column from year to month or days.

Now we will explain how to plot using the **Bokeh** library. First, we will plot a simple plot. At the end, we will learn about callbacks and the sophisticated functionalities of **Bokeh**.

Bokeh Basics

Bokeh is an interactive visualization library. It is able to handle large amounts of data and streaming data as well. Apart from Python, `Bokeh` can be used with R, Scala, Lua, and other programming languages.

For a simple graph, many interactivity tools come built-in with `Bokeh`, for example, pan, box zoom, and wheel zoom. Since we will be visualizing our output in a Jupyter Notebook, we need to import and initialize the required settings. Bokeh is essentially used for the following:

- Plots: Plots are containers that hold tools, data to show the figure, and maps to `bokeh.plotting.figure`. This is used to make a plot.

- Glyphs: Basic visual marks that Bokeh can display, for example, lines and circles.

- *Guides*: Help us to judge distances, angles, and so on. Examples include axes, grid lines, and ticks.

- *Annotations*: Visual aids that label certain points on a figure, such as the title and legends.

Advantages of Using Bokeh

The advantages of using `bokeh` are:

- `Bokeh` is fast and can handle a large amount of data. Complex visualizations can be drawn using the available commands.

- It has intuitive parameter names and usable defaults.
  `Bokeh` can output in various formats according to requirements, such as Jupyter Notebook, server response, and `html` files.

- Output from `matplotlib` and `seaborn` can be easily rendered into `bokeh`

- By default, many interactive tools are available, such as wheel zoom and box zoom.

Let's look at an example of adding interactivity on static plots using the `bokeh` library.

Example 3: Adding Zoom in and out Functionality on a Line Plot Using Bokeh

In this example, we'll add interactive features such as pan and zoom in and out on a static line plot using the `Bokeh` library. To do this, let's go through the following steps:

1. Import the necessary modules and functions:

```
import numpy as np from bokeh.plotting import output_notebook,
figure, show
```

2. Import the required modules and functions, importing figure, show, output_
    notebook, output_file:from bokeh.plotting import output_notebook, figure, show.

3. Set the output mode as output_notebook():

    ```
    output_notebook()
    ```

4. Load the data from pandas, SQL, from a URL, or from any other sources:

    ```
    #prepare some data
    x = np.arange(5)
    y = [6, 7, 2, 4, 5]
    ```

5. Create a figure and add glyphs to it:

    ```
    # create a new plot specifying plot_height, plot_width, with a title
    and axis labels.
    p = figure(plot_height=300, plot_width=700,title="simple line
    example", x_axis_label='x', y_axis_label='y')
    ```

6. Add a line renderer with legend and line thickness:

    ```
    # add a line renderer with legend and line thickness
    p.line(x, y, legend="Temp", line_width=3)
    ```

7. Show the visualization:

    ```
    # show the results
    show(p)
    ```

    The output is as follows:

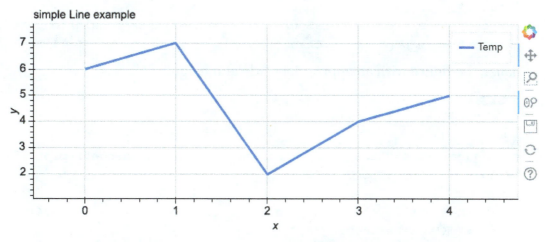

Figure 5.28: Zoomed-out line plot (L) and zoomed-in line plot (R)

Now, let's add more interactive functionalities to the plot through an exercise.

Exercise 42: Adding Interactivity to Static Line Plots Using Bokeh

In this exercise, we'll create static line plots and add interactivity such as zooming in and out. We'll be using the **uk_europe_population_2005_2019.csv** dataset. To do this, let's go through the following steps:

1. Import the libraries and read the data from the **datasets/chap5_data** folder:

```
import pandas as pd
from pathlib import Path
import pandas as pd
from pathlib import Path
from bokeh.plotting import figure, show, output_file
from bokeh.plotting import figure, output_notebook, show,
ColumnDataSource
DATA_PATH = Path('datasets/chap5_data')
```

2. Set the output as a notebook:

```
output_notebook()
```

3. Read the data as a DataFrame. Filter the rows by **UK** and **France**. Make DataFrame as **ColumnDataSource** so that **Bokeh** can access it by column names:

```
uk_eu_population = pd.read_csv(DATA_PATH / "uk_europe_
population_2005_2019.csv")
uk_population = uk_eu_population[uk_eu_population.country == 'UK']
source_uk = ColumnDataSource(dict(year=uk_population.year,
change=uk_population.change))
france_population = uk_eu_population[uk_eu_population.country ==
'France']
source_france = ColumnDataSource(dict(year=france_population.year,
change=france_population.change))
```

4. Initialize the figure with an appropriate title and height:

```
TOOLTIPS = [
    ("population:", "@change")
]
r = figure(title="Line Plot comparing Population Change", plot_
height=450, tooltips=TOOLTIPS)

r.line(x="year", y="change", source=source_uk, color='#1F78B4',
legend='UK', line_color="red", line_width=3)
```

```
r.line(x="year", y="change", source=source_france, legend='France',
line_color="black", line_width=2)
r.grid.grid_line_alpha=0.3
show(r)
```

The output is as follows:

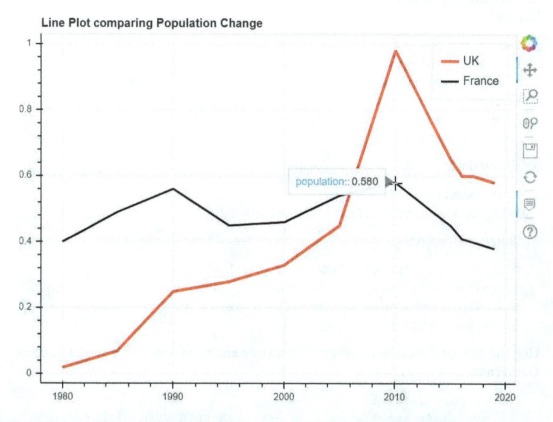

Figure 5.29: Line plot comparing population change for France

We have successfully added interactive features to a temporal static plot. We can see in the plots that in the **2000–2010** time period, the population in the UK increased a lot more than France.

Exercise 43: Changing the Line Color and Width on a Line Plot

In this exercise, we will change the line color and width of line plots. We will be using **microsoft_stock.csv** and **googlestock.csv**. To do so, let's go through the following steps:

1. Import the necessary Python modules and download the sample data from the library:

    ```python
    import pandas as pd
    from bokeh.plotting import figure, output_notebook, show,
    ColumnDataSource
    from bokeh.io import push_notebook, show, output_notebook
    from ipywidgets import interact
    output_notebook()
    ```

2. Read the data:

    ```python
    from pathlib import Path
    DATA_PATH = Path("../datasets/chap5_data/")
    ```

3. Initialize the figure:

    ```python
    TOOLTIPS = [ ("date", "@date"), ("value", "@close") ] p =
    figure(title="Interactive plot to change line width and color",
    plot_width=900, plot_height=400, x_axis_type="datetime",
    tooltips=TOOLTIPS)
    ```

4. Use the helper function to return the **microsoft_stock** and **google_stock** DataFrames:

    ```python
    def prepare_data():
        microsoft_stock = pd.read_csv(DATA_PATH / "microsoft_stock_ex6.
    csv")
        microsoft_stock["date"] = pd.to_datetime(microsoft_
    stock["date"])
        google_stock = pd.read_csv(DATA_PATH / "google_stock_ex6.csv")
        google_stock["date"] = pd.to_datetime(google_stock["date"])

        return microsoft_stock, google_stock
    ```

5. Call the helper function to get the DataFrames:

    ```python
    microsoft_stock, google_stock = prepare_data()
    ```

6. Add the lines for both DataFrames:

```
microsoft_line=p.line("date","close", source=microsoft_stock, line_
width=1.5, legend="microsoft_stock")
google_line = p.line("date", "close", source=google_stock, line_
width=1.5, legend="google_stock")
```

7. Define how to interact with user events:

```
def update(color, width=1):
    google_line.glyph.line_color = color
    google_line.glyph.line_width = width
    push_notebook()

interact(update, color=["red", "blue", "gray"], width=(1,5))
```

8. Show the output:

```
show(p, notebook_handle=True)
```

The output is as follows:

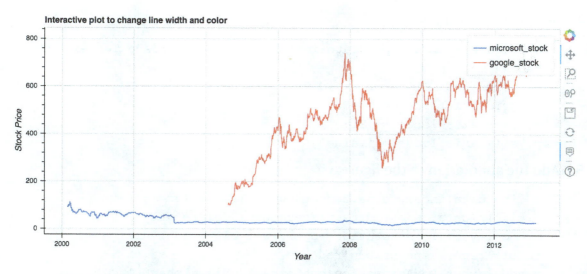

Figure 5.30: Interactive feature that changes the line color and width on a line plot

Exercise 44: Adding Box Annotations to Find Anomalies in a Dataset

In this exercise, we will add box annotations to link screen coordinates to specific plot regions in order to find anomalies in sea surface temperature. To do so, let's go through the following steps:

1. Import the necessary Python modules:

    ```
    from ipywidgets import interact
    import numpy as np
    from ipywidgets import interact
    from bokeh.io import push_notebook, show, output_notebook
    from ipywidgets import interact
    from bokeh.models import BoxAnnotation
    ```

2. Set the output as Jupyter Notebook:

    ```
    output_notebook()
    ```

3. Read the data:

    ```
    # data reading and filtering
    from bokeh.sampledata.sea_surface_temperature import sea_surface_
    temperature
    data = sea_surface_temperature.loc['2016-02-01':'2016-03-22']
    ```

4. Set the figure variables:

    ```
    p = figure(x_axis_type="datetime", title="Sea Surface Temperature
    Range")
    p.background_fill_color = "#dfffff"
    p.xgrid.grid_line_color=None
    p.xaxis.axis_label = 'Time'
    p.yaxis.axis_label = 'Value'
    ```

5. Add the annotation to the figure:

    ```
    p.line(data.index, data.temperature, line_color='grey')
    p.circle(data.index, data.temperature, color='grey', size=1)
    p.add_layout(BoxAnnotation(top=5, fill_alpha=0.1, fill_
    color='red', line_color='red'))
    p.add_layout(BoxAnnotation(bottom=4.5, fill_alpha=0.1, fill_
    color='red', line_color='red'))
    ```

6. Show the figure:

```
show(p)
```

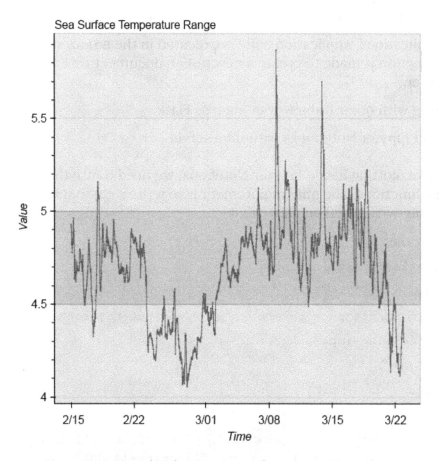

Figure 5.31: Line plot showing sea surface temperature change

As we can, during the time period of 1 Feb – 3 Mar in the year of 2016, the sea surface temperature increased from 5 to 5.5. In the next section, we'll explore interactivity using the **bokeh** library.

Interactivity in Bokeh

There are multiple ways in which we can achieve interactivity using the **Bokeh** library:

- *CustomJS callbacks*: Embedding JavaScript code inside Python. We create JavaScript code as strings that handle interactive events in the browser.

- Bokeh applications: Application code is executed in the **Bokeh** server each time a new connection is made to create a new **Bokeh** document that will be synced with the browser.

- Integrating with other frameworks, such as Flask.

- Running in Jupyter Notebooks without a server.

To do interactive plotting inside Jupyter Notebook, we need to use the **push_notebook** and **interact** functions. The only requirement is to write a custom function that will define the interactivity based on user events.

Let's implement this:

```
from ipywidgets import interact
import numpy as np
from bokeh.io import push_notebook, show, output_notebook
from bokeh.plotting import figure
output_notebook()
x = np.linspace(0, 4*np.pi, 1000)
y = np.sin(x)
p = figure(title="simple line example", plot_height=300, plot_
width=600, y_range=(-2,2), background_fill_color='#efffff')
r = p.line(x, y, color="#8888ff", line_width=1.5, alpha=0.8)
#custom function define how to interact for user event.
def update(f, w=1, A=1, phi=0):
if f == "sin": func = np.sin
elif f == "cos": func = np.cos
elif f == "tan": func = np.tan
```

```
r.data_source.data['y'] = A * func(w * x + phi)

push_notebook()

show(p, notebook_handle=True)

interact(update, f=["sin", "cos", "tan"], w=(0,50), A=(1,10), phi=(0,
20, 0.1))
```

The output is as follows:

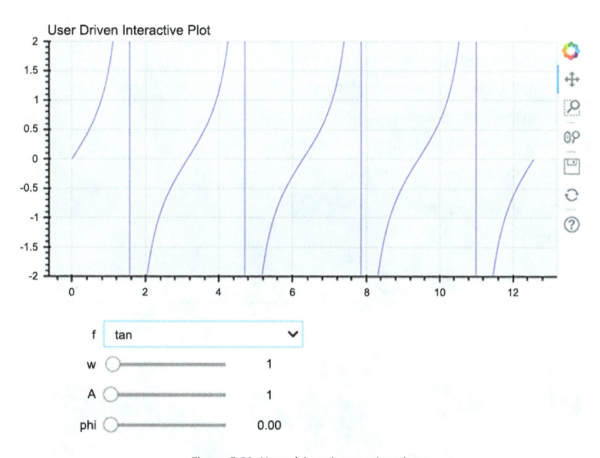

Figure 5.32: User-driven interactive plot

Activity 5: Create an Interactive Temporal Visualization

In this activity, we will analyze a large time-series dataset using **RangeTool**. **RangeTool** can be used to focus on a particular time slot. Then, you can also use the zoom feature to analyze in more depth. The next task is to create a plot that creates a drop-down list. Based on the aggregation level, it aggregates the data at runtime and renders the plot.

High-Level Steps

1. Import the necessary Python modules.

2. Read from the dataset.

3. Add the **RangeTool**.

4. Set up the values for the next plot.

5. Set up the libraries and read the data

6. Extract the x and y data from the DataFrame

7. Plot using the figure line method.

The output should look like:

After Step 3–

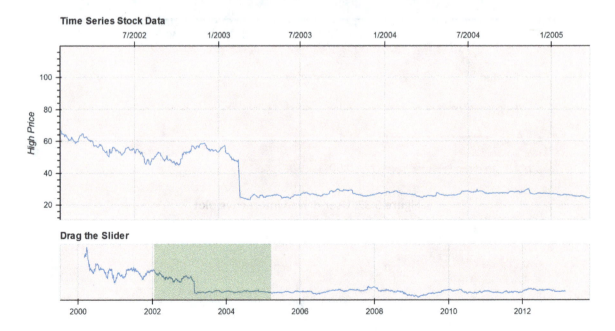

Figure 5.33: Time-series stock data

After Step 6:

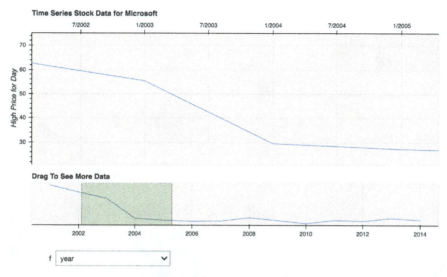

Figure 5.34: Stock price chart

> **Note**
>
> The solution steps can be found in page 272.

Summary

In this chapter, we focused on temporal data visualizations. Firstly, we learned the theory behind temporal data. Then, we covered the real-world applications of temporal data.

We used the **pandas** time function to learn about transforming date columns, such as setting time as an index value in line plots and analyzing data at different frequency levels. Time is sequential in nature, so we covered the **shift** and **tshift** functions, which can be used to compare current observations with past observations and to find out if there are any correlations.

We also looked at the **Bokeh** plotting interface. We plotted graphs using increasing levels of complexity and also explained how to add interactive annotations to play around with the time axis.

Finally, we covered the most important plots that will interact with users without running a server using the **ipywidgets.interact** and **push_notebook()** functions.

In the next chapter, we will see how to create interactive visualizations for data across geographical regions.

Interactive Visualization of Geographical Data

Learning Objectives

By the end of this chapter, you will be able to:

- Use choropleth maps to represent data across geographical regions

- Generate interactive choropleth maps, including choropleth maps depicting countries in the world and maps depicting states in the US, making layout changes to add functionality/aesthetic appeal, and adding animation

- Generate interactive scatter plots on maps, including scatter plots indicating geolocations of places of interest and interactive bubble plots on maps

- Generate interactive line plots on maps, including line plots indicating trajectories on a map

In this chapter, we'll learn about using interactive visualizations to depict data across geographical regions.

Introduction

In the previous chapters, you learned how to build interactive visualizations to present different features in a dataset across features that represent different strata and different time points. In this chapter, you are going to add another type of visualization to your skillset – plotting interactive visualizations with geographical data.

Most datasets generated in today's world involve some features depicting spatial or geographical aspects. For example, users of social media platforms are characterized by the different parts of the world they reside in, world development metrics are calculated for different countries in the world, transportation routes span many different locations across the globe, and so on. Therefore, it is essential to learn systematic ways to understand and present such information in a digestible yet insightful manner. This chapter will help you develop this ability by providing the necessary tools to generate a variety of plots depicting geographical data.

While `altair` and `geopandas` provide exciting possibilities in visualizing geographical data, `plotly` is especially great for generating a variety of geographical plots that are easy to build, debug, and customize. Therefore, in this chapter, we will be using `plotly` to demonstrate generating different classes of geographical plots with multiple publicly available datasets from a variety of contexts. We hope that, through this chapter, you will appreciate that `plotly` is (although arguably) one of the most powerful, intuitive, and easy-to-use libraries for the task of rendering interactive geographical plots, specifically, choropleth maps (which is one of the most widely used representations for geographical areas). We are going to explore choropleth maps in the succeeding sections.

> **Note**
>
> Some of the images in this chapter have colored notations, you can find high-quality color images used in this chapter at: https://github.com/TrainingByPackt/Interactive-Data-Visualization-with-Python/tree/master/Graphics/Lesson6.

Choropleth Maps

A **choropleth map** is a map of a region with different divisions colored to indicate the value of a specific feature in that division. This *division* may be a country, state, district, or any other well-documented area.

For example, you can visualize country-wise populations using a world map, state-wise populations on a country map, or the percentage of a population with access to a certain technology with a choropleth map.

Although the term choropleth map may or may not be familiar to you, as you go through the chapter, the concept of choropleth maps will become clearer.

Let's start exploring the different types of choropleth maps.

Worldwide Choropleth Maps

In the first visualization of this chapter, we are going to use the *internet usage statistics* published on **Our World in Data** (https://ourworldindata.org/internet) and present the percentage of the population using the internet in each country from **1990** to **2017**. The dataset is hosted on the book GitHub repository for easy access.

You can view the dataset using the code that follows:

```
import pandas as pd

internet_usage_url = "https://raw.githubusercontent.com/
TrainingByPackt/Interactive-Data-Visualization-with-Python/master/
datasets/share-of-individualsusing-the-internet.csv"

internet_usage_df = pd.read_csv(internet_usage_url)

internet_usage_df.head()
```

The output is as follows:

	Country	Code	Year	Individuals using the Internet (% of population)
0	Afghanistan	AFG	1990	0.000000
1	Afghanistan	AFG	2001	0.004723
2	Afghanistan	AFG	2002	0.004561
3	Afghanistan	AFG	2003	0.087891
4	Afghanistan	AFG	2004	0.105809

Figure 6.1: The Our World in Data dataset

Did you notice the feature called Code in the dataset? This refers to a code assigned to each country by a standard called ISO 3166-1. It is widely used so developers across the world have a common way to refer to and access country names in any data. You can learn more about the standard here: https://en.wikipedia.org/wiki/ISO_3166-1.The **Code** feature is also used by **plotly** to map data to the appropriate locations on the world map, as we will see soon.

Let's go ahead and generate our first world-wide choropleth map through an exercise.

Exercise 45: Creating a Worldwide Choropleth Map

In this exercise, we'll generate a world-wide choropleth map using the *Our World in Data* dataset, available here: https://raw.githubusercontent.com/TrainingByPackt/Interactive-Data-Visualization-with-Python/master/datasets/share-of-individuals-using-the-internet.csv. Since the DataFrame contains records from multiple years, let's first subset the data to one specific year, say, **2016**. We'll then use this subset to generate a world-wide map. To do so, let's go through the following steps:

1. Import the Python modules:

    ```
    import pandas as pd
    ```

2. Read the data from the **.csv** file:

    ```
    internet_usage_url = "https://raw.githubusercontent.com/
    TrainingByPackt/Interactive-Data-Visualization-with-Python/master/
    datasets/share-of-individuals-using-the-internet.csv"
    internet_usage_df = pd.read_csv(internet_usage_url)
    ```

3. Subset the data to one specific year since the DataFrame contains records from multiple years:

    ```
    internet_usage_2016 = internet_usage_df.query("Year==2016")
    internet_usage_2016.head()
    ```

    The output is as follows:

	Country	Code	Year	Individuals using the Internet (% of population)
16	Afghanistan	AFG	2016	10.595726
39	Albania	ALB	2016	66.363445
63	Algeria	DZA	2016	42.945527
85	Andorra	AND	2016	97.930637
107	Angola	AGO	2016	13.000000

    Figure 6.2: Subset of the Our World in Data dataset

For the next steps, we're going to use the *express module* (for its simplicity) from **plotly** and use the **choropleth** function from the module. The first argument passed to this function is the DataFrame that we want to visualize. The following parameters are set:

- *locations*: This is set to the name of the column in the DataFrame that contains the ISO 3166 country codes.

- *color*: This is set to the name of the column that contains the numerical feature using which the map is to be color-coded.

- *hover_name*: This is set to the name of the column that contains the feature to be displayed while hovering over the map.

- *color_continuous_scale*: This is set to a color scheme, such as *Blues | Reds | Greens | px.colors.sequential.Plasma*.

> **Note**
>
> For more options, see the **plotly** express documentation (https://www.plotly. express/plotly_express/colors/index.html).

4. Generate an interactive world-wide choropleth map using **choropleth** function of **plotly** library:

```
import plotly.express as px
fig = px.choropleth(internet_usage_2016,
                    locations="Code", # colunm containing ISO 3166
country codes
                    color="Individuals using the Internet (% of
population)", # column by which to color-code
                    hover_name="Country", # column to display in
hover information
                    color_continuous_scale=px.colors.sequential.Plasma)
fig.show()
```

The output is as follows:

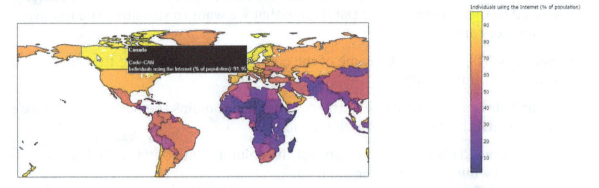

Figure 6.3a: World-wide choropleth map showing data for region=Canada

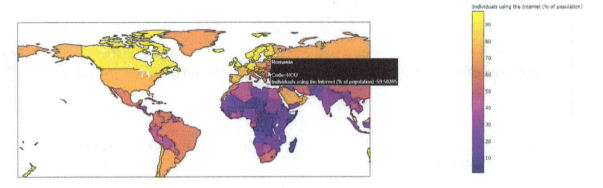

Figure 6.3b: World-wide choropleth map showing data for region=Romania

That was a quick way to get a beautiful plot!

Let's look at the plot carefully and see whether the observations match with our general knowledge. As you would expect, internet usage in the western world is higher than in the east.

Hover over the map a bit more. It is interesting to see, from Figure 6.3a and Figure 6.3b, that a higher percentage of the population (~91.6) in **Australia** and **Canada** have access to the internet than in the **US** and most **European** countries(~59.5).

What else does the plot show? Did you look at the sidebar at the top right of the plot? There you will see options for *selection types, zooming in and out, resetting the plot*, and even taking a *snapshot* of the plot in your choice of configuration.

It's worth playing around with the options a bit. Let's explore the interactivity of a choropleth map through the following exercise.

Exercise 46: Tweaking a Worldwide Choropleth Map

In this exercise, we will make some simple changes to the layout of the choropleth map, such as changing the map projection from **flat** to **natural earth**, zooming into a specific region, adding text to the map using the **update_layout** function, and adding a **rotation** feature. The following code demonstrates how to add these functionalities to the map. We'll use the dataset available here: [https://raw.githubusercontent.com/ TrainingByPackt/Interactive-Data-Visualization-with-Python/master/datasets/share-of-individuals-using-the-internet.csv](https://raw.githubusercontent.com/TrainingByPackt/Interactive-Data-Visualization-with-Python/master/datasets/share-of-individuals-using-the-internet.csv). To do so, let's look at the following steps:

1. Import the Python modules:

    ```
    import pandas as pd
    ```

2. Read the data from the **.csv** file:

    ```
    internet_usage_url = "https://raw.githubusercontent.com/
    TrainingByPackt/Interactive-Data-Visualization-with-Python/master/
    datasets/share-of-individuals-using-the-internet.csv"
    internet_usage_df = pd.read_csv(internet_usage_url)
    ```

3. Subset the data to one specific year since the DataFrame contains records from multiple years:

    ```
    internet_usage_2016 = internet_usage_df.query("Year==2016")
    ```

4. Add title text to the choropleth map setting the **title_text** parameter:

    ```
    import plotly.express as px
    fig = px.choropleth(internet_usage_2016,
                        locations="Code",
                        color="Individuals using the Internet (% of
    population)", # column by which to color-code
                        hover_name="Country", # column to display in
    hover information                    color_continuous_scale=px.
    colors.sequential.Plasma
    )

    fig.update_layout(
        # add a title text for the plot
        title_text = 'Internet usage across the world (% population) -
    2016'
    )
    fig.show()
    ```

The output is as follows:

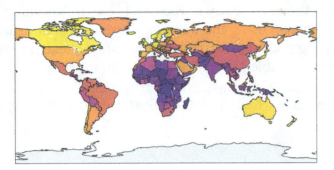
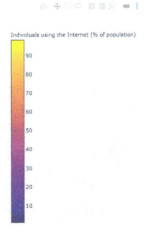

Figure 6.4: Adding text to the choropleth map

That's nice. But let's say, we are only interested in seeing internet usage across the continent of Asia.

5. Set **geo_scope** to **asia** in the **update_layout** function to zoom into the **asia** region. We can quickly do so with the following code:

```
import plotly.express as px
fig = px.choropleth(internet_usage_2016,
                    locations="Code",
                    color="Individuals using the Internet (% of
population)", # column by which to color-code
                    hover_name="Country", # column to display in
hover information
                    color_continuous_scale=px.colors.sequential.
Plasma)

fig.update_layout(
    # add a title text for the plot
    title_text = 'Internet usage across the Asian Continent (%
population) - 2016',
    geo_scope = 'asia' # can be set to north america | south america
| africa | asia | europe | usa
)

fig.show()
```

The output is as follows:

Internet usage across the Asian Continent (% population) - 2016

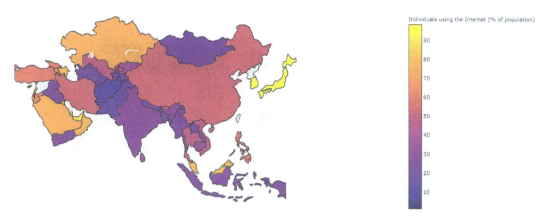

Figure 6.5: Choropleth map displaying the Asia region

Did you try dragging the plot and notice that it can move up and down or left and right? Wouldn't it be nice if the plot could rotate like a real globe? Well, that's easily possible too. All you need to do is to change the projection style of the map.

6. Set **projection type** to **natural earth**:

```
import plotly.express as px
fig = px.choropleth(internet_usage_2016,
                    locations="Code",
                    color="Individuals using the Internet (% of
population)", # column by which to color-code
                    hover_name="Country", # column to display in
hover information
                    color_continuous_scale=px.colors.sequential.
Plasma)

fig.update_layout(
    # add a title text for the plot
    title_text = 'Internet usage across the world (% population) -
2016',
    # set projection style for the plot
    geo = dict(projection={'type':'natural earth'}) # by default,
projection type is set to 'equirectangular'
)

fig.show()
```

The output is as follows:

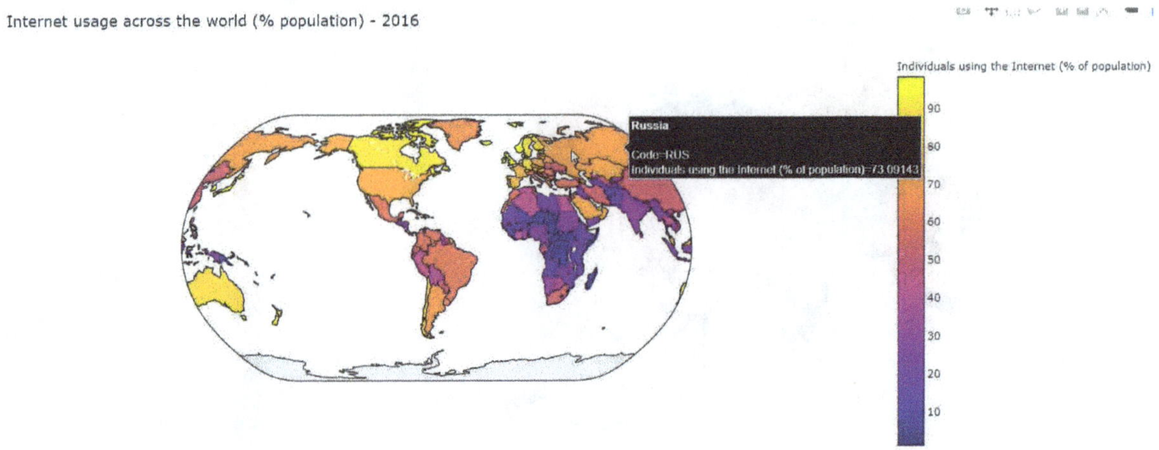

Figure 6.6: Choropleth map with projection type=natural earth

Try dragging the map now. The rotation gives the plot a much more realistic touch! **plotly** offers many such options to tweak visualizations. To experiment with other projection styles apart from the ones we have seen in our examples, visit the official **plotly** documentation here: https://plot.ly/python/reference/#layout-geo-projection.

It's now time to up the game! So far, we have been generating all our plots for the records in a single year, **2016**. *What about all the other timepoints?* While it is definitely possible to generate plots individually for each year we are interested in, that is not the most optimal use of a developer's time.

We'll see how to use animation, in such cases, on a choropleth map in the next section.

Animation in **plotly** choropleth maps is surprisingly easy. We simply need to set a parameter called **animation_frame** to the name of the column whose values we wish to animate our visualization for. Let's go through an exercise to understand how animation works on a choropleth map.

Exercise 47: Adding Animation to a Choropleth Map

In this exercise, we'll animate a world-wide choropleth map. First, we'll choose a column. We'll then go ahead and add a slider component to the map to view records at different timepoints. We'll be using the dataset on the share of populations using the internet, which is available here: https://github.com/TrainingByPackt/Interactive-Data-Visualization-with-Python/blob/master/datasets/share-of-individuals-using-the-internet.csv. Let's go through the following steps:

1. Import the Python modules:

   ```
   import pandas as pd
   ```

2. Read the data from the **.csv** file:

   ```
   internet_usage_url = "https://raw.githubusercontent.com/
   TrainingByPackt/Interactive-Data-Visualization-with-Python/master/
   datasets/share-of-individuals-using-the-internet.csv"
   internet_usage_df = pd.read_csv(internet_usage_url)
   ```

3. Add an animation to the **year** column using **animation_frame=year**:

   ```
   import plotly.express as px
   fig = px.choropleth(internet_usage_df, locations="Code",
                       color="Individuals using the Internet (% of
   population)", # lifeExp is a column of gapminder
                       hover_name="Country", # column to add to hover
   information
                       animation_frame="Year", # column on which to
   animate
                       color_continuous_scale=px.colors.sequential.
   Plasma)

   fig.update_layout(
       # add a title text for the plot
       title_text = 'Internet usage across the world (% population)',
       # set projection style for the plot
       geo = dict(projection={'type':'natural earth'}) # by default,
   projection type is set to 'equirectangular'
   )
   fig.show()
   ```

The output is as follows:

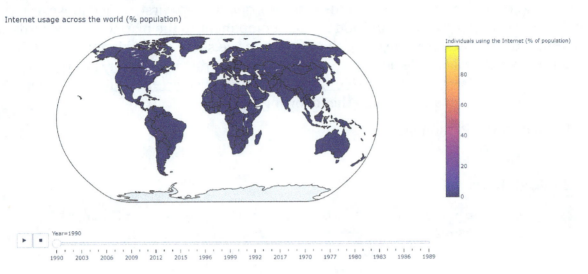

Figure 6.7: Choropleth map with a slider on the year column

Notice that the first argument to our **choropleth** function is the **internet_usage_df** DataFrame, which contains records for all the years between **1970–2017**, and not **internet_usage_2016**, which we had been using until now. If we used the **internet_usage_2016** DataFrame, we would get a *static plot* with no slider, since there would be nothing to animate with records only for a single year.

The animation functionality is really cool and the slider is a simple way to get a quick view of how internet usage has grown in different countries of the world over the years. However, something about the slider is funny! The years on the slider are not in the right order – it starts with **1990**, then goes all the way up to **2015**, and then goes back to **1970** and so on. The easiest way to fix this issue is to sort the DataFrame by time (the **Year** feature).

4. Sort the dataset by **Year** using the following code:

```
internet_usage_df.sort_values(by=["Year"],inplace=True)
internet_usage_df.head()
```

The output is as follows:

	Country	Code	Year	Individuals using the Internet (% of population)
5347	Syrian Arab Republic	NaN	1960	0.0
718	Burundi	BDI	1960	0.0
5493	Togo	TGO	1960	0.0
572	Botswana	BWA	1960	0.0
3414	Maldives	MDV	1960	0.0

Figure 6.8: Sorted internet usage dataset

5. Generate the animated plot again now that the sorting is done:

```
import plotly.express as px
fig = px.choropleth(internet_usage_df, locations="Code",
                    color="Individuals using the Internet (% of
population)", # lifeExp is a column of gapminder
                    hover_name="Country", # column to add to hover
information
                    animation_frame="Year", # column on which to
animate
                    color_continuous_scale=px.colors.sequential.
Plasma)

fig.update_layout(
    # add a title text for the plot
    title_text = 'Internet usage across the world (% population)',
    # set projection style for the plot
    geo = dict(projection={'type':'natural earth'}) # by default,
projection type is set to 'equirectangular'
)
fig.show()
```

The output is as follows:

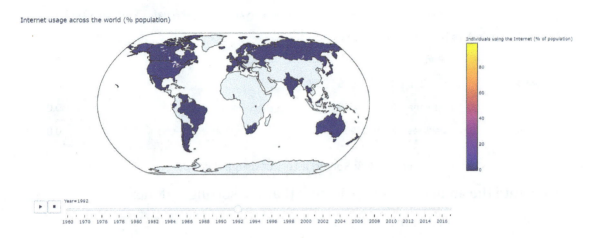

Figure 6.9a: First plot – choropleth map for the year 1992

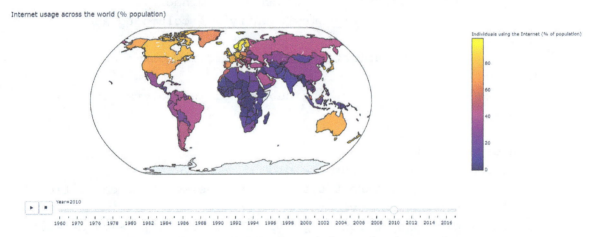

Figure 6.9b: Second plot – choropleth map for the year 2010

And this time, it's right! First plot shows internet usage across the world in the year **1992** while second plot shows the results for the year **2010**. We can see there was definitely an increase in internet usage between **1992** and **2010**.

There is one more point that needs to addressed before we close our discussion on worldwide choropleth maps. In your work, you may come across datasets that would be interesting to visualize on a geographical map but do not have a column that indicates their ISO 3166-1 code. In such cases, you can download the country codes from the official ISO website: https://www.iban.com/country-codes. For easy access, we have also uploaded these country codes to the book repository.

You'll be able to view the **country codes** dataset using the following code:

```
# get the country codes data stored at the github repository
import pandas as pd
country_codes_url = "https://raw.githubusercontent.com/
TrainingByPackt/Interactive-Data-Visualization-with-Python/master/
country_codes.tsv"
country_codes = pd.read_csv(country_codes_url, sep='\t')
country_codes.head()
```

The output is as follows:

	Country	Alpha-2 code	Alpha-3 code	Numeric
0	Afghanistan	AF	AFG	4
1	Albania	AL	ALB	8
2	Algeria	DZ	DZA	12
3	American Samoa	AS	ASM	16
4	Andorra	AD	AND	20

Figure 6.10: Country codes dataset

USA State Maps

While the goal of many visualizations is to compare and contrast specific features across countries, there are often also contexts in which we need to analyze features across smaller regions – such as states within a country. To generate choropleth maps for states in the US, we will be using the state-wise population data made available on the US census website: https://www.census.gov/newsroom/press-kits/2018/pop-estimates-national-state.html. We have also made the data available on the book's GitHub repository: https://github.com/TrainingByPackt/Interactive-Data-Visualization-with-Python/blob/master/datasets/us_state_population.tsv.

Exercise 48: Creating a USA State Choropleth Map

In this exercise, we'll be using the **USA state population** dataset. We'll tweak the dataset and use it to plot a state-wide choropleth map. Then, we'll change the layout of this map to show the US population across states. Let's go through the following steps to do so:

1. Import the Python module:

   ```
   import pandas as pd
   ```

2. Read the dataset from the URL:

   ```
   us_population_url = 'https://raw.githubusercontent.com/
   TrainingByPackt/Interactive-Data-Visualization-with-Python/master/
   datasets/us_state_population.tsv'
   df = pd.read_csv(us_population_url, sep='\t')
   df.head()
   ```

   The output is as follows:

	State	Code	2010	2011	2012	2013	2014	2015	2016	2017	2018
0	Alabama	AL	4785448	4798834	4815564	4830460	4842481	4853160	4864745	4875120	4887871
1	Alaska	AK	713906	722038	730399	737045	736307	737547	741504	739786	737438
2	Arizona	AZ	6407774	6473497	6556629	6634999	6733840	6833596	6945452	7048876	7171646
3	Arkansas	AR	2921978	2940407	2952109	2959549	2967726	2978407	2990410	3002997	3013825
4	California	CA	37320903	37641823	37960782	38280824	38625139	38953142	39209127	39399349	39557045

Figure 6.11:USA state population dataset

It is nice that this dataset also has the state codes available in the **Code** feature. However, the data is not in the format we would want it to be – it's in the wide format, and we need it to be long. Now is the time to hark back to the material covered in the very first chapter of this book!

3. Use the **melt** function to convert the data to the desired format:

```
df = pd.melt(df, id_vars=['State', 'Code'], var_name="Year", value_
name="Population")
df.head()
```

The output is as follows:

	State	Code	Year	Population
0	Alabama	AL	2010	4785448
1	Alaska	AK	2010	713906
2	Arizona	AZ	2010	6407774
3	Arkansas	AR	2010	2921978
4	California	CA	2010	37320903

Figure 6.12: Dataset after using the melt function

Once you know how to generate a choropleth map for countries in the world, a choropleth map of US states is quite straight-forward. Unlike the case of generating a worldwide choropleth map where we used the **plotly express** module, we'll use the **graph_objects** module to generate the choropleth map for states in the US. There are a few simple steps involved in drawing the US choropleth:

4. Import the **graph_objects** module:

```
import plotly.graph_objects as go
```

5. Initialize the figure with the **Figure** function in **graph_objects**. Specifically, the **data** argument needs to be an instance of the **Choropleth** class with the following parameters:

*   **locations**: This is set to the column of the DataFrame that contains the state name codes.

*   **z**: This is set to the column containing the numerical feature using which the map is to be color-coded.

*   **locationmode**: This is set to **USA-states**.

*   **colorscale**: This is set to a color scheme, such as **Blues | Reds | Greens**. For more options, see the **plotly** official documentation: https://plot.ly/python/reference/.

- **colorbar_title**:This is set to the title of the color bar on the right, indicating the correspondence of color and feature values. Refer to the following code:

```
# initialize the figure
fig = go.Figure(
    data=go.Choropleth(
        locations=df['Code'], # Code for US states
        z = df['Population'].astype(int), # Data to be color-coded
        locationmode = 'USA-states', # set of locations match
entries in 'locations'
        colorscale = 'Blues',
        colorbar_title = "Population",
    )
)
```

6. Make changes to the layout with **update_layout()** – set **title_text** and **geo_scope**:

```
# update layout
fig.update_layout(
    title_text = 'US Population across states',
    geo_scope='usa', # limit map scope to USA
)
fig.show()
```

The output is as follows:

US Population across states

Figure 6.13: State map with updated layout

Choropleth maps are an effective way to visualize aggregate statistics across divisions of a geographical region. Two modules from **plotly express** and **graph_objects** – can be used to generate interactive choropleth maps. The modules map records of divisions such as countries and states to locations on geographical maps using a system of standardized country and state code names.

In the next section, we'll explore how to create scatter plots and bubble plots on geographical maps.

Plots on Geographical Maps

While the previous plots were great for visualizing more global trends – such as countries or states – what if we want to represent features in smaller regions, say within individual states? In this section, you will learn how to draw scatter plots and bubble plots on maps. The most intuitive plot of this type is one that simply pinpoints certain locations of interest on the map.

Scatter Plots

We will be plotting the locations of Walmart stores on a map of the US. This dataset is publicly available at: https://github.com/plotly/datasets/ on the **plotly** website, and has been made available on the GitHub book repository. Let's look at an exercise on how to do so.

Exercise 49: Creating a Scatter Plot on a Geographical Map

In this exercise, we'll use the Walmart store openings dataset from **1962-2006** (available at: https://raw.githubusercontent.com/TrainingByPackt/Interactive-Data-Visualization-with-Python/master/datasets/1962_2006_walmart_store_openings.csv). To create a scatter plot from this dataset, we'll be using the **graph_objects** module. We'll find a location of interest on the map and we'll assign longitudes and latitudes on that map and find out the number of Walmart store openings for different parts of the US. To do so, let's go through the following steps:

1. Import Python modules:

    ```
    import pandas as pd
    ```

2. Read the data from the URL:

```
walmart_locations_url = "https://raw.githubusercontent.com/
TrainingByPackt/Interactive-Data-Visualization-with-Python/master/
datasets/1962_2006_walmart_store_openings.csv"
walmart_loc_df = pd.read_csv(walmart_locations_url)
walmart_loc_df.head()
```

The output is as follows:

	storenum	OPENDATE	date_super	conversion	st	county	STREETADDR	STRCITY	STRSTATE	ZIPCODE	type_store	LAT	LON	MONTH	DAY	YEAR
0	1	7/1/62	3/1/97	1.0	5	7	2110 WEST WALNUT	Rogers	AR	72756	Supercenter	36.342235	-94.07141	7	1	1962
1	2	8/1/64	3/1/96	1.0	5	9	1417 HWY 62/65 N	Harrison	AR	72601	Supercenter	36.236984	-93.09345	8	1	1964
2	4	8/1/65	3/1/02	1.0	5	7	2901 HWY 412 EAST	Siloam Springs	AR	72761	Supercenter	36.179905	-94.50208	8	1	1965
3	8	10/1/67	3/1/93	1.0	5	29	1621 NORTH BUSINESS 9	Morrilton	AR	72110	Supercenter	35.156491	-92.75858	10	1	1967
4	7	10/1/67	NaN	NaN	5	119	3801 CAMP ROBINSON RD.	North Little Rock	AR	72118	Wal-Mart	34.813269	-92.30229	10	1	1967

Figure 6.14: Walmart store opening dataset showing data from 1962-2006

We will again be using the **graph_objects** module to generate our scatter plot on the US map. As for the choropleth map, we will use the **Figure** function from **graph_objects** and the **update_layout()** function. However, this time, we will be assigning an instance of the **Scattergeo** class as the argument to **Figure()**. We will be passing the longitudes and latitudes of our locations of interest using the **lon** and **lat** parameters.

3. Plot the scatter plot using the **update_layout** function:

```
import plotly.graph_objects as go

fig = go.Figure(data=go.Scattergeo(
        lon = walmart_loc_df['LON'], # column containing longitude
information of the locations to plot
        lat = walmart_loc_df['LAT'], # column containing latitude
information of the locations to plot
        text = walmart_loc_df['STREETADDR'], # column containing
value to be displayed on hovering over the map
        mode = 'markers' # a marker for each location
        ))
```

```
fig.update_layout(
        title = 'Walmart stores across world',
        geo_scope='usa',
    )
fig.show()
```

The output is as follows:

Walmart stores across USA

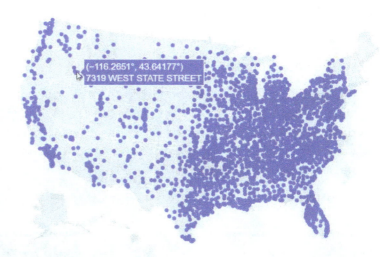

Figure 6.15: Scatter plot for Walmart stores across the US

And that's it – a scatter plot on a map. A striking observation is that Walmart is much more prominent in the east of the US than the west of the US.

Let's go ahead a look at bubble plots on geographical maps.

Bubble Plots

Since the eastern side of the map of the USA appears very densely populated with Walmart stores, it might be a good idea to show an aggregate feature, such as the count of Walmart stores across the different states. **Bubble plots** are designed for exactly this kind of visualization. In the current context of visualizing geographical data, bubble plots are plots with as many bubbles as regions of interest, where the bubble sizes depend on the value they are indicating – the bigger the value, the bigger the bubble.

Exercise 50: Creating a Bubble Plot on a Geographical Map

In this exercise, we'll use the Walmart store openings dataset from **1962–2006**(available at https://raw.githubusercontent.com/TrainingByPackt/Interactive-Data-Visualization-with-Python/master/datasets/1962_2006_walmart_store_openings.csv) and generate a bubble plot to see the number of Walmart stores across different states in the USA. Then, we'll look at another context and generate a bubble plot using the **internet_usage** dataset to find out the number of internet users across the world. We'll also animate the bubble plot to show the increase in the number of internet users across the world. To do so, let's go through the following steps:

1. Import the Python modules:

    ```
    import pandas as pd
    ```

2. Read the data from the URL:

    ```
    walmart_locations_url = "https://raw.githubusercontent.com/
    TrainingByPackt/Interactive-Data-Visualization-with-Python/master/
    datasets/1962_2006_walmart_store_openings.csv"
    walmart_loc_df = pd.read_csv(walmart_locations_url)
    walmart_loc_df.head()
    ```

    The output is as follows:

	storenum	OPENDATE	date_super	conversion	st	county	STREETADDR	STRCITY	STRSTATE	ZIPCODE	type_store	LAT	LON	MONTH	DAY	YEAR
0	1	7/1/62	3/1/97	1.0	5	7	2110 WEST WALNUT	Rogers	AR	72756	Supercenter	36.342235	-94.07141	7	1	1962
1	2	8/1/64	3/1/96	1.0	5	9	1417 HWY 62/65 N	Harrison	AR	72601	Supercenter	36.236984	-93.09345	8	1	1964
2	4	8/1/65	3/1/02	1.0	5	7	2901 HWY 412 EAST	Siloam Springs	AR	72761	Supercenter	36.179905	-94.50208	8	1	1965
3	8	10/1/67	3/1/93	1.0	5	29	1621 NORTH BUSINESS 9	Morrilton	AR	72110	Supercenter	35.156491	-92.75858	10	1	1967
4	7	10/1/67	NaN	NaN	5	119	3801 CAMP ROBINSON RD.	North Little Rock	AR	72118	Wal-Mart	34.813269	-92.30229	10	1	1967

Figure 6.16: Walmart store opening dataset

3. Use the **groupby** function to compute the number of Walmart stores per state. If you don't remember how to do this, it might be a good idea to revise the relevant concepts from the first chapter:

    ```
    walmart_stores_by_state = walmart_loc_df.groupby('STRSTATE').count()
    ['storenum'].reset_index().rename(columns={'storenum':'NUM_STORES'})
    walmart_stores_by_state.head()
    ```

The output is as follows:

	STRSTATE	NUM_STORES
0	AL	90
1	AR	81
2	AZ	55
3	CA	159
4	CO	56

Figure 6.17: Truncated Walmart store openings dataset

4. To generate the bubble plots, we will use the **plotly express** module and the **scatter_geo** function. Notice how the **locations** parameter is set to the name of the column that contains state codes, and the **size** parameter is set to the **NUM_STORES** feature:

```
import plotly.express as px
fig = px.scatter_geo(walmart_stores_by_state,
                     locations="STRSTATE", # name of column which
contains state codes
                     size="NUM_STORES", # name of column which
contains aggregate value to visualize
                     locationmode = 'USA-states',
                     hover_name="STRSTATE",
                     size_max=45)

fig.update_layout(
    # add a title text for the plot
    title_text = 'Walmart stores across states in the US',
    # limit plot scope to USA
    geo_scope='usa'
)
fig.show()
```

The output is as follows:

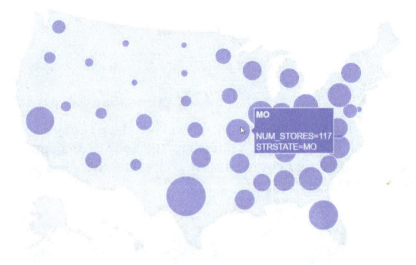

Walmart stores across states in the US

Figure 6.18: Bubble plot

Can you think of any other contexts where a bubble plot may be useful for visualization? How about revisiting the internet usage data (on the percentages of the population using the internet in each country) to generate a world-wide bubble plot? However, bubble plots are more suitable and intuitive for presenting counts/numbers, rather than percentages in individual regions.

It turns out that the count of individuals using the internet in each country is also available from the same resource (Our World in Data: https://ourworldindata. org/internet) that we used to collect our previous data. We have made the data available on the book repository.

5. Use the following code to read data from the **internet users by country** dataset:

```
import pandas as pd
internet_users_url = "https://raw.githubusercontent.com/
TrainingByPackt/Interactive-Data-Visualization-with-Python/master/
datasets/number-of-internet-users-by-country.csv"
internet_users_df = pd.read_csv(internet_users_url)
internet_users_df.head()
```

The output is as follows:

	Country	Code	Year	Number of internet users (users)
0	Afghanistan	AFG	1990	0
1	Afghanistan	AFG	2001	990
2	Afghanistan	AFG	2002	1003
3	Afghanistan	AFG	2003	20272
4	Afghanistan	AFG	2004	25520

Figure 6.19: Internet users dataset

6. Sort the DataFrame by the `Year` feature:

```
internet_users_df.sort_values(by=['Year'],inplace=True)
internet_users_df.head()
```

The output is as follows:

	Country	Code	Year	Number of internet users (users)
0	Afghanistan	AFG	1990	0
1257	Eritrea	ERI	1990	0
1236	Equatorial Guinea	GNQ	1990	0
4016	Timor	TLS	1990	0
1214	El Salvador	SLV	1990	0

Figure 6.20: Internet users dataset after sorting by year

7. Plot the number of users using the internet across the world in **2016**:

```
import plotly.express as px

fig = px.scatter_geo(internet_users_df.query("Year==2016"),
                    locations="Code", # name of column indicating
country-codes
                    size="Number of internet users (users)", # name
of column by which to size the bubble
```

```
                        hover_name="Country", # name of column to be
displayed while hovering over the map
                        size_max=80, # parameter to scale all bubble
sizes
                        color_continuous_scale=px.colors.sequential.
Plasma)

fig.update_layout(
    # add a title text for the plot
    title_text = 'Internet users across the world - 2016',
    # set projection style for the plot
    geo = dict(projection={'type':'natural earth'}) # by default,
projection type is set to 'equirectangular'
)
fig.show()
```

The output is as follows:

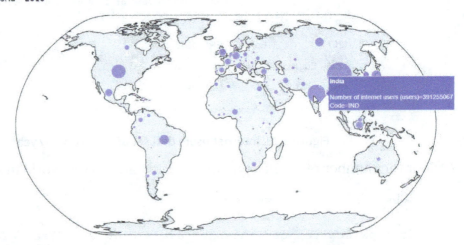

Figure 6.21: Bubble plot to see the number of internet users across the world

Notice how the largest numbers of users come from India and China? Since we know from our previous dataset that the percentage of the population using the internet in these countries is low, this large user group can be attributed to the vast population of these countries.

8. Animate the bubble plot to show the increase in the number of internet users over the years by using the **`animation_frame`** parameter:

```
import plotly.express as px

fig = px.scatter_geo(internet_users_df,
                     locations="Code", # name of column indicating
country-codes
                     size="Number of internet users (users)", # name
of column by which to size the bubble
                     hover_name="Country", # name of column to be
displayed while hovering over the map
                     size_max=80, # parameter to scale all bubble
size
                     animation_frame="Year",
                     )

fig.update_layout(
    # add a title text for the plot
    title_text = 'Internet users across the world',
    # set projection style for the plot
    geo = dict(projection={'type':'natural earth'}) # by default,
projection type is set to 'equirectangular'
    )
fig.show()
```

The output is as follows:

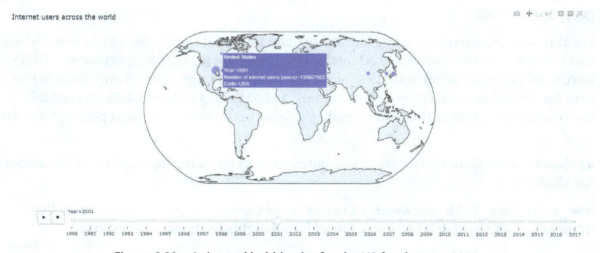

Figure 6.22a: Animated bubble plot for the US for the year 2001

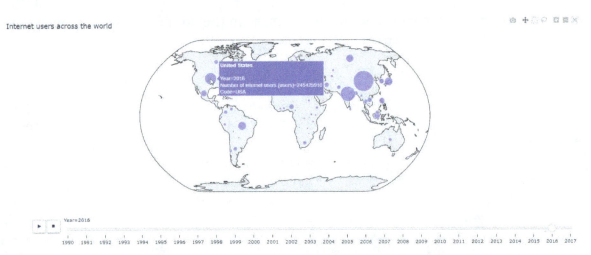

Figure 6.22b: Animated bubble plot for the US for the year 2016

We can see from the preceding two plots how the number of internet users increased between **2001** and **2016** for **USA**.

Scatter plots on maps can be used to show specific locations of interest on geographical maps, whereas bubble maps are a nice way to present count data across different divisions of a geographical region. The `Scattergeo` function from `plotly graph_objects` and the `scatter_geo` function from `plotly express` are generally used to generate interactive scatter plots and bubble plots on maps.

In the next section, we'll look at a few line plots on geographical maps.

Line Plots on Geographical Maps

Line plots rendered on maps are another important class of visualization for geographical data.

For this section, we will be using the airport and flight data from the **2015** Flight Delays and Cancellations dataset released by the **U.S. Department of Transportation**'s (**DOT**) Bureau of Transportation Statistics. Since the dataset is huge, we will only include the data for all flights with airline delays on `Jan 1,2015`. This reduced dataset contains the records of `1,820` flights and is made available in the book GitHub repository as two files:

`airports.csv`: Contains location attributes such as latitude and longitude information for all airports

`new_year_day_2015_delayed_flights.csv`: Contains flight details such as flight numbers, origin, and destination airports for all flights in the selected subset.

Exercise 51: Creating Line Plots on a Geographical Map

1. In this exercise, we'll use the **airports** dataset (available at: https://raw. githubusercontent.com/TrainingByPackt/Interactive-Data-Visualization-with-Python/master/datasets/airports.csv) and first generate a scatter plot to find out the locations of all airports in the US. We'll then merge the two DataFrames (**flights** and **airport_record**) together to obtain longitude and latitudes for the origin airports of all flights and draw line plots from the origin airport to the destination airport for each flight using this merged dataset. Let's go through the following steps:

2. Load the **airports** dataset first:

```
import pandas as pd
us_airports_url = "https://raw.githubusercontent.com/
TrainingByPackt/Interactive-Data-Visualization-with-Python/master/
datasets/airports.csv"
us_airports_df = pd.read_csv(us_airports_url)
us_airports_df.head()
```

The output is as follows:

	IATA_CODE	AIRPORT	CITY	STATE	COUNTRY	LATITUDE	LONGITUDE
0	ABE	Lehigh Valley International Airport	Allentown	PA	USA	40.65236	-75.44040
1	ABI	Abilene Regional Airport	Abilene	TX	USA	32.41132	-99.68190
2	ABQ	Albuquerque International Sunport	Albuquerque	NM	USA	35.04022	-106.60919
3	ABR	Aberdeen Regional Airport	Aberdeen	SD	USA	45.44906	-98.42183
4	ABY	Southwest Georgia Regional Airport	Albany	GA	USA	31.53552	-84.19447

Figure 6.23:Airports dataset

3. Generate a scatter plot on the US map to indicate the locations of all airports in our dataset, using the **graph_objects** module:

```
import plotly.graph_objects as go
fig = go.Figure()
fig.add_trace(go.Scattergeo(
    locationmode = 'USA-states',
    lon = us_airports_df['LONGITUDE'],
    lat = us_airports_df['LATITUDE'],
    hoverinfo = 'text',
    text = us_airports_df['AIRPORT'],
    mode = 'markers',
    marker = dict(size = 5,color = 'black')))
```

```
fig.update_layout(
    title_text = 'Airports in the USA',
    showlegend = False,
    geo = go.layout.Geo(
        scope = 'usa'
    ),
)
fig.show()
```

The output is as follows:

Airports in the USA

Figure 6.24: Number of airports in the US

That is neat! When you hover over a datapoint, you'll get the name of the US airport. The preceding plot shows **Central Illinois Regional Airport at Bloomington-Normal**.

Did you notice that there is an **add_trace()** function in addition to the usual instance creation of the **Scattergeo** class? The **add_trace** function is used because we are about to superimpose our flight data in the form of lines on top of this scatter plot on the map. The **add_ trace** allows **plotly** to treat the scatter plot and the line plots as multiple layers on the map.

4. Load the file containing the flight records:

```
new_year_2015_flights_url = "https://raw.githubusercontent.com/
TrainingByPackt/Interactive-Data-Visualization-with-Python/master/
datasets/new_year_day_2015_delayed_flights.csv"
new_year_2015_flights_df = pd.read_csv(new_year_2015_flights_url)
new_year_2015_flights_df.head()
```

The output is as follows:

	YEAR	MONTH	DAY	DAY_OF_WEEK	AIRLINE	FLIGHT_NUMBER	TAIL_NUMBER	ORIGIN_AIRPORT	DESTINATION_AIRPORT
0	2015	1	1	4	HA	17	N389HA	LAS	HNL
1	2015	1	1	4	B6	2134	N307JB	SJU	MCO
2	2015	1	1	4	B6	2276	N646JB	SJU	BDL
3	2015	1	1	4	US	425	N174US	PDX	PHX
4	2015	1	1	4	AA	89	N3KVAA	IAH	MIA

Figure 6.25: Dataset with flight records

5. Along with the origin and destination airports for each flight, we need to have the longitude and latitude information of the corresponding airports. To do this, we need to merge the DataFrames containing the airport and flight data. Let's first merge the two datasets to obtain the longitudes and latitudes for the origin airports of all flights:

```
# merge the DataFrames on origin airport codes
new_year_2015_flights_df = new_year_2015_flights_df.merge(us_airports_
df[['IATA_CODE','LATITUDE','LONGITUDE']], \
                              left_on='ORIGIN_AIRPORT', \
                              right_on='IATA_CODE', \
                              how='inner')

# drop the duplicate column containing airport code
new_year_2015_flights_df.drop(columns=['IATA_CODE'],inplace=True)

# rename the latitude and longitude columns to reflect that they
correspond to the origin airport
new_year_2015_flights_df.rename(columns={"LATITUDE":"ORIGIN_AIRPORT_
LATITUDE", "LONGITUDE":"ORIGIN_AIRPORT_LONGITUDE"},inplace=True)
new_year_2015_flights_df.head()
```

The output is as follows:

	YEAR	MONTH	DAY	DAY_OF_WEEK	AIRLINE	FLIGHT_NUMBER	TAIL_NUMBER	ORIGIN_AIRPORT	DESTINATION_AIRPORT	SCHEDULED_DEPARTURE	...
0	2015	1	1	4	HA	17	N389HA	LAS	HNL	145	...
1	2015	1	1	4	HA	7	N395HA	LAS	HNL	900	...
2	2015	1	1	4	AA	1623	N438AA	LAS	DFW	905	...
3	2015	1	1	4	DL	1530	N954DN	LAS	MSP	920	...
4	2015	1	1	4	WN	1170	N902WN	LAS	ELP	950	...

Figure 6.26: Dataset with flight records

6. Now, we will perform a similar merging to get the latitude and longitude data for the destination airports of all flights:

```
# merge the DataFrames on destination airport codes
new_year_2015_flights_df = new_year_2015_flights_df.merge(us_airports_
df[['IATA_CODE','LATITUDE','LONGITUDE']], \
                           left_on='DESTINATION_AIRPORT', \
                           right_on='IATA_CODE', \
                           how='inner')

# drop the duplicate column containing airport code
new_year_2015_flights_df.drop(columns=['IATA_CODE'],inplace=True)

# rename the latitude and longitude columns to reflect that they
correspond to the destination airport
new_year_2015_flights_df.rename(columns={'LATITUDE':'DESTINATION_
AIRPORT_LATITUDE', 'LONGITUDE':'DESTINATION_AIRPORT_
LONGITUDE'},inplace=True)
new_year_2015_flights_df.head()
```

The output is as follows:

	YEAR	MONTH	DAY	DAY_OF_WEEK	AIRLINE	FLIGHT_NUMBER	TAIL_NUMBER	ORIGIN_AIRPORT	DESTINATION_AIRPORT	SCHEDULED_DEPARTURE	...
0	2015	1	1	4	HA	17	N389HA	LAS	HNL	145	...
1	2015	1	1	4	HA	7	N395HA	LAS	HNL	900	...
2	2015	1	1	4	UA	253	N768UA	IAH	HNL	920	...
3	2015	1	1	4	UA	328	N210UA	DEN	HNL	1130	...
4	2015	1	1	4	UA	1173	N56859	SFO	HNL	805	...

5 rows × 35 columns

Figure 6.27: Merged flights dataset

7. Now, we will draw our line plots. For each flight, we need to draw a line between the origin airport and the destination airport. This is done by providing the latitude and longitude values of the destination and origin airports to the **lon** and **lat** parameters of **Scattergeo** and setting **mode** to *lines* instead of *markers*. Also, notice that we are using another **add_trace** function here. It may take a few minutes for the plot to show the flight routes:

```python
for i in range(len(new_year_2015_flights_df)):
    fig.add_trace(
        go.Scattergeo(
            locationmode = 'USA-states',
            lon = [new_year_2015_flights_df['ORIGIN_AIRPORT_
LONGITUDE'][i], new_year_2015_flights_df['DESTINATION_AIRPORT_
LONGITUDE'][i]],
            lat = [new_year_2015_flights_df['ORIGIN_AIRPORT_
LATITUDE'][i], new_year_2015_flights_df['DESTINATION_AIRPORT_
LATITUDE'][i]],
            mode = 'lines',
            line = dict(width = 1,color = 'red')
        )
    )

fig.update_layout(
    title_text = 'Delayed flight on Jan 1, 2015 in USA',
    showlegend = False,
    geo = go.layout.Geo(
        scope = 'usa'
    ),
)
fig.show()
```

The output is as follows:

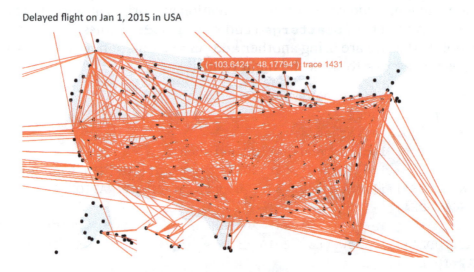

Delayed flight on Jan 1, 2015 in USA

(−103.6424°, 48.17794°) trace 1431

Figure 6.28: Line plot for all the delayed flights

And that is all for this section. Enjoy your newly gained skill and create a variety of wonderful geographical plots!

Line plots on geographical maps can be generated using the `graph_objects` module from `plotly`. Generally, a layering technique is used, with the help of the `add_trace()` function to superimpose two plots together on the map – the locations being connected as a scatter plot, and the routes connecting various locations as line plots.

Activity 6: Creating a Choropleth Map to Represent Total Renewable Energy Production and Consumption across the World

We will be working with the `Renewable Energy Consumption and Production` datasets from Our World in Data https://ourworldindata.org/renewable-energy). These datasets are made available on the book's GitHub repository as `share-of-electricity-production-from-renewable-sources.csv` (the production dataset) and `renewable-energy-consumption-by-country.csv` (the consumption dataset). Your task is to create choropleth maps for the total renewable energy production and consumption across different countries in the world animated based on the production/consumption years between (excluding) 2007 and 2017.

High-level steps

1. Load the **renewable energy production** dataset.

2. Sort the **production** DataFrame based on the **Year** feature.

3. Generate a choropleth map for renewable energy production using the **plotly express** module animated based on **Year**.

4. Update the layout to include a suitable projection style and title text, then display the figure.

5. Load the **renewable energy consumption** dataset.

6. Convert the **consumption** DataFrame to a suitable format for visualization.

7. Sort the **consumption** DataFrame based on the **Year** feature.

8. Generate a choropleth map for renewable energy consumption using the **plotly express** module animated based on **Year**.

9. Update the layout to include a suitable projection style and title text, then display the figure.

The output should be:

After Step 1–

	Country	Code	Year	Renewable electricity (% electricity production)
0	Afghanistan	AFG	1990	67.730496
1	Afghanistan	AFG	1991	67.980296
2	Afghanistan	AFG	1992	67.994310
3	Afghanistan	AFG	1993	68.345324
4	Afghanistan	AFG	1994	68.704512

Figure 6.29: Renewable sources dataset

After Step 2:

	Country	Code	Year	Renewable electricity (% electricity production)
0	Afghanistan	AFG	1990	67.730496
1668	France	FRA	1990	13.369879
1643	Finland	FIN	1990	29.451790
1618	Fiji	FJI	1990	82.441113
1593	Faeroe Islands	FRO	1990	35.545024

Figure 6.30: Renewable sources dataset after sorting by year

After Step 4-

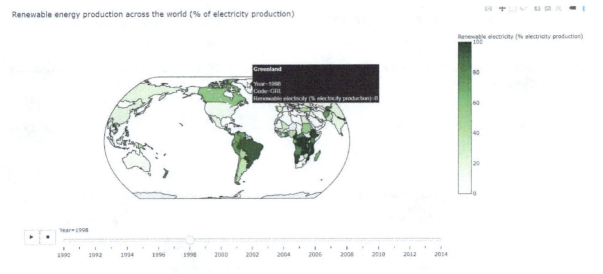

Figure 6.31a: Choropleth map showing the renewable energy production
of Greenland in the year 1998

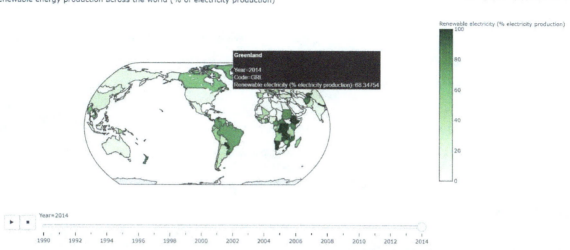

Figure 6.31b: Choropleth map showing the renewable energy production of Greenland in the year 2014

After Step 5-

	Country	Code	Year	Traditional biofuels	Other renewables (modern biofuels, geothermal, wave & tidal)	Wind	Solar PV	Hydropower	Total
0	Algeria	DZA	1965	NaN		0.0	0.0	0.0	NaN	0.0
1	Algeria	DZA	1966	NaN		0.0	0.0	0.0	NaN	0.0
2	Algeria	DZA	1967	NaN		0.0	0.0	0.0	NaN	0.0
3	Algeria	DZA	1968	NaN		0.0	0.0	0.0	NaN	0.0
4	Algeria	DZA	1969	NaN		0.0	0.0	0.0	NaN	0.0

Figure 6.32: Renewable energy consumption dataset

After Step 6-

	Country	Code	Year	Energy Source	Consumption (terrawatt-hours)
0	Algeria	DZA	1965	Energy Source	Traditional biofuels
1	Algeria	DZA	1966	Energy Source	Traditional biofuels
2	Algeria	DZA	1967	Energy Source	Traditional biofuels
3	Algeria	DZA	1968	Energy Source	Traditional biofuels
4	Algeria	DZA	1969	Energy Source	Traditional biofuels

Figure 6.33: The desired dataset after conversion

After Step 7-

	Country	Code	Year	Energy Source	Consumption (terrawatt-hours)
0	Algeria	DZA	1965	Traditional biofuels	NaN
4240	Finland	FIN	1965	Other renewables (modern biofuels, geothermal,...	0.0
17252	Chile	CHL	1965	Total	0.0
4292	France	FRA	1965	Other renewables (modern biofuels, geothermal,...	0.0
4344	Germany	DEU	1965	Other renewables (modern biofuels, geothermal,...	0.0

Figure 6.34: The dataset after sorting by year

After Step 8-

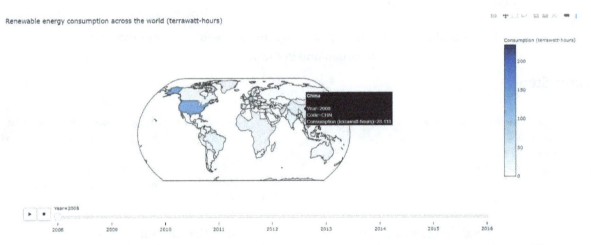

Figure 6.35a: Choropleth map showing renewable energy consumption across the world

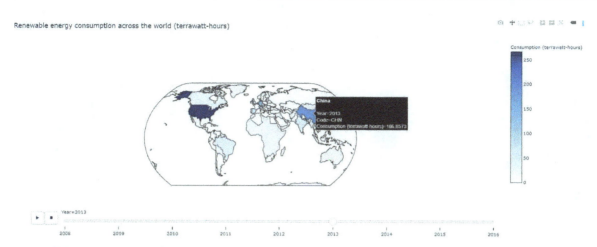

Figure 6.35b: Choropleth map showing renewable energy consumption across the world

> **Note**
>
> The solution steps can be found on page 275.

Summary

In this chapter, we presented three different types of visualization using geographical data choropleth maps, scatter plots and bubble plots on geographical maps, and line plots on geographical maps. Choropleth maps present aggregate statistics across different regions on geographical maps. Scatter plots are effective at indicating details regarding specific locations of interest, whereas bubble plots are useful for presenting count data per region on a map. Line plots are helpful in visualizing the routes of transportation systems, for instance.

These plots can easily be generated using the `plotly express` and `graph_objects` modules. Animation can be performed with respect to a discrete numeric feature in a dataset.

In the next chapter, we'll look at a few common pitfalls faced while creating visualizations and how to avoid them. Along with that, we'll also look at a cheat sheet for generating interactive visualizations.

Avoiding Common Pitfalls to Create Interactive Visualizations

Learning Objectives

By the end of this chapter, you will be able to:

- Identify the errors that are made when creating visualizations

- Apply techniques to correct the errors and create effective visualizations

- Select and design the appropriate visualizations for specific types of data

- Describe the different libraries and tools that are available for creating visualizations

In this chapter, we'll learn how to avoid common pitfalls while creating interactive visualizations. This chapter also gives an overview of some of the quick tricks when it comes to creating context-based visualizations.

Introduction

The previous chapters of this book have progressed from static to interactive data visualizations and described various interactive features (such as sliders and hover tools) and types of plots (such as grouped bar graphs, line plots, and choropleth world maps) pertaining to specific types of data, such as temporal and geographical. This chapter lists and explains the possible mistakes and errors that are made during various stages of the data visualization process – such as visualizing uncorrelated elements from a dataset to display a relationship or creating an inapt interactive feature – and discusses how to ensure that the final visualization is appropriate, informative, and simple. Additionally, there is a cheat sheet at the end of this chapter that describes the libraries and the types of visualizations you should use when performing data visualization.

The process of data visualization may seem simple – take some data, plot some graphs, add some interactive features, and voila! Your job is done. Or, maybe it's not – there could be several places during the journey where mistakes may be made. These mistakes ultimately result in a faulty visualization that is unable to easily and efficiently convey what the data is saying, thus making it completely useless to the audience who's viewing it.

Let's break the data visualization process into two parts – data formatting and interpretation and data visualization – so that we can understand what mistakes can be made where, and how to best avoid them.

> **Note**
>
> Some of the images in this chapter have colored notations, you can find high-quality color images used in this chapter at: https://github.com/ TrainingByPackt/Interactive-Data-Visualization-with-Python/tree/master/Graphics/ Lesson7.

Data Formatting and Interpretation

The purpose of interactive data visualization is to visually and interactively present data so that it is easy to comprehend. Thus, naturally, data is the most important factor of any visualization. Hence, the first phase of data visualization is understanding the data in front of you – understanding what it is, what it means, and what it's conveying. Only when you understand the data will you be able to design a visualization that will help others understand it.

Additionally, it is important to ensure that your data makes sense and contains enough information – be it categorical, numerical, or a mix of both – to be visualized. So, if you are dealing with erroneous or dirty data, you're bound to end up with a faulty visualization.

In the next section, we'll look at a few ways to avoid common mistakes that are typically made in this phase of data and how to avoid them.

Avoiding Common Pitfalls while Dealing with Dirty Data

Garbage In, Garbage Out – this is a popular saying in the field of data science, especially with respect to data visualization. It basically means that if you use messy and noisy data, you're going to get a flawed and uninformative visualization.

Messy, noisy, and dirty data corresponds to an array of problems found in data. Let's discuss the problems one by one and ways to deal with this kind of data.

Outliers

Data containing inaccurate values or instances that are significantly different from the rest of the data in a dataset are called **outliers**.

These are the data points that are distinctly different from the majority of the data points in your dataset. These outliers can either be *genuine*, that is, they seem incorrect but are actually not, or are mistakes that are made while collecting or storing the data.

Let's look at an example of a mistake that was made while collecting or storing data. The following table lists the **age**, **weight**, and **sex** of clients who visit a particular gym. The **sex** column consists of three discrete values – **0**, **1**, and **2** – that all correspond to a class – **male**, **female** and **other** respectively. The **age** column is in years and the **weight** column is in kilograms. Let's look at the dataset:

	age	weight	sex
0	29	88	2
1	45	96	1
2	35	91	0
3	37	790	1
4	27	62	0

Figure 7.1: The head of a DataFrame displaying an error in storing data

Everything seems fine until we reach the fourth instance (index **3**), where `weight` is listed as **790** kg. That seems odd because nobody can actually weigh **790** kg, especially someone whose height is **5** feet and **7** inches. Whoever stored this data must have meant **79** kg and added a **0** by mistake. This is an instance of an outlier in the dataset. This may seem trivial right now, however, this can result in flawed visualizations, insights, and machine learning model predictions or patterns, especially if there are multiple repetitions of such data.

Now, let's look at an example of a *genuine outlier* in the following table:

	age	weight	sex
0	29	88	2
1	45	96	1
2	35	91	0
3	37	167	1
4	27	62	0

Figure 7.2: The head of a DataFrame displaying a genuine outlier

The weight in the fourth instance (index **3**) is **167** kilograms, which does seem oddly high. However, this is still a plausible value – it is possible that someone has a medical condition and does in fact weigh **167** kilograms at the age of **37**. Therefore, this is a **genuine outlier**.

While, in the preceding examples, it is easy to spot the outlier as there are only **5** instances, in reality, our datasets are massive, and so checking each instance for outliers is a tedious and impractical task. Hence, in real-life scenarios, we can use basic static data visualizations, such as box plots, to observe the existence of outliers.

Box plots are simple yet informative data visualizations that can tell us a lot about the way our data is distributed. They display the range of our data based on five key values:

- The minimum value in the column
- The first quartile
- The median
- The third quartile
- The maximum value in the column

This is what makes them great at displaying outliers as well, along with describing the symmetry of the data, how tightly it's grouped (whether all the values are close together or are spread out over a large range), and whether or not it's skewed.

Exercise 52: Visualizing Outliers in a Dataset with a Box Plot

In this exercise, we are going to create a box plot to check whether our dataset contains outliers. We are going to use the **gym.csv** dataset, which contains information about the clients of a certain gym. The following steps will help you with the solution:

1. Download the .csv file titled **gym** from this book's GitHub repository into the folder where you will be creating the interactive data visualization

> **Note**
>
> The datasets can be found here https://github.com/TrainingByPackt/Interactive-Data-Visualization-with-Python/tree/master/datasets.

2. Open **cmd** or a terminal, depending on your operating system

3. Navigate to the folder where you have stored the **.csv** files and use the following command to initiate a Jupyter notebook:

```
jupyter notebook
```

4. Import the **pandas** library:

```
import pandas as pd
```

5. Import the **numpy** library:

```
import numpy as np
```

6. Import the **plotly.express** library:

```
import plotly.express as px
```

7. Store the **gym.csv** file in a DataFrame called **gym**, and print the first five rows of it to see what the data looks like:

```
pd.read_csv('https://raw.githubusercontent.com/TrainingByPackt/
Interactive-Data-Visualization-with-Python/master/datasets/gym.csv')
gym.head()
```

The output is as follows:

	age	weight	sex
0	29	88	2
1	45	96	1
2	35	91	0
3	37	790	1
4	27	62	0

Figure 7.3: The first five rows of the gym DataFrame

As you can see, our data has three columns – **age**, **weight**, and **sex**. The **sex** column consists of three discrete values that correspond to three discrete classes – **0** is male, **1** is female, and **2** is other.

8. Create a box plot with the x axis as the **sex** column and the y axis as the **weight** column:

```
fig = px.box(gym, x = 'sex', y = 'weight', notched = True)
```

9. Display the figure:

```
fig.show()
```

The output is as follows:

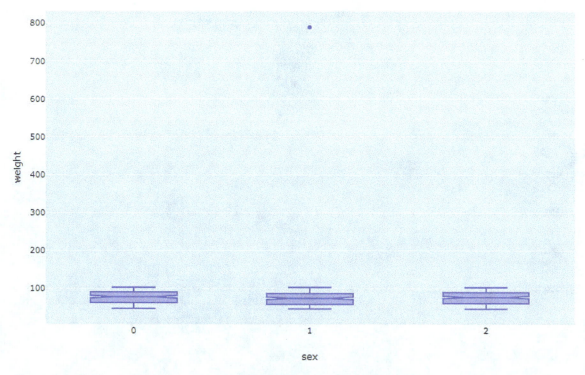

Figure 7.4: The box plot of the gym DataFrame, showing the outlier as a blue dot in the sex = 1 box

The scale of the y axis seems strangely large since all the box plots are compressed in the bottom 1/8th of the plot, thus not presenting a clear visualization of the data. This is due to the outlier in the fourth instance of our DataFrame -790 kg. If you hover near the point, you'll see the following:

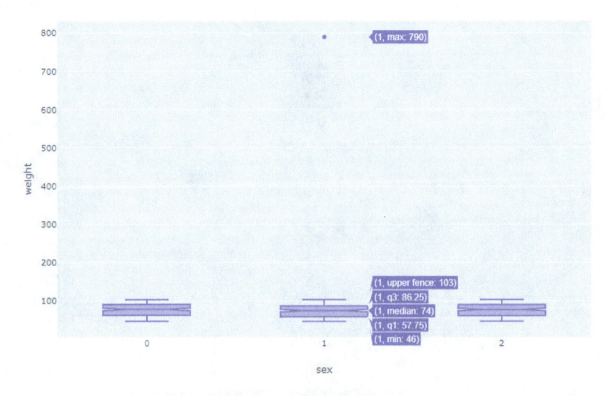

Figure 7.5: The result of hovering over the outlier

All the values seem fine except for that one outlier at the top of the plot with **max=790**.

Now, we'll look at the ways of dealing with outliers.

Dealing with Outliers

There are three main ways of dealing with outliers:

Deletion: If there are only a few instances (rows) that possess outliers then those instances can be completely removed from the dataset, thus leaving you with a dataset with zero outliers. There are also times when a certain feature (column) contains a large number of outliers. In such a case, that particular feature can be removed from the dataset, but only if that feature is insignificant. However, deleting data isn't always the best idea.

Imputation: Imputation is a better option than deletion, especially if there are many outliers in the dataset.

This can be done in three ways:

- The most common way is to impute the outliers with the mean, median, or mode of the column. In the case of many outliers, though, these values may not be good enough, since each outlier will be replaced by the same value (either the mean, median, or mode).

- The other method to arrive at better values for outliers, especially in the case of time series analysis, is linear interpolation, that is, using linear polynomials to create new data points within a defined range of known data points to replace outlier values.

- A linear regression model can also be used to predict a missing value if it is numerical, and in the case that the missing value is categorical, a logistic regression model can be used. Linear regression and logistic regression are supervised machine learning algorithms, that is, they learn from labeled data to make predictions for new unlabeled data. *Linear regression* is used to predict numerical values, while logistic regression is used to predict categories.

- For example, let's say you have a dataset from which you need to display a relationship between height and weight. The height column has several missing values but, since it is a significant feature, you can't delete it, nor can you impute the mean of the column since that might lead to a false relationship. The dataset can be split into two datasets:

  (a) The training dataset, which contains instances without missing values

  (b) The new dataset, which contains only those instances where there are missing values in the `height` column

  A linear regression model can then be used on the training dataset. The model will learn from this data, and then, when the new dataset is provided as input, it will be able to predict values for the height column. Now, the two datasets can be merged together and be used to create visualizations since there are no missing values.

Transformation: This is the process of transforming the outliers by building up the column of data wherein the outlier lies, for example, converting the values into percentages and using that column as a feature instead of the original column.

In the following section, we'll look at an exercise to understand how we can deal with outliers.

Exercise 53: Dealing with Outliers

In this exercise, we are going to delete the instance that contains the outlier from the dataset we used in *Exercise 52, Visualizing Outliers in a Dataset with a Box Plot* and visualize the dataset again by generating a box plot based on the new dataset. Let's get started:

1. Import the **pandas** and **numpy** libraries:

   ```
   import pandas as pd
   import numpy as np
   ```

2. Import the **plotly.express** library:

   ```
   import plotly.express as px
   ```

3. Store the **gym.csv** file in a DataFrame called **gym** and print the first five rows of it to see what the data looks like:

   ```
   gym = pd.read_csv('gym.csv')
   ```

4. Create a boxplot with the x axis as the **sex** column and the y axis as the **weight** column:

   ```
   fig = px.box(gym, x = 'sex', y = 'weight', notched = True)
   ```

5. Display the figure:

   ```
   fig.show()
   ```

The output is as follows:

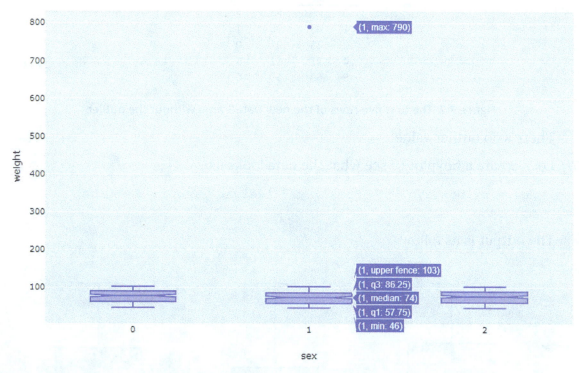

Figure 7.6:The box plot with the outlier

Upon hovering over the box of **sex = 1**, we can see that the upper fence is **103**. Therefore, we know that the maximum value that's present in the **weight** column is **103**.

6. Modify the **gym** DataFrame so that it only consists of those instances where the **weight** is less than **103** and print the first five rows:

```
gym = gym[gym['weight'] <104]
gym.head()
```

The output is as follows:

	age	weight	sex
0	29	88	2
1	45	96	1
2	35	91	0
4	27	62	0
5	58	55	0

Figure 7.7: The first five rows of the new DataFrame without the outlier

There's no outlier value!

7. Let's create a boxplot to see what the data looks like:

```
fig1 = px.box(gym, x = 'sex', y = 'weight', notched = True)
fig1.show()
```

The output is as follows:

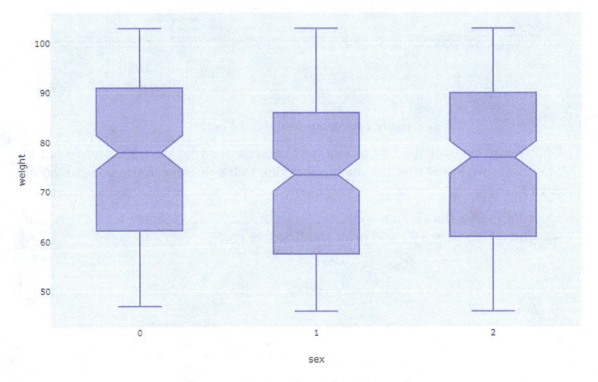

Figure 7.8: The box plot without the outlier

Now our visualization looks good! There are no outlier values and so the scale of the y axis is appropriate. Now that we've looked at how to deal with outliers, we'll look at the other problems that exist in data that can lead to flawed visualizations.

Missing Data

Missing data is as its name states – values that are blank (**NaN**, **-**, **0** when they shouldn't be **0**, and so on). Just like outliers, missing values can be problematic in the case of visualizations as well as machine learning models. Missing values in visualizations may display a trend that doesn't actually exist or fail to portray a relationship between two variables that, in reality, is significant. While it is possible to create visualizations with a dataset that contains missing values, this isn't recommended. In doing this, the instances wherein those missing values are found are ignored, thus creating a visualization based on some of the data but not all of it. Therefore, dealing with missing values is of utmost importance.

There are two main approaches for dealing with missing values – deletion and imputation – both of which have been discussed in terms of dealing with outliers. The same logic applies to missing values.

Exercise 54: Dealing with Missing Values

In this exercise, we are going to work on a dataset that has seven missing values in the form of **0**s. First, we will remove the instances containing these missing values and generate a box plot to see the impact that the deletion of a large number of instances has on our visualization. Then, we will impute the median value of the column that contains the missing values to the said missing values and generate a box plot based on this imputed dataset. Let's get started:

1. Download the **.csv** file titled **weight** from this book's GitHub repository into the folder where you will be creating the interactive data visualization.

2. Navigate to the folder where you have stored the .csv files and use the following command to initiate a Jupyter notebook:

   ```
   jupyter notebook
   ```

3. Import the **pandas** library:

   ```
   import pandas as pd
   ```

4. Import the **numpy** library:

   ```
   import numpy as np
   ```

5. Import the `plotly.express` library:

```
import plotly.express as px
```

6. Store the .csv file in a DataFrame and use the `.describe()` function to display information about it:

```
w = pd.read_csv('https://raw.githubusercontent.com/TrainingByPackt/
Interactive-Data-Visualization-with-Python/master/datasets/weight.
csv')
w.describe()
```

The output is as follows:

	weight	sex
count	62.000000	62.000000
mean	38.200000	0.838710
std	9.870307	0.813685
min	21.000000	0.000000
25%	31.250000	0.000000
50%	38.100000	1.000000
75%	46.000000	1.750000
max	56.000000	2.000000

Figure 7.9: Statistical information about the weight DataFrame

As we can see, the minimum `weight` value in our dataset is 0; however, nobody can weigh 0kgs, which means we have missing values in the form of 0s. Let's try deleting these instances.

7. Create a new DataFrame that consists of only those instances where the weight is not equal to **0**. Display information about this new DataFrame:

```
doc_w = w[w['weight'] != 0]
doc_w.describe()
```

The output is as follows:

	weight	sex
count	55.00000	55.000000
mean	38.20000	0.836364
std	10.49056	0.811118
min	21.00000	0.000000
25%	31.00000	0.000000
50%	36.00000	1.000000
75%	46.50000	1.500000
max	56.00000	2.000000

Figure 7.10: Statistical information about the DataFrame post deletion

8. Create a boxplot with this new DataFrame, with the x axis as **sex** and the y axis as **weight**. Then, display the figure:

```
fig1 = px.box(doc_w, x = 'sex', y = 'weight', notched = True)
fig1.show()
```

The output is as follows:

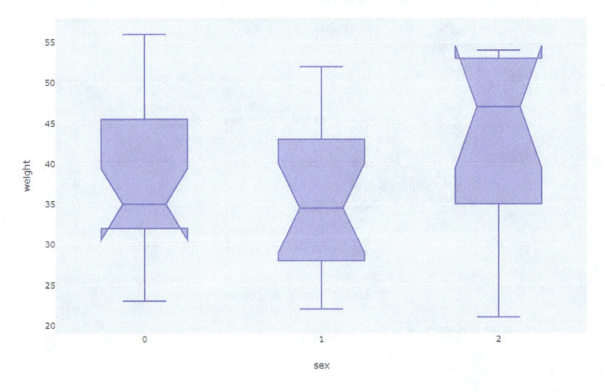

Figure 7.11: The box plot that was generated on the DataFrame post deletion

Now, the minimum weight value is **21**, which makes more sense. However, our count has reduced to **55** from **62**, which means we've deleted **7** instances from our dataset. This may seem small in this example, but in reality, this may have serious repercussions on the insights gained. Also, in the preceding box plot, the lower end of the box for **0** sex and the upper end of the box for **2** sex is slightly abnormal. Therefore, let's replace the **0** values in the **weight** column with the mean value of the column. Remember that we need to calculate the mean of the column without considering those **0** values! If we take those into account, then our mean will be incorrect.

9. Calculate the mean of the **weight** column from the DataFrame that consists of only non-zero weight values:

    ```
    mean_w = doc_w['weight'].mean()
    ```

    The mean should be **38.2**.

10. Use the `.replace()` function to replace the **0** values present in the **weight** column of the original DataFrame with the mean of the **weight** column from the modified DataFrame. Store this in a new DataFrame:

```
w_new = w.replace({'weight': {0:mean_w}})
```

11. Display the information of the new DataFrame:

```
w_new.describe()
```

The output is as follows:

	weight	sex
count	62.000000	62.000000
mean	33.887097	0.838710
std	15.683451	0.813685
min	0.000000	0.000000
25%	25.000000	0.000000
50%	35.000000	1.000000
75%	46.000000	1.750000
max	56.000000	2.000000

Figure 7.12: Statistical information of the DataFrame post imputation

Our count is **62**, which means we have all the instances, and our minimum weight is **21**, which means we have no **0** values!

12. Create a box plot with this new DataFrame, with the x axis as **sex** and the y axis as **weight**. Then, display the figure:

```
fig2 = px.box(w_new, x = 'sex', y = 'weight', notched = True)
fig2.show()
```

The output is as follows:

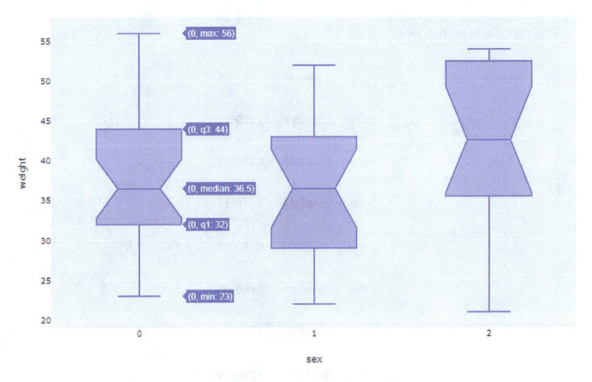

Figure 7.13: The box plot that's generated on the DataFrame post imputation

Now, we have a visualization that has no missing values and represents all the instances that are present in the dataset!

Let's look at the third problem that can generate faulty visualization.

Duplicate Instances and/or Features

The third problem is the presence of duplicate instances and/or features in a dataset.

These are unnecessary elements in the dataset and if they are not removed, they can impact the trends and insights that are displayed by a visualization. For example, you can create a visualization that displays the relationship between the gender of a teenager and whether they play the piano. With a dataset devoid of outliers, anomalies, or missing values, you will get a great visualization. From the visualization, you will also be able to conclude that more females play the piano than males do. However, let's say that the following information is from the dataset that was used to create this visualization:

	Name	Gender	Play the Piano	Age
1	Pooja Rajesh	F	Yes	17
2	Pooja Rajesh	F	Yes	17
3	Pooja Rajesh	F	Yes	17
4	Nita Thadaka	F	No	19
5	Nita Thadaka	F	No	19
6	Shubhangi Hora	F	Yes	14

Table 7.14: The relationship between gender and playing the piano

There are two instances for `Nita Thadaka` and three instances for `Pooja Rajesh`, which means there are three duplicate instances in total! This means that the insights your visualization is providing are inaccurate.

The way to deal with duplicates is simple – *drop them*.

Bad Feature Selection

With respect to a dataset, a feature is a column in the dataset while an instance is a row in the dataset. For example, in the preceding table, `name`, `gender`, `play the piano`, and `age` are features, while `Pooja Rajesh`, `F`, `Yes`, and `17` is an instance.

Since the aim of a visualization is to show a trend, pattern, relationship, or some link between two or more features in a dataset, it is important that the selection of those features is done carefully. Therefore, this is a crucial point in the data visualization journey.

If the goal is to convey that a strong relationship exists between two features, then you must ensure that they are correlated strongly before going ahead with visualizing them. Selecting insignificant features will result in a pointless visualization and it won't end up conveying any concrete information. For example, in terms of the `co2.csv` dataset, the dataset contains information regarding carbon dioxide emissions per person per country and the GDP per country. We checked for a correlation between CO2 emissions and the GDP before visualizing the dataset, guaranteeing that we were going to create a worthwhile visualization.

Activity 7: Determining Which Features to Visualize on a Scatter Plot

You are given the `co2.csv` dataset and are asked to provide insights on it, such as what kind of patterns exist, are there any trends between the features, and so on. You need to ensure that your end visualization conveys meaningful information. To achieve this, you are going to create visualizations for different feature pairings to understand how to select features that are correlated and, thus, worth visualizing.

High-Level Steps

1. Import the necessary libraries.
2. Recreate the DataFrame. From the `gm` DataFrame include the `population`, `fertility`, and `life` columns.
3. Visualize the relationship between `co2` and `life` using a scatter graph, with the country name as information in the hover tool and the year as a slider.
4. Check the correlation between `co2` and `life`.

5. Visualize the relationship between **co2** and **fertility** using a scatter graph, with the country name as information in the hover tool and the year as a slider.

6. Check the correlation between **co2** and **fertility**.

The output is as follows:

After Step 4:

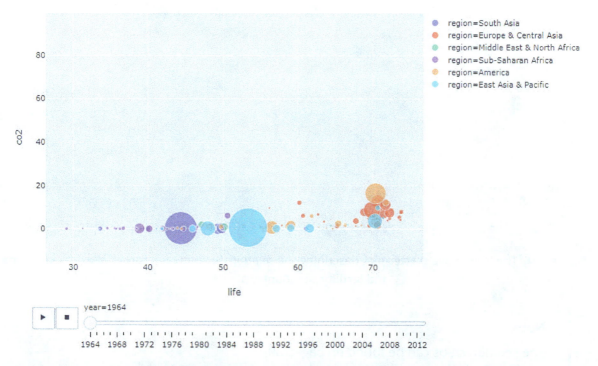

Figure 7.15: The interactive scatter plot describing the relationship between carbon dioxide emissions and life per country per year

After Step 5:

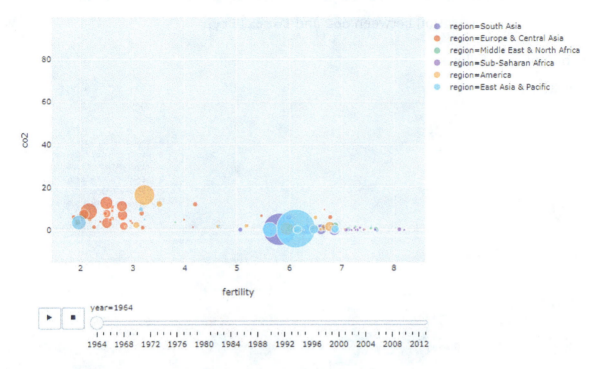

Figure 7.16: The interactive scatter plot describing the relationship between carbon dioxide emissions and fertility per country per year

> **Note**
>
> The solution steps can be found on page 280.

In this activity, we have a weak negative correlation, which is why we can't observe much from our visualization. Therefore, it is always important to select features properly so that we create an insightful visualization. Let's see how we can choose a visualization wisely and the common pitfalls that are faced during this process.

Data Visualization

The actual visualization is as important as the data that is being visualized, obviously, since it is the end product of the process. Thus, paying close attention to creating the best possible visualization for the data at hand is crucial.

Interactive visualizations have multiple elements/parts. Let's take a closer look at each element to understand what can go wrong and how to prevent such mistakes.

Choosing a Visualization

Once your data has been cleaned and prepared, and the features that you want to visualize have been chosen, the first step in creating a visualization is selecting the graph or plot that is going to display your data. This decision impacts the efficiency and ease with which your visualization can explain your data, and thus you need to ensure that you're picking a visualization that can accurately explain and describe your data.

In the previous chapters, we looked at three types of data – stratified, temporal, and geographical – and used different visualizations to describe them. Hence, you already know that there are particular types of visualizations that are best suited for specific types of data; for example, using a world map to describe the relationship between gender and playing the piano in one particular school is quite pointless.

Let's take a look at the different visualizations that we can use to accurately explain and represent our data.

> **Note**
>
> As we saw in *Chapter 3, From Static to Interactive Visualization*, the basic plot is always a static one; interactive features are added to this static plot. Therefore, all the plots that we will mention here are static.

The visualization you choose for your data also depends on what you want to show. Therefore, the data and what you want to convey can be categorized, making it easier for you to decide which visualization you need to use to efficiently describe your data. The categories are as follows:

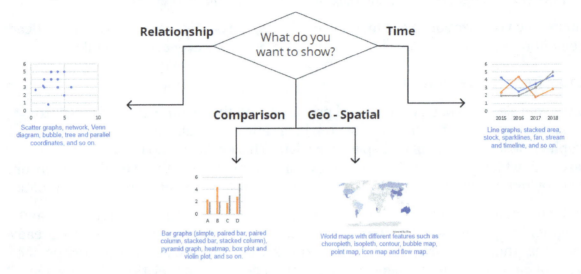

Figure 7.17: The broad types of visualizations

Relationship

These visualizations are used when showing a link between two or more variables. For example, in *Chapter 3, From Static to Interactive Visualization*, we described the relationship between the carbon dioxide emissions per person per country and the GDP per country.

The plots that are used to depict relationships include network graphs, scatter plots, Venn diagrams, bubble charts, trees, and parallel coordinates, among others.

Comparison

Comparison visualizations are used when you want to show the differences or similarities between two or more variables.

The plots that are used to depict comparisons include all the types of bar graphs (simple, paired bar, paired column, stacked bar, and stacked column), pyramid graphs, heatmaps, box plots, and violin plots, among others.

Geo-spatial

Geo-spatial visualizations are specific to data that is geographical in nature. Therefore, location is a feature that must exist in the data. Only then should this visualization be used.

The plots we used in *Chapter 6, Interactive Visualization of Geographical Data*, to depict geo-spatial data include world maps with different features, such as choropleth maps, isopleth maps, contour maps, bubble maps, point maps, icon maps, and flow maps, among others.

Time

When data consists of dates and/or times, these visualizations are used to track the necessary changes.

The plots that are used to depict temporal data include variations of line graphs, stacked area charts, stock charts, sparklines, fan charts, stream charts, and timeline charts, among others.

As we mentioned previously, these are all static plots to which interactive features are added. However, the key thing to remember is when your data comes under more than one of the aforementioned categories – what visualization should you choose then?

As an example, let's take the `co2.csv` dataset – we wanted to create a visualization that depicts the relationship between the carbon dioxide emissions per person per country and the GDP per country, over the span of a few decades. Therefore, this data technically comes under three categories – relationship, geo-spatial, and time.

The great thing about interactive features is that they can sometimes deal with the problem of our data falling under several categories. As you may remember, we used a slider to show the change in the data points over the time period of the dataset. Therefore, the time aspect of the data was taken care of by this interactive feature.

However, we still have the problem of choosing between a relationship visualization or a geo-spatial visualization:

- When deciding between two visualizations, it is important to remind yourself of what you actually want to convey with your visualization. In this case, we want to show the relationship between the carbon dioxide emissions per person per country and the GDP per country, not the relationship between carbon dioxide emissions and country, or GDP and country. This means that the two main features are carbon dioxide emissions and GDP, and so one needs to be the x axis and the other needs to be the y axis. Therefore, we chose a relationship visualization – the scatter graph.

- If we wanted to depict just how carbon dioxide emissions changed over time per country, we would pick a geo-spatial visualization.

- Also, an important thing to keep in mind is that to create a geo-spatial visualization, you need to have a location, and this location feature needs to be recognizable by the library you are using and the visualization that you are creating. For example, in our DataFrame, we have a `country` column. For us, that is a location feature and so we should be able to create a geo-spatial visualization using it. However, this is not recognized by the map visualizations in `plotly.express`. Features such as longitude and latitude or `iso_alpha` codes are required for the visualizations to understand where on the world map or country map a particular data point belongs.

Let's take a look at some of the other mistakes that can be made after choosing a visualization.

Common Pitfalls While Visualizing Data

Visualizing Too Much Information

While visualizations are great at simplifying data and conveying important insights, forcing them to convey too much information results in them becoming too complicated, and so, ultimately, the viewer isn't able to understand anything by looking at them. Too much information basically means incorporating more than four or five features in your visualization, thereby introducing more than 5 colors and having too many words.

Inconsistent Scales

Each feature has its own range within which all its data falls; if it's a numerical feature, then all the values fall within this range, while if it is a categorical feature, then there is a discrete set of classes.

When visualizing more than one or two features in a single plot, the problem of scales often arises because each feature has its own scale. Not considering the scale of each feature often leads to confusing visualizations that show trends where there are none. Inconsistent scales also often force relationships that do not exist. Additionally, some visualizations also show elements of a plot that don't scale with respect to each other. This misleads viewers into believing something is true when it is not.

Mislabeling Elements

Labels are often overlooked and considered as trivial elements of a visualization. Only in their absence do we realize their importance. Visualizations without labels become very confusing as the viewer doesn't know what they're seeing.

Exercise 55: Creating a Confusing Visualization

In this exercise, we're going to use the dataset from *Chapter 3, From Static to Interactive Visualization*, and the one we used in this chapter in *Activity 7, Determining Which Features to Visualize on a Scatter Plot*, to create a visualization that's hard to understand, thus explaining to you what you shouldn't be doing. Our visualization will aim to display the changes in carbon dioxide emissions per region every decade, starting in **1970** and ending in **2010**. Let's get started:

1. Download the .csv file titled **weight** from this book's GitHub repository into the folder where you will be creating the interactive data visualization.

2. Navigate to the folder where you have stored the .csv files and use the following command to initiate a Jupyter Notebook:

   ```
   jupyter notebook
   ```

3. Import the **pandas** library:

   ```
   import pandas as pd
   ```

4. Import the **numpy** library:

   ```
   import numpy as np
   ```

5. Import the **chart_studio.plotly** and **plotly.graph_objs** packages:

   ```
   import chart_studio.plotly as py
   import plotly.graph_objs as go
   ```

   > **Note**
   >
   > Please install chart_studio using pip install chart_studio

6. Create the DataFrame we used in *Activity 7, Determining Which Features to Visualize on a Scatter Plot*:

   ```
   co2 = pd.read_csv('../datasets/co2.csv')
   gm = pd.read_csv('../datasets/gapminder.csv')
   df_gm = gm[['Country', 'region']].drop_duplicates()
   df_w_regions = pd.merge(co2, df_gm, left_on='country', right_on='Country', how='inner')
   df_w_regions = df_w_regions.drop('Country', axis='columns')
   ```

```
new_co2 = pd.melt(df_w_regions, id_vars=['country', 'region'])
columns = ['country', 'region', 'year', 'co2']
new_co2.columns = columns
df_co2 = new_co2[new_co2['year'].astype('int64') > 1963]
df_co2 = df_co2.sort_values(by=['country', 'year'])
df_co2['year'] = df_co2['year'].astype('int64')
df_g = gm[['Country', 'Year', 'gdp', 'population', 'fertility',
'life']]
df_g.columns = ['country', 'year', 'gdp', 'population', 'fertility',
'life']
data = pd.merge(df_co2, df_g, on=['country', 'year'], how='left')
data = data.dropna()
```

7. Create a stacked bar graph per region per decade – each bar will correspond
    to one region, and will consist of carbon dioxide emissions per country for that
    particular year. Therefore, each bar will have 5 stacks. The x axis will be the region
    while the y axis will be the carbon dioxide emissions in **1970, 1980, 1990,
    2000, and 2010**:

```
source = [
    go.Bar(x = data['region'],
           y = data.co2[data['year'] == 1970]),
    go.Bar(x = data['region'],
           y = data.co2[data['year'] == 1980]),
    go.Bar(x = data['region'],
           y = data.co2[data['year'] == 1990]),
    go.Bar(x = data['region'],
           y = data.co2[data['year'] == 2000]),
    go.Bar(x = data['region'],
           y = data.co2[data['year'] == 2010]),
]
```

8. Set the layout as a stacked bar graph:

```
layout = go.Layout(barmode = 'stack')
```

9. Plot the figure and display it:

```
fig = go.Figure(source, layout)
fig.show()
```

The output is as follows:

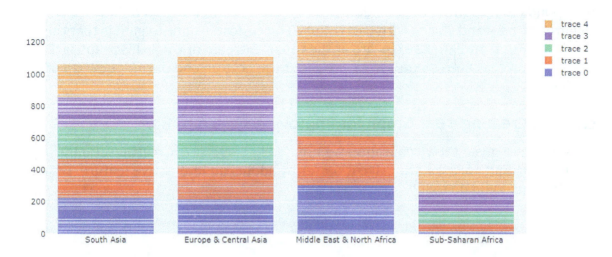

Figure 7.18: The stacked bar graph supposedly displaying the carbon dioxide emissions per region per decade

It's a little hard to understand this graph, isn't it? The axes aren't labeled, so other than you no one else is going to know what has been visualized. The legend just describes the different stacks (colors) as traces:

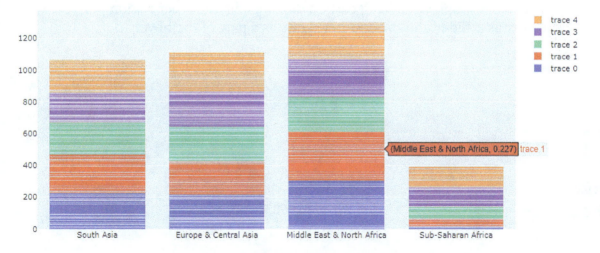

Figure 7.19: Hovering over one of the stacks

When you hover over the stacks, you see some numbers, but you aren't told what those numbers mean. Maybe you can figure out that each individual line in a stack corresponds to a country, but you don't know which country. It's even difficult to compare the bars and stacks with each other. The easiest insight to gain is that the `Middle East & North Africa` are at the top of extreme of what this graph is displaying and that `Sub-Saharan Africa` is at the bottom end during the span of five decades.

Activity 8: Creating a Bar Graph for Improving a Visualization

Let's say you're given the visualization we created in *Exercise 4, Creating a Confusing Visualization*, and are asked to make it better by adding an interactive feature. How do you think you could do that?

> **Note**
>
> This activity is a continuation of Exercise 55, so carry out the tasks in the same Jupyter notebook.

High-Level Steps

1. Import the necessary libraries.

2. Create a bar graph visualizing carbon dioxide emissions per region per year with the year as a slider and the country name as a part of the hover tool.

The expected output is:

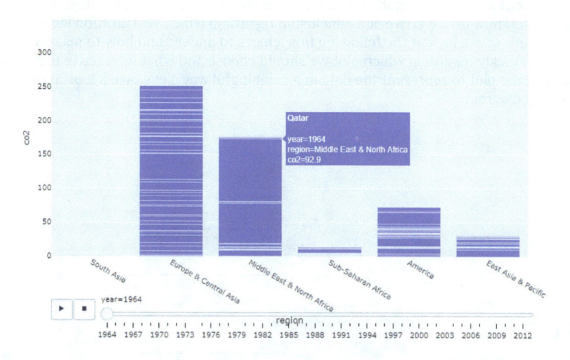

Figure 7.20: The interactive visualization in the form of a stacked bar graph depicting the carbon dioxide emissions per region over the span of five decades

> **Note**
>
> The solution steps can be found on page 284.

We shifted the time information to a sliding bar and added the country information to the hover tool. This has made our visualization so much better! There are labels on the axes, and the scale of the y axis isn't abnormally high. With this, we are able to get a better idea of what's going on. It is easier to compare the total carbon dioxide emissions per region per year now than it was in the earlier visualization.

Cheat Sheet for the Visualization Process

We have looked at various static and interactive visualization plots. But when we look at a dataset, how do we arrive at a conclusion regarding which visualization suits our needs? Let's take a look at the following flow charts to understand how to make a decision quickly regarding which plot we should choose and what interactive features to add to the plot to represent the data in a meaningful way. Let's take a look at the following diagram:

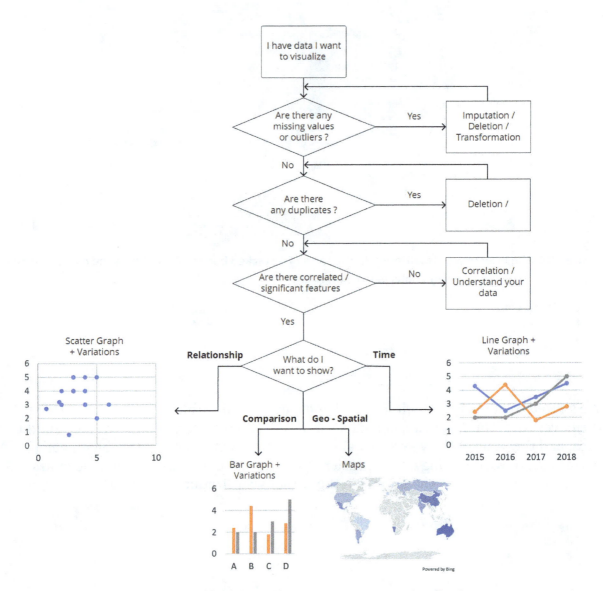

Figure 7.21a: Guideline of how to create a great visualization

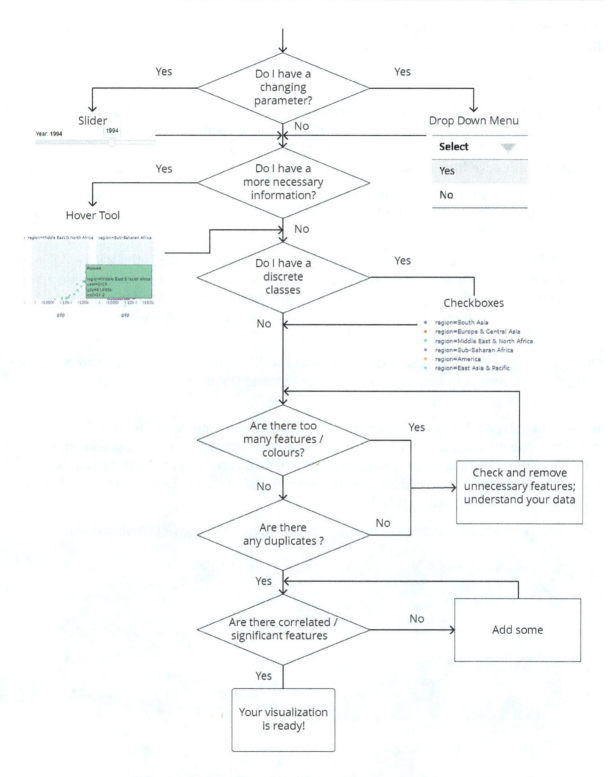

Figure 7.21b: Guideline of how to create a great visualization

This flow chart acts as a cheat sheet so that you can arrive at a conclusion regarding how to create a quick visualization based on a dataset.

Summary

In this book, we learned about the benefits of creating interactive data visualizations and how to build on static data visualizations to make them interactive. Simply incorporating features such as sliders, hover tools, and checkboxes can have an immensely positive impact on the way data is understood and how insights are gained.

We looked at different Python libraries and what visualizations and situations they are best suited for. For example, `bokeh` is preferred when creating visualizations for web-based applications.

Data and what you wish to show can be classified into four broad categories – comparisons, relationships, geo-spatial, and temporal. Each category has a wide array of graphs that suit that type of data best, but interactive features can help when data or what you want to show fall under more than one category – that's why interactive data visualizations are so great!

We also created context-based visualizations for different types of data – temporal, geographical, and data across strata – to understand the differences in the visualizations.

In this chapter, we learned about the various errors that can be made in different phases of the visualization process – right from the formatting of data (anomalies, missing values, and duplicates) to creating the visualizations (inconsistent scales, too many features, uncorrelated features, missing labels, and choosing the correct visualization), and how to avoid/deal with them.

Now, you're ready to create beautiful and meaningful interactive visualizations!

Appendix

About

This section is included to assist the readers to perform the activities in the book.
It includes detailed steps that are to be performed by the readers to achieve the objectives of the activities.

Chapter 1: Introduction to Visualization with Python – Basic and Customized Plotting

Activity 1: Analyzing Different Scenarios and Generating the Appropriate Visualization

Solution

1. Download the dataset hosted on the book GitHub repository, and format it as a **pandas** DataFrame:

```
# load necessary modules
import pandas as pd
import seaborn as sns
from numpy import median, mean
```

2. Read the dataset as a **pandas** DataFrame:

```
# download file 'athlete_events.csv' from course GitHub repository:
https://github.com/TrainingByPackt/Interactive-Data-Visualization-
with-Python/datasets
# read the dataset as a pandas DataFrame
olympics_df = pd.read_csv('..../Interactive-Data-Visualization-with-
Python/datasets/athlete_events.csv')
# preview DataFrame
olympics_df.head()
```

The output is as follows:

	ID	Name	Sex	Age	Height	Weight	Team	NOC	Games	Year	Season	City	Sport	Event	Medal
0	1	A Dijiang	M	24.0	180.0	80.0	China	CHN	1992 Summer	1992	Summer	Barcelona	Basketball	Basketball Men's Basketball	NaN
1	2	A Lamusi	M	23.0	170.0	60.0	China	CHN	2012 Summer	2012	Summer	London	Judo	Judo Men's Extra-Lightweight	NaN
2	3	Gunnar Nielsen Aaby	M	24.0	NaN	NaN	Denmark	DEN	1920 Summer	1920	Summer	Antwerpen	Football	Football Men's Football	NaN
3	4	Edgar Lindenau Aabye	M	34.0	NaN	NaN	Denmark/Sweden	DEN	1900 Summer	1900	Summer	Paris	Tug-Of-War	Tug-Of-War Men's Tug-Of-War	Gold
4	5	Christine Jacoba Aaftink	F	21.0	185.0	82.0	Netherlands	NED	1988 Winter	1988	Winter	Calgary	Speed Skating	Speed Skating Women's 500 metres	NaN

Figure 1.32: Olympics dataset

3. Filter the DataFrame to contain only medal winners of the year 2016:

```
# filter the DataFrame to contain medal winners only (for
non-winners, the Medal feature is NaN)
# note use of the inplace parameter
olympics_winners = olympics_df.dropna(subset=['Medal'])
olympics_winners.head()
```

The output is as follows:

	ID	Name	Sex	Age	Height	Weight	Team	NOC	Games	Year	Season	City	Sport	Event	Medal
3	4	Edgar Lindenau Aabye	M	34.0	NaN	NaN	Denmark/Sweden	DEN	1900 Summer	1900	Summer	Paris	Tug-Of-War	Tug-Of-War Men's Tug-Of-War	Gold
37	15	Arvo Ossian Aaltonen	M	30.0	NaN	NaN	Finland	FIN	1920 Summer	1920	Summer	Antwerpen	Swimming	Swimming Men's 200 metres Breaststroke	Bronze
38	15	Arvo Ossian Aaltonen	M	30.0	NaN	NaN	Finland	FIN	1920 Summer	1920	Summer	Antwerpen	Swimming	Swimming Men's 400 metres Breaststroke	Bronze
40	16	Juhamatti Tapio Aaltonen	M	28.0	184.0	85.0	Finland	FIN	2014 Winter	2014	Winter	Sochi	Ice Hockey	Ice Hockey Men's Ice Hockey	Bronze
41	17	Paavo Johannes Aaltonen	M	28.0	175.0	64.0	Finland	FIN	1948 Summer	1948	Summer	London	Gymnastics	Gymnastics Men's Individual All-Around	Bronze

Figure 1.33: Filtered Olympics DataFrame

4. Print the number of medals awarded in each sport in 2016:

```
# print records for each value of the feature 'Sport'
olympics_winners_2016 = olympics_winners[(olympics_winners.Year ==
2016)]
olympics_winners_2016.Sport.value_counts()
```

The output is as follows:

```
                   Athletics               192
                   Swimming                191
                   Rowing                  144
                   Football                106
                   Hockey                   99
                   Handball                 89
                   Cycling                  84
                   Canoeing                 82
                   Water Polo               78
                   Rugby Sevens             74
                   Basketball               72
                   Volleyball               72
                   Wrestling                72
                   Gymnastics               66
                   Fencing                  65
                   Judo                     56
                   Boxing                   51
                   Sailing                  45
                   Equestrianism            45
                   Shooting                 45
                   Weightlifting            45
                   Diving                   36
                   Taekwondo                32
                   Synchronized Swimming    32
                   Table Tennis             24
                   Badminton                24
                   Tennis                   24
                   Archery                  24
                   Rhythmic Gymnastics      18
                   Beach Volleyball         12
                   Modern Pentathlon         6
                   Trampolining              6
                   Golf                      6
                   Triathlon                 6
                   Name: Sport, dtype: int64
```

Figure 1.34: The number of medals awarded

5. Note the top five sports based on the largest number of medals awarded in the year 2016, and then create a DataFrame to include only these sports:

```
# list the top 5 sports
top_sports = ['Athletics', 'Swimming', 'Rowing', 'Football',
'Hockey']
# subset the DataFrame to include data from the top sports
olympics_top_sports_winners_2016 = olympics_winners_2016[(olympics_
winners_2016.Sport.isin(top_sports))]
olympics_top_sports_winners_2016.head()
```

The output is as follows:

	ID	Name	Sex	Age	Height	Weight	Team	NOC	Games	Year	Season	City	Sport	Event	Medal
158	62	Giovanni Abagnale	M	21.0	198.0	90.0	Italy	ITA	2016 Summer	2016	Summer	Rio de Janeiro	Rowing	Rowing Men's Coxless Pairs	Bronze
814	465	Matthew "Matt" Abood	M	30.0	197.0	92.0	Australia	AUS	2016 Summer	2016	Summer	Rio de Janeiro	Swimming	Swimming Men's 4 x 100 metres Freestyle Relay	Bronze
1228	690	Chantal Achterberg	F	31.0	172.0	72.0	Netherlands	NED	2016 Summer	2016	Summer	Rio de Janeiro	Rowing	Rowing Women's Quadruple Sculls	Silver
1529	846	Valerie Kasanita Adams-Vili (-Price)	F	31.0	193.0	120.0	New Zealand	NZL	2016 Summer	2016	Summer	Rio de Janeiro	Athletics	Athletics Women's Shot Put	Silver
1847	1017	Nathan Ghar-Jun Adrian	M	27.0	198.0	100.0	United States	USA	2016 Summer	2016	Summer	Rio de Janeiro	Swimming	Swimming Men's 50 metres Freestyle	Bronze

Figure 1.35: Olympics DataFrame

6. Generate a bar plot of 2016 medal winners across the top five sports:

```
# generate bar plot indicating count of medals awarded in each of
the top sports
g = sns.catplot('Sport', data=olympics_top_sports_winners_2016,
kind="count", aspect=1.5)
```

The output is as follows:

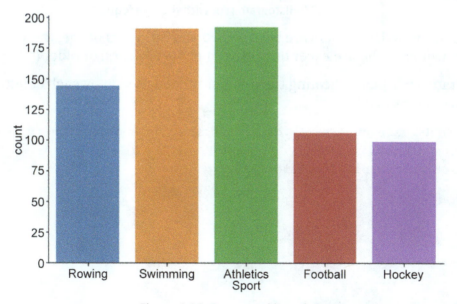

Figure 1.36: Generated bar plot

7. Generate a histogram for the **Age** feature of all athletes who competed in the top five sports in 2016:

    ```
    sns.distplot(olympics_top_sports_winners_2016.Age, kde=False)
    ```

The output is as follows:

```
<matplotlib.axes._subplots.AxesSubplot at 0x1ab5e1058d0>
```

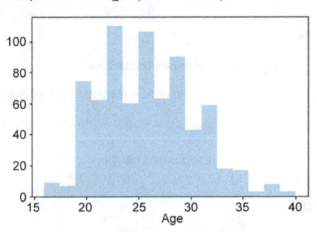

Figure 1.37: Histogram plot with the Age feature

While most medal winners are between **20** and **30** years of age, there are also medal winners who are exceptionally younger (~**16** years) or older (~**40** years).

8. Generate a bar plot indicating the number of medals won by each country in the top five sports in 2016:

    ```
    g = sns.catplot('Team', data=olympics_top_sports_winners_2016,
    kind="count", aspect=3)
    g.set_xticklabels(rotation=90)
    ```

The output is as follows:

```
<seaborn.axisgrid.FacetGrid at 0x1ab5e1a0208>
```

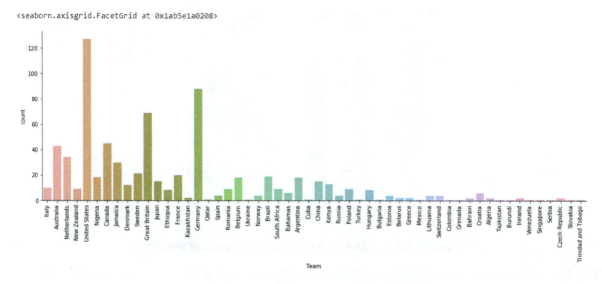

Figure 1.38: Bar plot with the number of medals won

Considering the five sports, the US won the most medals, followed by *Germany*, *Great Britain*, *Canada*, and *Australia*.

9. Generate a bar plot indicating the average weight of players, categorized as male and female, winning in the top five sports in 2016:

```
sns.set(style="whitegrid")
sns.barplot(x="Sport", y="Weight", data=olympics_top_sports_
winners_2016, estimator=mean, hue='Sex')
```

The output is as follows:

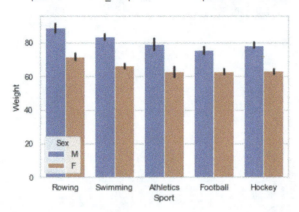

`<matplotlib.axes._subplots.AxesSubplot at 0x1ab5e8488d0>`

Figure 1.39: Bar plot with the average weight of players

The bar plot indicates the highest athlete weight in rowing, followed by swimming, and then the other remaining sports. The trend is similar across both male and female players.

Chapter 2: Static Visualization – Global Patterns and Summary Statistics

Activity 2: Design Static Visualization to Present Global Patterns and Summary Statistics

Solution

1. Load the necessary python modules and download the **Olympic History** dataset hosted in the book's GitHub repository, and format it as a **pandas** DataFrame:

```
# load necessary modules
import pandas as pd
import seaborn as sns
from numpy import median, mean
# download file 'athlete_events.csv' from course GitHub repository:
https://github.com/TrainingByPackt/Interactive-Data-Visualization-
with-Python/datasets
# read the dataset as a pandas DataFrame
olympics_df = pd.read_csv('../Interactive-Data-Visualization-with-
Python-master/datasets/athlete_events.csv')
# preview DataFrame
olympics_df.head()
```

The output is as follows:

	ID	Name	Sex	Age	Height	Weight	Team	NOC	Games	Year	Season	City	Sport	Event	Medal
0	1	A Dijiang	M	24.0	180.0	80.0	China	CHN	1992 Summer	1992	Summer	Barcelona	Basketball	Basketball Men's Basketball	NaN
1	2	A Lamusi	M	23.0	170.0	60.0	China	CHN	2012 Summer	2012	Summer	London	Judo	Judo Men's Extra-Lightweight	NaN
2	3	Gunnar Nielsen Aaby	M	24.0	NaN	NaN	Denmark	DEN	1920 Summer	1920	Summer	Antwerpen	Football	Football Men's Football	NaN
3	4	Edgar Lindenau Aabye	M	34.0	NaN	NaN	Denmark/Sweden	DEN	1900 Summer	1900	Summer	Paris	Tug-Of-War	Tug-Of-War Men's Tug-Of-War	Gold
4	5	Christine Jacoba Aaftink	F	21.0	185.0	82.0	Netherlands	NED	1988 Winter	1988	Winter	Calgary	Speed Skating	Speed Skating Women's 500 metres	NaN

Figure 2.22: Olympic History dataset

2. Filter the DataFrame to contain only the medal winners of the year 2016 for the sports mentioned in the activity description:

```
# filter the DataFrame to contain medal winners only (for
non-winners, the Medal feature is NaN)
# note use of the inplace parameter
olympics_winners = olympics_df.dropna(subset=['Medal'])
# list the top 5 sports
top_sports = ['Athletics', 'Swimming', 'Rowing', 'Football',
'Hockey']
# filter dataframe to include 2016 records of specified sports
olympics_top_sports_winners_2016 = olympics_winners[(olympics_
winners.Sport.isin(top_sports)) & (olympics_winners.Year == 2016)]
olympics_top_sports_winners_2016.head()
```

The output is as follows:

	ID	Name	Sex	Age	Height	Weight	Team	NOC	Games	Year	Season	City	Sport	Event	Medal
158	62	Giovanni Abagnale	M	21.0	198.0	90.0	Italy	ITA	2016 Summer	2016	Summer	Rio de Janeiro	Rowing	Rowing Men's Coxless Pairs	Bronze
814	465	Matthew "Matt" Abood	M	30.0	197.0	92.0	Australia	AUS	2016 Summer	2016	Summer	Rio de Janeiro	Swimming	Swimming Men's 4 x 100 metres Freestyle Relay	Bronze
1228	690	Chantal Achterberg	F	31.0	172.0	72.0	Netherlands	NED	2016 Summer	2016	Summer	Rio de Janeiro	Rowing	Rowing Women's Quadruple Sculls	Silver
1529	846	Valerie Kasanita Adams-Vili (-Price)	F	31.0	193.0	120.0	New Zealand	NZL	2016 Summer	2016	Summer	Rio de Janeiro	Athletics	Athletics Women's Shot Put	Silver
1847	1017	Nathan Ghar-Jun Adrian	M	27.0	198.0	100.0	United States	USA	2016 Summer	2016	Summer	Rio de Janeiro	Swimming	Swimming Men's 50 metres Freestyle	Bronze

Figure 2.23: Olympics history dataset with the medal winners

Look at the features in the dataset and note their data type – are they *categorical* or *numerical*?

3. The **Sport** feature, the **Team** feature, the **Medal** feature, and the **Sex** feature are all categorical, while the **Age**, **Height**, and **Weight** features are numerical. However, we should also note the range of values taken by the numerical features to get a sense of the data. This can be done using the **describe** function, as seen in *Chapter 1, Introduction to Visualization with Python– Basic and Customized Plotting* like so:

```
olympics_top_sports_winners_2016[['Age', 'Height', 'Weight']].
describe()
```

The output is as follows:

	Age	Height	Weight
count	732.000000	729.000000	727.000000
mean	25.577869	180.023320	73.720770
std	4.451373	10.076398	14.279014
min	16.000000	150.000000	40.000000
25%	22.000000	173.000000	64.000000
50%	25.000000	180.000000	72.000000
75%	29.000000	187.000000	82.000000
max	40.000000	207.000000	136.000000

Figure 2.24: Olympics history dataset with the top sport winners

4. Based on the output above, we are going to visualize the **Height** and **Weight** features, depicting their global pattern:

```
# import the seaborn library
import matplotlib.pyplot as plt
import seaborn as sns

fig1 = plt.figure()
ax = fig1.add_subplot(111)
ax = sns.scatterplot(x="Height", y="Weight", data=olympics_top_
sports_winners_2016)
plt.show()
```

The output is as follows:

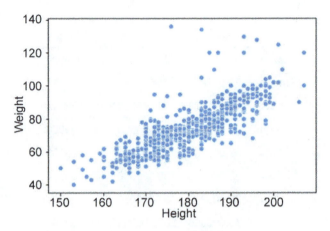

Figure 2.25: Scatter plot

It is interesting to note that there is an almost linear relationship between the **Height** and **Weight** features of the medal winners, with a few outliers. However, since this is a fairly dense plot with many universities in certain ranges we will draw a hexbin plot to represent the data.

5. Draw a hexbin plot:

```
sns.set(style="ticks")
## hexbin plot
sns.jointplot(olympics_top_sports_winners_2016.Height, olympics_top_
sports_winners_2016.Weight, kind="hex", color="#4CB391")
```

The output is as follows:

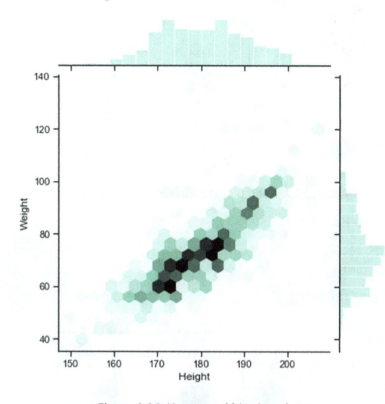

Figure 2.26: Hexagonal binning plot

6. Now let's visualize the **height** and **weight** features, depicting the medal-wise summary statistics, segregated by athlete gender:

```
sns.set_style('white')
ax1 = sns.violinplot(x='Medal', y='Weight', data=olympics_top_
sports_winners_2016, hue='Sex')
```

The output is as follows:

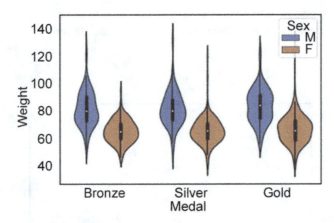

Figure 2.27: Violin plot showing medal versus weight

7. Set the y axis to `Height` like so:

```
ax2 = sns.violinplot(x='Medal', y='Height', data=olympics_top_
sports_winners_2016, hue='Sex')
```

The output is as follows:

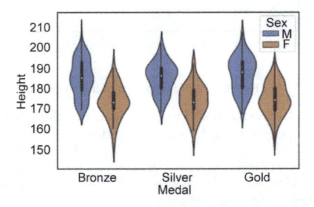

Figure 2.28: Violin plot showing medal versus height

As expected, we see that the `Height` and `Weight` features do not differ significantly across the different medal winners. Also, `Height` and `Weight` are substantially lower for female medal winners than for male winners.

Chapter 3: From Static to Interactive Visualization

Activity 3: Creating Different Interactive Visualizations Using Plotly Express

Solution

1. Open a new Jupyter notebook.

2. Import the necessary Python libraries and packages:

   ```
   import pandas as pd
   import plotly.express as px
   ```

3. Recreate the carbon dioxide emissions and **GDP** DataFrame from Exercise 22 in this notebook:

   ```
   url_co2 = 'https://raw.githubusercontent.com/TrainingByPackt/
   Interactive-Data-Visualization-with-Python/master/datasets/co2.csv'
   url_gm = 'https://raw.githubusercontent.com/TrainingByPackt/
   Interactive-Data-Visualization-with-Python/master/datasets/
   gapminder.csv'
   co2 = pd.read_csv(url_co2)
   gm = pd.read_csv(url_gm)
   df_gm = gm[['Country', 'region']].drop_duplicates()
   df_w_regions = pd.merge(co2, df_gm, left_on='country', right_
   on='Country', how='inner')
   df_w_regions = df_w_regions.drop('Country', axis='columns')
   new_co2 = pd.melt(df_w_regions, id_vars=['country', 'region'])
   columns = ['country', 'region', 'year', 'co2']
   new_co2.columns = columns
   df_co2 = new_co2[new_co2['year'].astype('int64') > 1963]
   df_co2 = df_co2.sort_values(by=['country', 'year'])
   df_co2['year'] = df_co2['year'].astype('int64')
   df_gdp = gm[['Country', 'Year', 'gdp']]
   df_gdp.columns = ['country', 'year', 'gdp']
   data = pd.merge(df_co2, df_gdp, on=['country', 'year'], how='left')
   data = data.dropna()
   ```

4. Create a scatter plot with the x- and y-axes as **year** and **co2** respectively. Let the region determine the color of the datapoints. Add a box plot for the **co2** values with the **marginaly_y** parameter:

```
scat = px.scatter(data, x = 'year', y = 'co2', color = 'region',
marginal_y = 'box')
```

5. Display the scatter plot:

```
scat.show()
```

The output is as follows:

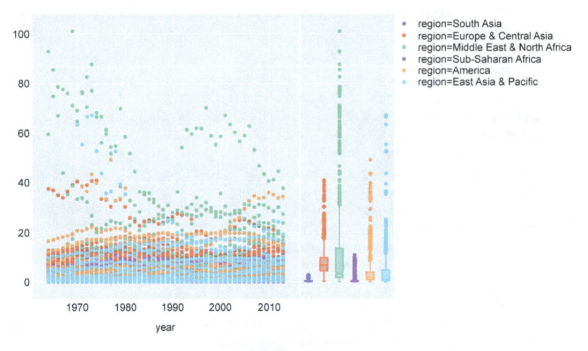

Figure 3.31: Scatter plot of CO2 emissions per year

This plot is interactive because of the following reasons:

You can hover over a datapoint to receive more information. You can also select and deselect the regions to observe data that's specific to a particular region/set of regions.

6. Create a scatter plot with the x and y axes as **gdp** and **co2** respectively. Let the region determine the color of the datapoints. Add a box plot for the **co2** values with the **marginal_y** parameter and a rug plot for the **gdp** values with the **marginal_x** parameter. Add the animation parameters on the **year** column:

```
scat1 = px.scatter(data, x = 'gdp', y = 'co2', color = 'region',
marginal_y = 'box', marginal_x = 'rug', animation_frame = 'year',
animation_group = 'country')
```

7. Display the scatter plot:

```
scat1.show()
```

The output should be as follows:

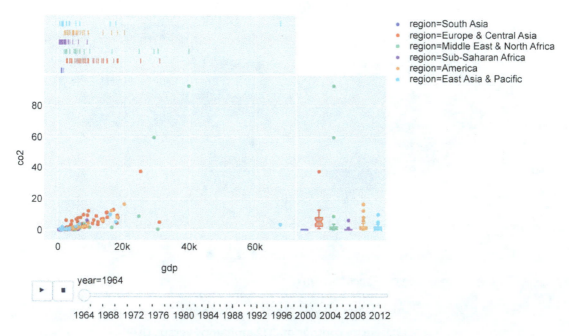

Figure 3.32: Scatter plot of CO2 emissions versus GDP

This plot is interactive because of the following reasons:

You can hover over a datapoint to receive more information about it; you can also select and deselect the regions to observe data specific to a particular region/set of regions; you can slide the bar to observe the datapoints in different years.

8. Create a density contour with the x and y axes as **gdp** and **co2** respectively. Let the region determine the color of the datapoints. Add a histogram for the **co2** values with the **marginal_y** parameter and a rug plot for the **gdp** values with the **marginal_x** parameter. Add the animation parameters on the **year** column:

    ```
    dens1 = px.density_contour(data, x="gdp", y="co2", color="region",
    marginal_x="rug", marginal_y="histogram", animation_frame = 'year',
    animation_group = 'region')
    ```

9. Display the density contour:

    ```
    dens1.show()
    ```

    The output is as follows:

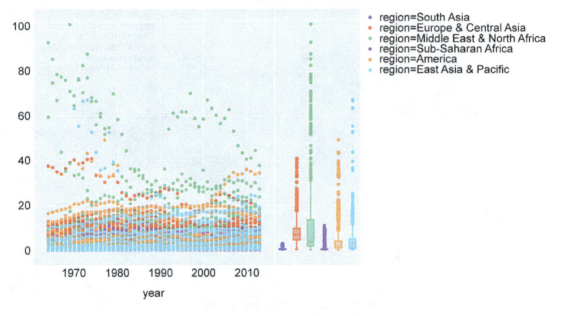

Fig 3.33: Density contour of CO2 emissions versus GDP

This plot is interactive because of the following reasons:

You can hover over a contour to receive more information about it ; you can select and deselect the regions to observe data that's specific to a particular region/set of regions; you can slide the bar to observe the contours in different years.

Chapter 4: Interactive Visualization of Data across Strata

Activity 4: Generate a Bar Plot and a Heatmap to Represent Content Rating Types in the Google Play Store Apps Dataset

Solution

1. Load the necessary Python modules and download the dataset hosted in the book GitHub repository and format it as a **pandas** DataFrame:

```
# load pandas library
Import pandas as pd
# download file 'googleplaystore.csv' from course GitHub repository
# read the dataset as a pandas DataFrame
gps_apps_df =pd.read_csv('https://raw.githubusercontent.com/
TrainingByPackt/Interactive-Data-Visualization-with-Python/master/
datasets/googleplaystore.csv')
#worldrank_df = pd.read_csv('https://raw.githubusercontent.com/
TrainingByPackt/Interactive-Data-Visualization-with-Python/master/
datasets/googleplaystore.csv')
# preview DataFrame
gps_apps_df.head()
```

The output is as follows:

	App	Category	Rating	Reviews	Size	Installs	Type	Price	Content Rating	Genres	Last Updated	Current Ver	Android Ver
0	Photo Editor & Candy Camera & Grid & ScrapBook	ART_AND_DESIGN	4.1	159	19M	10,000+	Free	0	Everyone	Art & Design	January 7, 2018	1.0.0	4.0.3 and up
1	Coloring book moana	ART_AND_DESIGN	3.9	967	14M	500,000+	Free	0	Everyone	Art & Design;Pretend Play	January 15, 2018	2.0.0	4.0.3 and up
2	U Launcher Lite – FREE Live Cool Themes, Hide ...	ART_AND_DESIGN	4.7	87510	8.7M	5,000,000+	Free	0	Everyone	Art & Design	August 1, 2018	1.2.4	4.0.3 and up
3	Sketch - Draw & Paint	ART_AND_DESIGN	4.5	215644	25M	50,000,000+	Free	0	Teen	Art & Design	June 8, 2018	Varies with device	4.2 and up
4	Pixel Draw - Number Art Coloring Book	ART_AND_DESIGN	4.3	967	2.8M	100,000+	Free	0	Everyone	Art & Design;Creativity	June 20, 2018	1.1	4.4 and up

Figure 4.30: Google Play Store dataset apps

2. Remove the entries in the DataFrame that have feature values of **NA**:

```
gps_apps_df = gps_apps_df.dropna()
```

3. Create the required bar chart of the number of apps in each **Content Rating** category of the app; that is, whether the app is rated by **Adults only 18+/ Everyone/Everyone 10+/Mature 17+/Teen/Unrated**:

```
#import altair
Import altair as alt
alt.data_transformers.enable('default',max_rows=None)
# create bar plot
alt.Chart(gps_apps_df).mark_bar().encode(
x='Content Rating:N',
y='count():Q'
).properties(width=200)
```

The output is as follows:

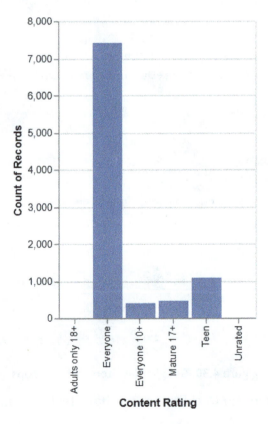

Figure 4.31: Bar plot

4. Create the required heatmap indicating the number of apps across the app **Category** and **Rating** ranges:

```
# create heatmap
alt.Chart(gps_apps_df).mark_rect().encode(
alt.X('Category:N'),
alt.Y('Rating:Q',bin=True),
alt.Color('count()',
scale=alt.Scale(scheme='greenblue'),
legend=alt.Legend(title='Total Apps')
)
).properties(
width=600
)
```

The output is as follows:

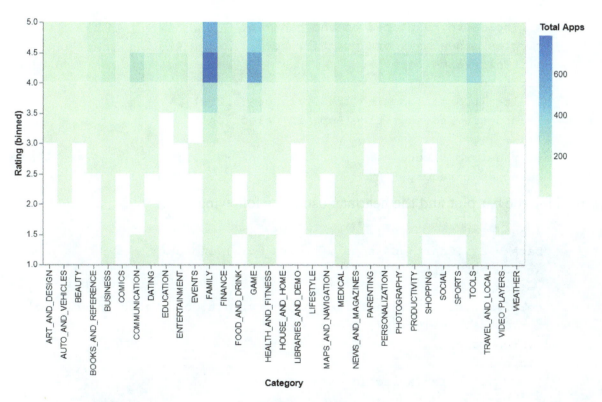

Figure 4.32: Heatmap

5. Merge the code for the bar chart and heatmap and create a visualization with both plots linked dynamically to each other such that the selection in the bar chart is reflected in the changes on the heatmap:

```
# define selection
selected_category = alt.selection(type="single", encodings=['x'])
# heatmap
heatmap = alt.Chart(gps_apps_df).mark_rect().encode(
alt.X('Category:N'),
alt.Y('Rating:Q', bin=True),
alt.Color('count()',
scale=alt.Scale(scheme='greenblue'),
legend=alt.Legend(title='Total Apps')
)
).properties(
width=600
)
# circles to be placed on the heatmap
circles = heatmap.mark_point().encode(
alt.ColorValue('grey'),
alt.Size('count()',
scale=alt.Scale(domain=(1,600),range=(1,200)),
legend=alt.Legend(title='Apps in Selection')
)
).transform_filter(
selected_category)
```

6. Link the bar plot and the heatmap using the following code:

```
# bar plot
bars = alt.Chart(gps_apps_df).mark_bar().encode(
x='Content Rating:N',
y='count()',
color=alt.condition(selected_category, alt.ColorValue("steelblue"),
alt.ColorValue("grey"))
).properties(
width=200
).add_selection(selected_category)
# layering and hconcat
heatmap+circles|bars
```

The output is as follows:

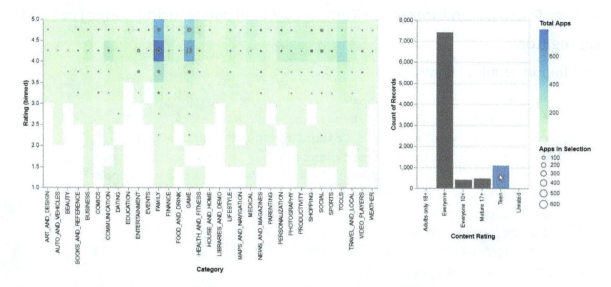

Figure 4.33: Linked bar plot and heatmap

And that's it. Congratulations!

Chapter 5: Interactive Visualization of Data across Time

Activity 5: Create an Interactive Temporal Visualization using RangeTool and Aggregator

1. Import required libraries:

```
from bokeh.io import show
from bokeh.layouts import column
from bokeh.models import ColumnDataSource, RangeTool
from bokeh.plotting import figure
from bokeh.io import push_notebook, show, output_notebook
from pathlib import Path
import pandas as pd
import numpy as np
from ipywidgets import interact
%matplotlib inline
```

2. Setup the output to Jupyter Notebook:

```
DATA_PATH = Path("../datasets/chap5_data/")
output_notebook()
```

3. Create a DataFrame **microsoft_df** and parse the **date** column:

```
microsoft_df = pd.read_csv(DATA_PATH / "microsoft_stock.csv", parse_
dates=['date'])
```

4. Set the **index** as **date**:

```
microsoft_df.index = microsoft_df.date
```

5. Create **date numpy** array and source as **ColumnDataSource**. We will use these to draw line plot:

```
dates = np.array(microsoft_df['date'], dtype=np.datetime64)
source = ColumnDataSource(data=dict(date=dates, close=microsoft_
df['high']))
```

6. Initialize the figure and draw the line:

```
p = figure(plot_height=300, plot_width=800, tools="xpan", toolbar_
location=None, title="Time Series Stock Data",
            x_axis_type="datetime", x_axis_location="above",
```

```
                background_fill_color="#ffefef", x_range=(dates[1000],
dates[1800]))
r = p.line('date', 'close', source=source)
p.yaxis.axis_label = 'High Price'
```

7. Create range slider using **RangeTool**:

```
select = figure(title="Drag To See More Data",plot_width=800, y_
range=p.y_range,
                x_axis_type="datetime", y_axis_type=None, plot_
height=130,
                tools="", background_fill_color="#ffefef", toolbar_
location=None,)
range_tool = RangeTool(x_range=p.x_range)
range_tool.overlay.fill_color = "green"
range_tool.overlay.fill_alpha = 0.2
```

8. Write a custom update function which aggregate data by **month**, **year** and **day**:

```
def update(f):
    if   f == "day":
        r.data_source.data = dict({
            'date': microsoft_df.index,
            'high': microsoft_df.high
        })
    elif f == "month":
        month = microsoft_df.groupby(pd.Grouper(freq="M"))
[['high']].mean()
        r.data_source.data = dict({
            'date': month.index,
            'high': month.high
        })
    elif f == "year":
        year = microsoft_df.groupby(pd.Grouper(freq="Y"))[['high']].
mean()
        r.data_source.data = dict({
            'date': year.index,
            'high': year.high
        })
```

```
    push_notebook()

select.line('date', 'high', source=source)
select.ygrid.grid_line_color = None
select.add_tools(range_tool)
select.toolbar.active_multi = range_tool
show(column(p, select), notebook_handle=True)
```

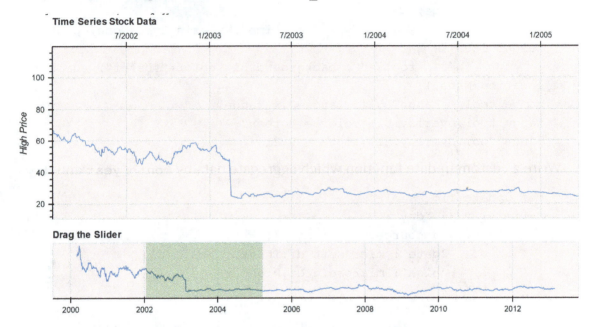

Figure 5.33: Time-series Microsoft stock data

9. Plot both range slider and aggregator on the plot:

```
select.line('date', 'high', source=source)
select.ygrid.grid_line_color = None
select.add_tools(range_tool)
select.toolbar.active_multi = range_tool
show(column(p, select), notebook_handle=True)
interact(update, f=["day", "month", "year"])
```

The output is as follows:

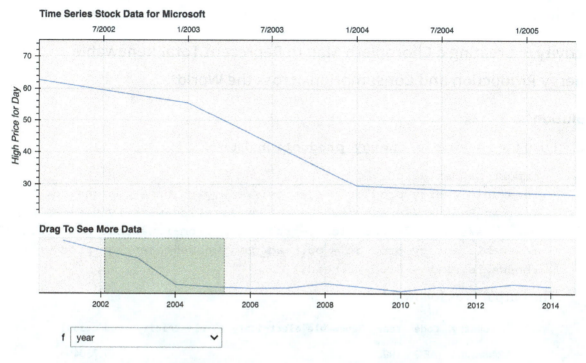

Figure 5.34: Microsoft stock price chart with range slider and aggregator

We can now change the plot to show month, day, and year. In this section, we have delved into interactive temporal visualizations using **bokeh**. We've looked at basic interactive plots in **bokeh** and used box annotations to highlight regions.

Chapter 6: Interactive Visualizations of Data across Geographical Regions

Activity 6: Creating a Choropleth Map to Represent Total Renewable Energy Production and Consumption across the World

Solution

1. Load the **renewable energy production** dataset:

```
import pandas as pd
renewable_energy_prod_url = "https://raw.githubusercontent.com/
TrainingByPackt/Interactive-Data-Visualization-with-Python/master/
datasets/share-of-electricity-production-from-renewable-sources.csv"
renewable_energy_prod_df = pd.read_csv(renewable_energy_prod_url)
renewable_energy_prod_df.head()
```

The output is as follows:

	Country	Code	Year	Renewable electricity (% electricity production)
0	Afghanistan	AFG	1990	67.730496
1	Afghanistan	AFG	1991	67.980296
2	Afghanistan	AFG	1992	67.994310
3	Afghanistan	AFG	1993	68.345324
4	Afghanistan	AFG	1994	68.704512

Figure 6.29: Renewable sources dataset

2. Sort the production DataFrame based on the **Year** feature:

```
renewable_energy_prod_df.sort_values(by=['Year'],inplace=True)
renewable_energy_prod_df.head()
```

The output is as follows:

	Country	Code	Year	Renewable electricity (% electricity production)
0	Afghanistan	AFG	1990	67.730496
1668	France	FRA	1990	13.369879
1643	Finland	FIN	1990	29.451790
1618	Fiji	FJI	1990	82.441113
1593	Faeroe Islands	FRO	1990	35.545024

Figure 6.30: Renewable sources dataset after sorting by year

3. Generate a choropleth map using the **plotly express** module animated based on **Year**:

```
import plotly.express as px
renewable_energy_prod = renewable_energy_prod_df.query('Year<2017
and Year>2007')
fig = px.choropleth(renewable_energy_prod_df, locations="Code",
color="Renewable electricity (% electricity production)",
hover_name="Country",
animation_frame="Year",
color_continuous_scale='Greens')
```

4. Update the layout to include a suitable projection style and title text, then display the figure:

```
fig.update_layout(
# add a title text for the plot
title_text = 'Renewable energy production across the world (% of
electricity production)',
# set projection style for the plot
geo = dict(projection={'type':'natural earth'}) # by default,
projection type is set to 'equirectangular'
)
fig.show()
```

The output is as follows:

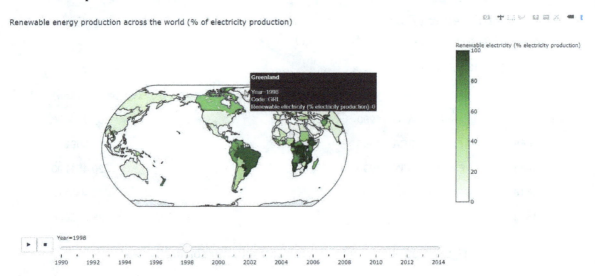

Figure 6.31a: Choropleth map showing the renewable energy production of Greenland in the year 1998

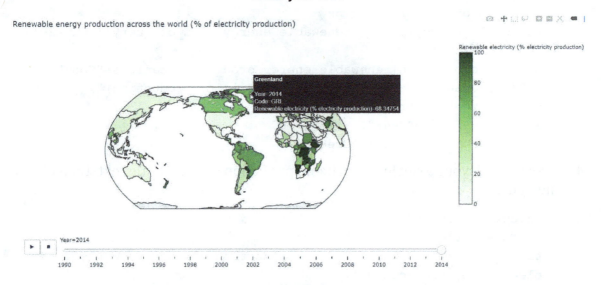

Figure 6.31b: Choropleth map showing the renewable energy production of Greenland in the year 2014

5. Load the **renewable energy consumption** dataset:

```
import pandas as pd
renewable_energy_cons_url = "https://raw.githubusercontent.com/
TrainingByPackt/Interactive-Data-Visualization-with-Python/master/
datasets/renewable-energy-consumption-by-country.csv"
renewable_energy_cons_df = pd.read_csv(renewable_energy_cons_url)
renewable_energy_cons_df.head()
```

The output is as follows:

	Country	Code	Year	Traditional biofuels	Other renewables (modern biofuels, geothermal, wave & tidal)	Wind	Solar PV	Hydropower	Total
0	Algeria	DZA	1965	NaN		0.0	0.0	0.0	NaN	0.0
1	Algeria	DZA	1966	NaN		0.0	0.0	0.0	NaN	0.0
2	Algeria	DZA	1967	NaN		0.0	0.0	0.0	NaN	0.0
3	Algeria	DZA	1968	NaN		0.0	0.0	0.0	NaN	0.0
4	Algeria	DZA	1969	NaN		0.0	0.0	0.0	NaN	0.0

Figure 6.32: Renewable energy consumption dataset

6. Convert the DataFrame to the desired format:

```
#renewable_energy_long_df = pd.wide_to_long(renewable_energy_df,
stubnames='Consumption', i=['Country', 'Code','Year'], j='Energy_
Source')
#renewable_energy_long_df.head()
renewable_energy_cons_df = pd.melt(renewable_energy_cons_df, \
id_vars=['Country', 'Code','Year'], \
var_name="Energy Source", \
value_name="Consumption (terrawatt-hours)")
renewable_energy_cons_df.head()
```

The output is as follows:

	Country	Code	Year	Energy Source	Consumption (terrawatt-hours)
0	Algeria	DZA	1965	Energy Source	Traditional biofuels
1	Algeria	DZA	1966	Energy Source	Traditional biofuels
2	Algeria	DZA	1967	Energy Source	Traditional biofuels
3	Algeria	DZA	1968	Energy Source	Traditional biofuels
4	Algeria	DZA	1969	Energy Source	Traditional biofuels

Figure 6.33: The desired dataset after conversion

7. Sort the consumption DataFrame based on the **Year** feature:

```
renewable_energy_cons_df.sort_values(by=['Year'], inplace=True)
renewable_energy_cons_df.head()
```

The output is as follows:

	Country	Code	Year	Energy Source	Consumption (terrawatt-hours)
0	Algeria	DZA	1965	Traditional biofuels	NaN
4240	Finland	FIN	1965	Other renewables (modern biofuels, geothermal,...	0.0
17252	Chile	CHL	1965	Total	0.0
4292	France	FRA	1965	Other renewables (modern biofuels, geothermal,...	0.0
4344	Germany	DEU	1965	Other renewables (modern biofuels, geothermal,...	0.0

Figure 6.34: The dataset after sorting by year

8. Generate a choropleth map for renewable energy consumption using the **plotly express** module animated based on **Year**:

```
import plotly.express as px
renewable_energy_total_cons = renewable_energy_cons_df[renewable_
energy_cons_df['Energy Source']=='Total'].query('Year<2017 and
Year>2007')
fig = px.choropleth(renewable_energy_total_cons, locations="Code",
color="Consumption (terrawatt-hours)",
hover_name="Country",
animation_frame="Year",
color_continuous_scale='Blues')
```

9. Update the layout of the consumption plot to include a suitable projection style and title text, then display the figure:

```
fig.update_layout(
# add a title text for the plot
title_text = 'Renewable energy consumption across the world
(terrawatt-hours)',
# set projection style for the plot
geo = dict(projection={'type':'natural earth'}) # by default,
projection type is set to 'equirectangular'
)
fig.show()
```

The output is as follows:

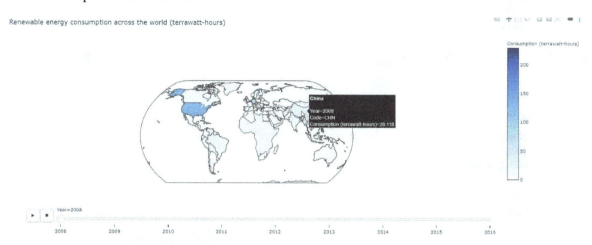

Figure 6.35a: Choropleth map showing renewable energy consumption across the world

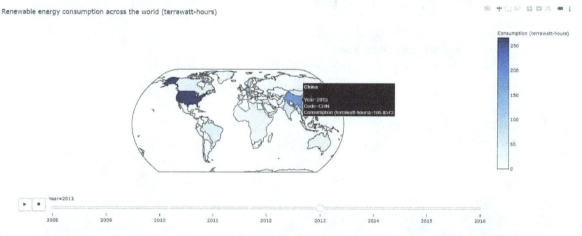

Figure 6.35b: Choropleth map showing renewable energy consumption across the world

So, from the preceding two plots we can deduce that China's renewable energy consumption increased between **2008** and **2013**.

Chapter 7: Avoiding Common Pitfalls to Create Interactive Visualizations

Activity 7: Determining Which Features to Visualize on a Scatter Plot

Solution

1. Navigate to the folder where you have stored the .csv files and initiate a Jupyter Notebook.

2. Import **pandas**, **numpy**, and **plotly.express**:

```
import pandas as pd
import numpy as np
import plotly.express as px
```

3. Create the same DataFrame, but instead of including only the **gdp** column from the **gm** DataFrame, include the **population**, **fertility**, and **life** columns as well:

```
co2 = pd.read_csv('co2.csv')
gm = pd.read_csv('gapminder.csv')
df_gm = gm[['Country', 'region']].drop_duplicates()
df_w_regions = pd.merge(co2, df_gm, left_on='country', right_
on='Country', how='inner')
df_w_regions = df_w_regions.drop('Country', axis='columns')
new_co2 = pd.melt(df_w_regions, id_vars=['country', 'region'])
columns = ['country', 'region', 'year', 'co2']
new_co2.columns = columns
df_co2 = new_co2[new_co2['year'].astype('int64') > 1963]
df_co2 = df_co2.sort_values(by=['country', 'year'])
df_co2['year'] = df_co2['year'].astype('int64')
df_g = gm[['Country', 'Year', 'gdp', 'population', 'fertility',
'life']]
df_g.columns = ['country', 'year', 'gdp', 'population', 'fertility',
'life']
data = pd.merge(df_co2, df_g, on=['country', 'year'], how='left')
data = data.dropna()
```

4. Print the head of this DataFrame. You should have eight columns, excluding the index column:

```
data.head()
```

The output is as follows:

	Country	Year	fertility	life	population	child_mortality	gdp	region
0	Afghanistan	1964	7.671	33.639	10474903.0	339.7	1182.0	South Asia
1	Afghanistan	1965	7.671	34.152	10697983.0	334.1	1182.0	South Asia
2	Afghanistan	1966	7.671	34.662	10927724.0	328.7	1168.0	South Asia
3	Afghanistan	1967	7.671	35.170	11163656.0	323.3	1173.0	South Asia
4	Afghanistan	1968	7.671	35.674	11411022.0	318.1	1187.0	South Asia

Figure 7.22: The first five rows of the final DataFrame

5. Visualize the relationship between co2 and life using a scatter graph with the following information:

The x axis as the life column, the y axis as the co2 column, the size parameter as the population column, the color parameter as the region column, the animation_frame parameter as the year column, the animation_group parameter as the country column, the hover_name parameter as the country column, the maximum size as 60 :

```
fig = px.scatter(data, x="life", y="co2", size="population",
color="region", animation_frame = 'year', animation_group =
'country', hover_name="country", size_max=60)
fig.show()
```

The following is the expected output:

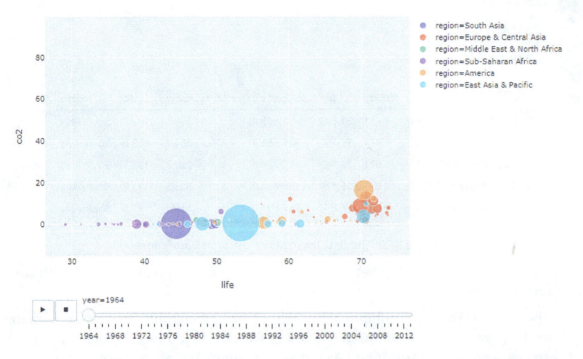

Figure 7.23: The interactive scatter plot describing the relationship between carbon dioxide emissions and life per country per year

If you press the play button or manually drag the sliding bar to different years, you'll notice that there isn't much of a trend or pattern emerging from this scatter plot. *But the whole point of a scatter plot is to display a relationship, so is there even a relationship here worth visualizing?* Let's check.

6. Create **numpy** arrays of the **co2** column and the **life** column:

```
np1 = np.array(data['co2'])
np2 = np.array(data['life'])
```

7. Calculate the correlation between the two arrays:

```
np.corrcoef(np1, np2)
```

The following is the expected output:

```
array([[1.        , 0.40288934],
       [0.40288934, 1.        ]])
```

There's barely any correlation here. Compare this with the correlation we found between **co2** and **gdp**.

8. Repeat steps 6 and 7 with the **co2** and **gdp** columns:

```
np1 = np.array(data['co2'])
np2 = np.array(data['gdp'])
np.corrcoef(np1, np2)
```

The following is the expected output:

```
array([[1..., 0.78219731],
       [0.78219731, 1...]])
```

That's a high correlation! That's why we were able to observe a trend when we plotted these two features together.

9. Visualize the relationship between **co2** and **fertility** using a scatter graph with the following information:

   The x axis as the **fertility** column, the y axis as the **co2** column, the **size** parameter as the **population** column, the **color** parameter as the **region** column, The **animation_frame** parameter as the **year** column, The **animation_group** parameter as the **country** column, the **hover_name** parameter as the **country** column, the maximum **size** as **60**:

```
fig = px.scatter(data, x="fertility", y="co2", size="population",
color="region", animation_frame = 'year', animation_group =
'country', hover_name="country", size_max=60)
fig.show()
```

The expected output is as follows:

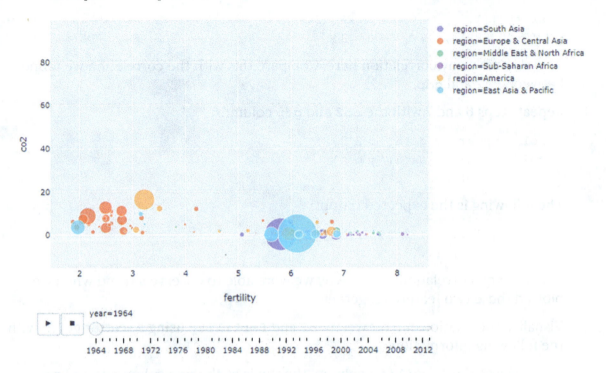

Figure 7.24: The interactive scatter plot describing the relationship between carbon dioxide emissions and fertility per country per year

Much like our previous graph, there doesn't seem to be much of a relationship between these two features. Let's check again.

10. Repeat steps 6 and 7 for the **co2** and **fertility** columns:

```
np1 = np.array(data['co2'])
np2 = np.array(data['fertility'])
np.corrcoef(np1, np2)
```

The output is as follows:

```
array([[ 1., -0.31439742],
       [-0.31439742,1.          ]])
```

Here, we have a weak negative correlation, which is why we can't observe much from our visualization. Therefore, it is always important to select features properly so that we create an insightful visualization. Let's see how we can choose a visualization wisely and the common pitfalls that are faced during this process.

Activity 8: Creating a Bar Graph for Improving a Visualization

Solution

1. Import **plotly.express**:

```
%run exercise55.ipynb
import plotly.express as px
```

2. Create a bar graph visualizing carbon dioxide emissions per region, per year with the following information:

The x-axis as the **region** column. The y-axis as the **co2** column. The **animation_frame** parameter as the **year** column. The **animation_group** parameter as the **country** column. The **hover_name** parameter as the **country** column.

```
fig3 = px.bar(data, x = 'region', y = "co2", animation_frame =
'year', animation_group = 'region', hover_name = 'country')
fig3.show()
```

The output is as follows:

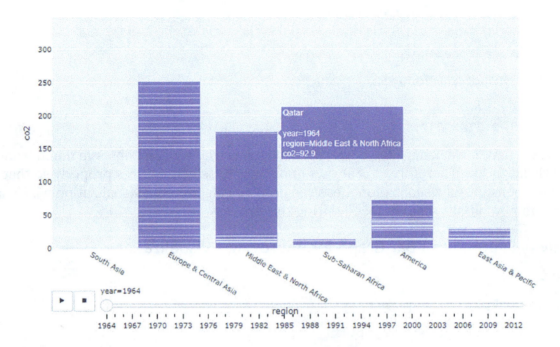

Fig 7.25: The interactive visualization in the form of a stacked bar graph depicting the carbon dioxide emissions per region over the span of five decades

We shifted the time information to a sliding bar and added the country information to the hover tool. This has made our visualization so much better! There are labels on the axes, and the scale of the y axis isn't abnormally high. With this, we are able to get a better idea of what's going on. It is easier to compare the total carbon dioxide emissions per region, per year now than it was in the earlier visualization.

Index